LEGISLATIVE POLITICS U.S.A.

Congress and the Forces that Shape It

LEGISLATIVE POLITICS U.S.A.

Readings Selected and Edited

by **THEODORE J. LOWI** *Cornell University*

Boston *Toronto*
LITTLE, BROWN AND COMPANY

LIBRARY OF CONGRESS CATALOG CARD NO. 62-14043

SECOND PRINTING

Published simultaneously in Canada
by Little, Brown & Company (Canada) Limited

PRINTED IN THE UNITED STATES OF AMERICA

Legislative Politics U.S.A.

TABLE OF CONTENTS

IV. CONGRESS AS AN INSTRUMENT OF GOVERNMENT

Chapter Seven

THE FORMULATION OF POLICY: Representation, Result

Chapter Eight

INQUIRY AS AN INSTRUMENT OF GOVERNMENT: Information, Supervision

V. THE MEANING OF MODERN REPRESENTATIVE GOVERNMENT

Chapter Nine

ASPECTS OF THE CONTROVERSY: Mobocracy, Power Elite, Benevolent Myth

Editor's Introduction

REPRESENTATION AND DECISION

In all forms of collective life there is at least one simple division of labor—leaders and followers. Most people accept the fact until it is called to their attention.

The first problem of popular government is to recognize the inevitability of leadership and power, not to deny it: to establish some fair and regular pattern for the selection of leaders and, further, to secure a minimum of control over leaders once they are granted a position of authority over others. "Representation" is such an attempt. Theories of representation are made for the purpose of *legitimizing* leadership. Obeisance to the proper rituals converts "leaders" into "representatives"; popular election converts "power" into "authority." Where doctrines of representation are accepted, there is a much higher probability that followers will do the bidding of representatives than that of leaders.

Constitutionally, the representation formula works a limitation on governmental power, along with other constitutional formulas such as Separation of Powers and Federalism. Our form of representation requires not only the periodic election of office-holders; it also requires that the law-making body be drawn from every geographical area of the country.[1] Thus we attempt to limit our legislators by making them electorally dependent *and* by placing in the assembly a very heterogeneous collection of leaders, giving our system several hundred "checks and balances."

Ideologically, acceptance of the doctrine impels the representative to act "in a representative way," to seek the perceived and even the unperceived needs of his following.[2] This is to say that mechanical accountability to an electorate is a necessary but, in itself, insufficient condition for representation. Without a widely shared acceptance of representation as a "good thing" the whole structure becomes a sham. A working system of representation brings forth a special type of leader, one who is generally flexible in ideology, outgoing in personality; a type, in short, that is groomed by the dictates of nomination and election and that makes the representative system work. It may be that John Stuart Mill's claims for representative government are overly optimistic (in "The Ideally Best Polity"), and that Gaetano Mosca's critique of the system as mere myth (in "Representation and Suffrage") is closer to the truth. But if the behavior of leaders is affected by a myth, the myth is real to that extent. Professor Friedrich (in "The Dual Nature of Representation") ably demonstrates that while representation may not be all that Mill claimed, it is far more than Mosca would allow.[3]

A government based on the principle of representation has a reality all its own, even if it is not the reality offered by its friends or its enemies. The most significant feature of representative government, indeed the determining characteristic, is its peculiar combination of two inconsistent norms: *representation* and *government*, or synonymously, participation and decision. The interplay between these two forces, representation versus decision, is the integrating theme of this volume. Achieving a balance between these two forces is the basic problem of all authoritative

[1] The "geographical constituency" is not the only method of representation, and it is not universally accepted as the best. Professor Friedrich discusses alternatives in his essay.

[2] Uncertainty as to the size of his following and that of alternative leaders, of course, makes the representative vulnerable to a far wider range of claims than merely his own following.

[3] Compare Mosca the young scholar at the turn of the century (in "Representation and Suffrage") with Mosca the elderly subject of Italian Fascist rule (in "Restoration of the Representative System").

institutions—American and non-American, democratic and non-democratic—for even an autocrat cannot depart too far or too long from the prevailing values of his subjects. The autocrat, feeling the pressures for representation, typically creates the myth of *virtual* representation—that he *is* the people or the vanguard of the people. But of course the significance lies in where the balance is struck. With the autocrat the reality is the overwhelming stress put on efficiency and decision. The problem of successful limited government is to balance the two forces without getting a maximum of either.

A healthy fear and hatred of autocracy and irresponsibility in the United States, as well as all Western democracies, led to a strong preference for government by representation, government that would be both limited and popularly based. But government can all too easily be made *too* representative; we can react too strongly to fear of irresponsible, unlimited government. In the immortal words of James Thurber, "You might just as well fall flat on your face as lean over too far backwards." A *perfectly representative* government would be virtually incapable of making a decision! The reformer's schemes of proportional or occupational representation, recall, or referendum are schemes that could, if employed meticulously, make the legislature an almost perfect replica of the society; but how would the members of such a legislature face the problem of agreement? If a majority vote is required, and a *two-thirds* majority must be ready for many controversial matters (in order to close debate and bring the question to a vote, as in our Senate), we can easily see that perfect representation would result in complete stalemate. It cannot be emphasized too strongly or too often that you can surround government with innumerable restraints but not to the extent of taking away its capacity to act. The answer to autocracy is not a completely popular government. Every degree of representativeness is likely to be paid for in inefficiency.

The problem of achieving a proper balance between these two forces is best seen in Congress; thus Congress becomes our focal point for studying the process of representative government. Beyond its intrinsic importance for study as an instrument of government, Congress serves as an excellent laboratory for the study of politics and the continuum that extends from perceived distress to organization to public policy and back again. Factors such as the committee and subcommittee system, the opposition or minority party, most of the parliamentary rules (dull and dry in themselves but politically potent—no rule is neutral!), seniority, floor debate, interest groups and regional blocs are almost constantly working for delay, for the fullest possible deliberation of one interest or another. Against those the (usually weaker) forces of the President and his immediate following in the executive branch, the President's party in Congress, the Speaker and other congressional officers, "gag rules" in the House, are supposedly at work molding the variety of interests into policy. (Of course, expediting decisions is not a synonym for "progress." A decision can amount to "turning the clock back.") To complicate matters further, the contribution of any one of these factors or participants to representation or decision depends upon the issue in question. For example, a committee chairman who strongly favors a piece of legislation becomes a strong force for result rather than "deliberation." The fight in January and February of 1961 to enlarge the Rules Committee was a struggle to convert that powerful committee from an instrument of delay into a lever of expedition. And the Congressman least involved in an issue usually supports its quick settlement in order to get on with business he deems most important. Thus, the process of representative government can be characterized abstractly in simple terms, but in practice it is very complex. Each factor must be assessed carefully.

It is the responsibility and need for making decisions that converts an otherwise somber debating society into a *power arena.* The constant attempt to put issues on the agenda for serious consideration and to reach agreement on them requires organization, skill, and compromise. In a collective decision-making body like Congress, agreement *equals* power. Every participant in the "legislative struggle" is seeking at least enough agreement or power either to enact a law or to prevent one from being enacted. Only a body without important decisions to make can afford the highest degree of representation, and only in such a body can the members afford to be perfectly straightforward and perfectly equal. Our representative institutions can afford neither. But the consequences of this, sometimes ludicrous, more often mystifying, are all too easily denounced. A representative system not only depends upon partisanship, compromise, manipulation; it could hardly work without them. The intelligent, sophisticated student of Congress is one who does not take any participant in the struggle at face value but tries instead to assess the participant's *functional* value in the total context of which he is only one part.

In an age of crisis, where we can survive only if we respond quickly to stress and disequilibrium—indeed to anticipate and prevent these maladies—we can afford poor representativeness if we gain an increment of efficiency thereby. For, in the face of crisis, if representation leads to stalemate, the need for remedies will become so great that some executive agency can be expected to take "discretionary action," if only to prevent a private group or social movement from taking matters into its own hands. Twentieth-century America is not a happy time or place for government by representative assembly. The technical complexities of modern society have forced Congress to delegate some of its powers to the executive agencies because of the need for *expertise* and continuous administration: Statutes are not self-executing. Further, the pace of modern life leaves Congress precious little time for full and fair deliberation, so that delegation to the executive also involves *delegation of conflict*, settlement of which is the most important function of Congress.

The twentieth century is an "executive-centered" era. We achieve productivity and abundance through specialization, but specialization leads to *interdependence*. Few men are now autonomous; all the rest are part of a very common destiny because each depends on others as well as himself for sustenance. The farmer lives by market patterns set by anonymous others. Laborer and manager alike have become part of a product over which they have no personal control, to which they contribute in only a minuscule way and in which they can take only the remotest pride. Informal ties such as family, community, and traditional values are weakening. An increasing number of class and intergroup relations must therefore be regularized by deliberate and formal procedures—*administered* social relations. Not all of these administered relationships are governmental—for example, trade associations and other interest groups, labor unions, civic groups, and "red feather" ("family service" and the like) agencies—but an increasing number *are* governmental. The growing burden of public management coupled with America's sudden exposure to the uncontrollable outside world make for an executive-centered government. All of the agencies of government are pushed to the very limits of their constitutional authority, and beyond. For we are operating under an essentially eighteenth-century body of constitutional doctrine.

Out of all this, the President has emerged as the most important legislator, the most important force for decision in our scheme of representative government. In the past, only "strong" Presidents have taken the initiative and set the agenda of Congress (in a "program"). Nowadays, this initiative is the norm; it is virtually thrust upon every President. (See Professor Neustadt's observations in "Planning the President's Program.") So often is this the case that the relations between the two branches have in large part been *reversed,* with the President proposing, in budget, State of the Union, and special messages, draft legislation and the like; and Congress exercising the powers of amendment and veto. But the President, with his advantageous position and vast resources, does not *legislate*. His powers, like congressional statutes, are not self-executing. The President is the most important but not the only participant in the legislative process. Modern problems have shifted the centers of power, but laws must still be made in Congress. Thus the struggle is not materially different from the struggle of earlier days. In the age-old way, a *majority must be created for every issue,* and every participant plays some role in the creation or the obstruction of that majority. The difference from earlier times lies in the need to bring each struggle sooner to a close. The potential role of each major participant is assessed in Section II (Chapter Three) and Section III (Chapters Four, Five, and Six).

There is no longer any controversy over the fact that the last generation has seen profound alterations in relations between President and Congress. But this is not to say that the power of Congress has declined. On the contrary, as an instrument of government it is clear that congressional power has actually increased. Secondly, as the relation of Congress to the executive branch has changed, the nature of its problem has changed; the power of Congress manifests itself in new ways. The new forms can easily be overlooked or underemphasized. Let us take up each of these points in turn.

The 1930's saw the end of one constitutional epoch and the beginning of another, in which the power of the national government over economic affairs was materially enhanced. By 1937 the

Supreme Court had recognized that developments in our economic system had all but completely abolished the meaning of state boundaries. A national market had been created; eventually every commodity became involved in interstate commerce. Most of the problems of combating economic instability and waste of natural and human resources appeared to be beyond the jurisdiction of a single state, and "states' rights" under the Tenth Amendment is a doctrine applicable only to local matters in one state that do not affect other states. Thus, the Supreme Court, in *N.L.R.B.* v. *Jones and Laughlin Steel Corporation,* adapted the Constitution to the new economic system (although by 1937, the system was at least a generation old). The case included in this reader, *Wickard* v. *Filburn,* is offered as an example of the degree to which national, therefore congressional, power was increased as a consequence.

The present, relatively comprehensive federal regulation of commerce, extending well into the domain traditionally considered exclusively state, is perfectly compatible with constitutional federalism. One may not like this or that program, and a good case might be made for the abolition of many of them on the ground that they do not contribute to a sound economy. But a good case cannot be made for their unconstitutionality. Every extension of trade beyond the borders of a single state reduces state jurisdiction and increases the reach of federal law. This enlargement of national power is rarely if ever due to "federal encroachment"; rather more simply it is due to the fact that economics recognizes no artificial state lines.

But Federalism, or "states' rights," has not been destroyed in the bargain. Only *economic* federalism was affected by the 1930's. Where practices are still essentially local, federalism remains a vital force, more specifically in civil rights. Perhaps one can say that federalism works where morally it should not. But it works, unquestionably. The Fourteenth Amendment failed in its attempt to nationalize citizenship (see *Civil Rights Cases,* still fairly good law after three quarters of a century); and all Congress can do is employ a few gentle subterfuges, subterfuge itself emphasizing limitation. (See "To Secure These Rights.")

In the field of foreign affairs, always considered executive business *par excellence,* congressional power has vastly increased. The charge that the executive has "usurped" the power of Congress by use of executive agreements rather than treaties[4] has been much too strongly emphasized. As a world leader, most of our international affairs involve money, or troops which involve money. And money involves Congress—not only the Senate but now the House of Representatives—in foreign policy as never before. The degree of congressional participation in foreign policy decisions depends, of course, on the nature of the decision. A quickly developing crisis might require an executive action with congressional approval only after the fact. But more often than not, some congressional leaders become involved in even the most urgent cases, as shown in "The Day We Didn't Go to War." On the longer range, more elaborately considered policies, Congress is intimately involved. Marshall Plan, NATO, and the other bulwarks of our international involvements were as much congressional as executive. The problem of enactment is about the same here as in the domestic field; presidential initiative is simply more frequent and presidential power is more telling. However, when a sufficient number of congressional leaders feel strongly enough on an issue, Congress can grab the initiative. Our Spanish policies, for instance, were shaped almost entirely by congressional influence.[5]

The second aspect of changing congressional power referred to above is that of the newer forms in which this power is manifest. Legislation remains the most important power of Congress, and without it Congress would possess no power at all. But even the

[4] Executive agreements have all the force and effect of treaties but do not require approval by two-thirds vote of the Senate.

[5] Between 1946 and 1950, the Administration was adamantly against close relations with Spain, particularly opposed to economic aid and military alliance. Due to the efforts of leaders such as Senators McCarran, McKellar, Taft, and Brewster and Congressman O'Konski, Multer, and Richards, our position shifted in 1951, and by 1953 we had a treaty with Spain which included millions in economic aid and several air bases. The following is an example of the congressional technique:

> *Senator McCarran* (in Hearings before the Subcommittee of the Senate Appropriations Committee for State Department Appropriations, 1949): Mr. Secretary (Dean Acheson), during the course of these hearings there will come up in this bill the matter of diplomatic items. I should like to ask you why it is that this country refuses to recognize Spain. . . . Let me say to you, Mr. Secretary, that so far as I am personally concerned as chairman of this subcommittee, I am not in favor of your policy with reference to Spain and until that policy is changed I am going to examine your appropriations with a fine-tooth comb.

(For the full story see Theodore J. Lowi, "Bases in Spain," *Twentieth Century Fund Studies in Civil-Military Relations*, published in 1962.)

problem of legislation has changed. In brief, the major problem and major focus of Congress is no longer simply that of prescribing the behavior of citizens but more often that of *affecting the behavior of administrators*. This is the constitutional implication of "executive-centered" government.

This aspect of the problem facing Congress is often dignified in the political rhetoric as the achievement of a "responsible bureaucracy," and indeed this would be the ideal outcome. But the workaday problem is one of power, electoral power versus the power of organization and specialization. Until the twentieth century there was no power in the West (where violence was not involved) to match electoral power. Wealth, status, monarchy fell before it. Now, however, it faces a sturdier foe in the esoteric authority of *expertise*. Almost every statute passes through the hands and the discretion of the full-time, expert administrator. As never before Congress faces the truth—that its laws are not self-executing. With the President, although too often at cross purposes with the President, Congress is concerned with the job of *reducing the discretion of the administrator*, if it is to enjoy its status as creator of law and not merely the enunciator of a pious, platitudinous public will.

The process of influencing administrative behavior begins with the statute, substantive and appropriations enactments; nothing, including presidential orders, influences administrative decisions like a statute, *if said statute is a clear expression*. But that is only a beginning even when the statute is unambiguous, which is almost never. In an executive-centered world it is not only the administrator but also Congress whose job is continuous. Thus more than ever before congressional government is government by committee and subcommittee. Most of the important legislative decisions are still made in committee as in the days of Woodrow Wilson's "Imperious Authority of the Standing Committees." Now these committees are almost exclusive agents of continuing congressional supervision ("oversight") and clarification of law: the new forms of congressional power.

The reader will note in Section IV there are two groups of readings, "The Formulation of Policy" and "Inquiry as an Instrument of Government." Here it should be emphasized again that without the power to make policy, Congress would not possess these additional powers; they are based on the possibility and eventuality of statutes. Inquiry includes hearings and investigations; the peculiar term "legislative oversight" is current usage for these procedures.

Hearings are used for a variety of purposes. The manifest purpose in all cases is that of collecting information from administrators, non-governmental experts, and interest-group leaders for the drafting and revision of proposed legislation. As such, hearings are intimately connected with the process of representation, a crudely systematic means of taking the largest possible number of views into account. But hearings are also used effectively as a strategy for building support or opposition in the legislative struggle. The chairman of a committee or subcommittee has the power to pick his witnesses, the order of their appearance, the amount of time to be devoted to the issue and most of the key questions. This includes the power to avoid witnesses if publicity is expected to bring adverse reactions (note Representative May's strategy in "A Law Is Passed—The Atomic Energy Act of 1946").

Most significantly, hearings are a lever for influencing the administrator. The Standing Committees are organized along departmental lines (e.g., Committee on Foreign Relations, Committee on Agriculture, Labor and Education), and the vital subcommittees of the House and Senate Appropriations Committees are organized in the same manner.[6] The occasion of a hearing can be a time of trepidation for the bureaucrats; no hearings are taken lightly. Many of these committee chairmen are old-timers who consider the bureaucrats either birds of passage (which is *true* of the top political appointees!) or their own servants. These old men get to know departmental business as well as any bureaucrat, and when one of them threatens to examine appropriations "with a fine-tooth comb" you can be sure that it is not an idle promise. These hearings can be effective even if no new laws are passed, and often it is understood that no important new legislation is even contemplated. Every administrator called as a witness can expect to defend last year's activities and to receive some instructions on expected practice for next year.[7] The hearings in

[6] Appropriations Subcommittee hearings are singled out for special treatment in MacMahon's "Congressional Oversight of Administration: The Power of the Purse." Although this essay is almost twenty years old, it still stands as the best on the subject.

[7] Of course, the administrators have their means of reprisal. Senator McCarran (Dem., Nevada) did not always get his way: In 1948 Congress—in effect,

general build up a record of "legislative intent," before *and* after the fact, that has great bearing on administrative conduct even if it does not, as is often hoped, influence the judiciary very much when their turn comes to interpret a statute.

The second tool of "oversight" is the investigation. Roughly the same as the hearings in outward appearance, the investigation covers a problem area (which can be co-extensive with one department or can include more or less than a department) rather than a specific piece of proposed legislation. For this reason, the investigation can be a more potent device, but it is also more slipshod in that it usually covers so much territory. Investigation has become a discredited technique in the estimation of many because of abuses of witnesses. But there is an important distinction to be made between investigation of the executive branch and investigation (*à la* grand jury) of the past and present conduct of private citizens. It is only in the latter case that constitutional problems of procedural due process arise.

Through hearings and investigations Congress carries the process of representation over into the bureaucracy. And it may well be that the most abiding role of Congress in the years to come will be its *service as a place where the needs of the bureaucracy are continually being balanced against the prevailing special interests in the community*. We call this our insurance against an irresponsible administrative government, but it is not quite so simple. We pay the price in decentralized and inefficient administration. Congress reaches down into the departments creating split loyalties

---

McCarran's Subcommittee on State, Commerce, and Judiciary Appropriations —reduced Commerce's appropriations for field offices in a fierce effort to effect budget reductions. In the 1949 hearings, here was the result:

> *Senator McCarran:* I notice the [Commerce] Secretary's statement this morning makes reference to the elimination of four field offices. That arrests my attention because he makes mention of the elimination of those four field offices in the West. Would you kindly tell me, if you know, what offices are to be eliminated?
>
> *Secretary Sawyer:* The basis of elimination is the volume of business done, and the ones indicated . . . are Reno, Cheyenne, Albuquerque and Phoenix. . . .
>
> *Senator McCarran:* You cannot do that to Reno, Mr. Secretary.
>
> *Secretary Sawyer:* After all, you are the doctor . . .
>
> *Mr. Gladieux* (Sawyer's Executive Assistant): . . . But under the House reductions this is the only alternative we have, to eliminate those particular offices. (From Hearings before the Subcommittee of the Committee on Appropriations, U.S. Senate, on H.R. 4016, 1949, p. 7.)

between the President and the Committees. Thus Congress builds into the executive its own problem of representation versus decision, creating many barriers to effective Presidential co-ordination. The continuing relations between Congress and the executive tend to create a kind of triangular trading pattern involving a Standing Committee or Appropriations Subcommittee (or both), an executive agency, and one or more agency clientele groups. The situation in Maass' "Congress and Water Resources" may be extreme but it is certainly not unique. Here again is the problem of balance. How centralized and efficient a bureaucracy can we afford?[8] How much interference by congressional committees (which, after all, are specialized much like the agencies and often are special pleaders on behalf of "their" agencies) can the system support and still maintain a continuous, consistent, rational posture?

These problems can only be raised; they cannot be solved. Every area of governmental activity challenges Congress in its own peculiar way. The balance between administrative autonomy and political control must be adjusted accordingly. In older, well-established activities Congress might, for instance, slacken its reins. In new and unplotted areas, where every administrative decision may be a "hard case," a precedent, closer congressional-administrative relations might follow. (Note the solution in Senator Jackson's "Congress and the Atom.")

I dwell on inquiry at some length because its importance is most likely to be overlooked. Inquiry is not a new device; it is as old as Congress itself, having developed along with the committee system. (See Professor McGeary's "The Development of Congressional Investigative Power.") Its growing importance stems from the increasing need of Congress to grant discretion to experts, therefore to delegate its intrinsic powers of legislation. What Congress gives away in chunks it tries to take back in bits.

In sum, the representative assembly performs a number of functions vital to the democratic political order. The making of laws is its manifest or constitutional function and is the most important if only because without it no other functions would follow. But legislation is not the only function of the assembly; if legislation

[8] Ironically, the sins associated with "bureaucracy" in its pejorative sense, such as inefficiency, waste, overlapping, duplication, etc., result from not enough bureaucratization! The perfect bureaucracy would have none of these.

were the only function, the assembly could hardly justify its existence. A totally bureaucratic organization, for instance, would be a much more efficient instrument and would probably be more rational and fair, however these ambiguous terms might be defined. It is the subsidiary, extraconstitutional or "latent" functions of the assembly that make it an indispensable feature of government.

The most important subsidiary or "latent" function of the representative assembly is, through its powers of policy, appropriation, inquiry, and supervision, that of balancing administrative needs against organized community desires. This extension of the representative principle into the bureaucracy may, so I have argued, prove to be its most abiding function as its legislative power atrophies into general, even if significant, policy expressions.

Finally, there are several equally significant functions that are not so directly involved in statutes or administrative control as such but are part of the legislative struggle itself. Exact assessment of these functions is impossible but their importance cannot be doubted. These will be briefly summarized:[9]

(1) *Communications.* The exposed deliberations of the assembly enlarge the area of conflict and widen public awareness of problems and proposed solutions. Wilson offers suggestions for improving this function.

(2) *Legitimacy.* The ritual of formulating public policy among 535 participants and hundreds of influential outsiders tends to reaffirm faith in democratic procedures. Modern civilizations never entirely eliminate the more primitive instincts, including the need for ritual. By acting out the social struggle before the world, Congress is the grandest of all stages for the political passion play. Furthermore, to commit the powerful to this *method* of settling conflicts tends also to commit them to the *outcomes*, even in adversity.[10] And, to be Machiavellian, with so many participants it is possible for dissatisfied groups to blame individual members *without losing faith in the institution itself*.

(3) *Power.* "Representation stabilizes the power structure by providing a mean between the extremes of concentration and dis-

[9] I have relied heavily upon Harold Lasswell and Abraham Kaplan, *Power and Society*. (Yale University Press, New Haven, 1950, pp. 161–169.)

[10] See Professor Friedrich's interesting notion of "recurrent integration."

persion of power." [11] The one is intolerable, the other is impractical. There may be more powerful men in the country than ordinary Congressmen, but they must eventually go to Congress to build greater support if their demands are to be made legitimate claims. Again to be Machiavellian, the size of the assembly makes it easier for the individual Congressman to hide his pursuit of the public interest when such pursuit conflicts with constituency interests. Thus the old British adage that "The Socialist Deputy is more deputy than Socialist."

Here then are some fragments and intimations of the total context of representative government. It is the responsible citizen's task to study and evaluate the inner workings of the system for himself. I have, in Section V, offered three somber but reflective interpretations of representative government today. I have deliberately juxtaposed differing views in hopes that the student might become cross-pressured sufficiently to undertake his own inquiry.

The materials in this anthology offer, I feel, an excellent basis for such an undertaking. They have been arranged in an order consistent with the theme set out above, that of representation *versus* government, and it was my aim in this introduction to give continuity and inter-relation to the essays.

A good case study can, of course, be the source of several morals. Many of the articles included here can, therefore, be used for purposes other than those for which they have been categorized. Perhaps it would be useful to offer a few suggestions for alternative uses:

In dealing with the topic of Chapter Three, "Internal Organization and Processes," all of the articles in Chapter Four are equally applicable. On the committee system, Chapter Eight is strongly relevant, as are the policy cases by James Landis and Byron Miller in Seven. Further emphasis on parties and elections can be gotten from Friedrich (in One), Goodwin (in Three), Mazo and Dexter (in Five) and Riker (in Six). On the role of the executive, Berdahl (in Four) and the Landis and Miller case studies (in Seven) make good additions. The articles by Shuman (in Three) and Maass and Mann (in Six) are excellent policy-making cases in addition to the three in Seven. Finally, all of the articles in Sections II through IV should be used as evidence to weigh

[11] Lasswell and Kaplan, *op. cit.*, p. 166.

against the bold interpretations of Section V. For example, does Mills' argument fit any of the cases on policy formulation, particularly "The Day We Didn't Go to War"? Theories and evaluations are hardly useful unless they can account for at least a clear majority of known cases.

Every reader and every teacher will discover gaps and weaknesses in subject-matter coverage. This is inevitable and unavoidable in anthologies and is likely to be especially evident here. This is the price I was willing to pay for a short and inexpensive volume with substantial pieces rather than fragments. For many purposes, including armchair study and introductory American Government courses, this anthology ought to be more than sufficient. For further work in the field, particularly for use in advanced courses in the legislative process, this volume is best used as supplementary reading—as a filler source—in conjunction with the *Congressional Quarterly* and any basic textbook on Congress.

I am grateful to the authors and publishers of the works included herein for granting their permissions. The words and ideas from here to the end remain those of the original authors, although I am alone responsible for all harm done in editing and in the creation of their setting.

ACKNOWLEDGMENTS

The editor, like the author, always carries to press a considerable burden of indebtedness to others. While my greatest debt is to the original authors and their publishers, there are others who have an important share in this volume. The hardy professionals on the staff of Little, Brown head the list, particularly Donald R. Hammonds whose advice was invaluable and whose carrot-and-stick strategies were brilliant. I would also like to thank Professors Murray Levin, Donald Matthews, Richard Fenno, Fred Greenstein, Raymond E. Wolfinger, and James David Barber for their many helpful criticisms and suggestions at various stages of preparation. Miss Anna Lane of the Cornell School of Industrial and Labor Relations is deserving of special mention not only because of her extraordinary stenographic talents but also because of her uncommon patience with my crude editorial markings. I am also deeply obliged to my sister Bettie for the sacrifice of many holiday hours. Finally, there were my students in Gov. 218 at Cornell, to whom I gratefully dedicate this little volume.

T. J. L.

SECTION I *Representative Government*

Chapter One REPRESENTATIVE GOVERNMENT: The More Perfect Union?

AFFIRMATIVE

The Ideally Best Polity

JOHN STUART MILL

There is no difficulty in showing that the ideally best form of government is that in which the sovereignty, or supreme controlling power in the last resort, is vested in the entire aggregate of the community; every citizen not only having a voice in the exercise of that ultimate sovereignty, but being, at least occasionally, called on to take an actual part in the government, by the personal discharge of some public function, local or general.

To test this proposition, it has to be examined in reference to the two branches into which . . . the inquiry into the goodness of a government conveniently divides itself, namely, how far it promotes the good management of the affairs of society by means of the existing faculties, moral, intellectual, and active, of its vari-

From John Stuart Mill, *Considerations on Representative Government* (pp. 141-151), Basil Blackwell edition, 1948.

ous members, and what is its effect in improving or deteriorating those faculties.

The ideally best form of government, it is scarcely necessary to say, does not mean one which is practicable or eligible in all states of civilization but the one which, in the circumstances in which it is practicable and eligible, is attended with the greatest amount of beneficial consequences, immediate and prospective. A completely popular government is the only polity which can make out any claim to this character. It is pre-eminent in both the departments between which the excellence of a political constitution is divided. It is both more favourable to present good government, and promotes a better and higher form of national character, than any other polity whatsoever.

Its superiority in reference to present well-being rests upon two principles of as universal truth and applicability as any general propositions which can be laid down respecting human affairs. The first is, that the rights and interests of every or any person are only secure from being disregarded when the person interested is himself able, and habitually disposed, to stand up for them. The second is, that the general prosperity attains a greater height, and is more widely diffused, in proportion to the amount and variety of the personal energies enlisted in promoting it.

Putting these two propositions into a shape more special to their present application; human beings are only secure from evil at the hands of others in proportion as they have the power of being, and are, self-protecting; and they only achieve a high degree of success in their struggle with Nature in proportion as they are self-dependent, relying on what they themselves can do, either separately or in concert, rather than on what others do for them.

The former proposition—that each is the only safe guardian of his own rights and interests—is one of those elementary maxims of prudence, which every person, capable of conducting his own affairs, implicitly acts upon, whatever he himself is interested. Many, indeed, have a great dislike to it as a political doctrine, and are fond of holding it up to obloquy, as a doctrine of universal selfishness. To which we may answer, that whenever it ceases to be true that mankind, as a rule, prefer themselves to others, and those nearest to them to those more remote, from the moment Communism is not only practicable, but the only defensible form of society; and will, when that time arrives, be assuredly carried into effect. For my own part, not believing in universal selfishness, I have no difficulty in admitting that Communism would even now be practicable among the élite of mankind, and may become so among the rest. But as this opinion is anything but popular with those defenders of existing institutions who find fault with the doctrine of the general predominance of self-interest, I am inclined to think they do in reality believe that most men consider themselves before other people. It is not, however, necessary to affirm even this much in order to support the claim of all to participate in the sovereign power. We need not suppose that when power resides in an exclusive class, that class will knowingly and deliberately sacrifice the other classes to themselves: it suffices that, in the absence of its natural defenders, the interest of the excluded is always in danger of being overlooked; and, when looked at, is seen with very different eyes from those of the persons whom it directly concerns. . . .

It is an adherent condition of human affairs that no intention, however sincere, of protecting the interests of others can make it safe or salutary to tie up their own hands. Still more obviously true is it, that by their own hands only can any positive and durable improvement of their circumstances in life be worked out. Through the joint influence of these two principles, all free communities have both been more exempt from social injustice and crime, and have attained more brilliant prosperity, than any others, or than they themselves after they lost their freedom. Contrast the free states of the world, while their freedom lasted, with the contemporary subjects of monarchical or oligarchical despotism: the Greek cities with the Persian satrapies; the Italian republics and the free towns of Flanders and Germany, with the feudal monarchies of Europe; Switzerland, Holland, and England, with Austria or anterevolutionary France. Their superior prosperity was too obvious ever to have been gainsaid: while their superiority in good government and social relations is proved by the prosperity, and is manifest besides in every page of history. If we compare, not one age with another, but the different governments which co-existed in the same age, no amount of disorder which exaggeration itself can pretend to have existed amidst the publicity of the free states can be compared for a moment with the contemptuous trampling upon the mass of the people which pervaded the whole life of the monarchical countries, or the disgusting individual tyranny which was of more than daily occurrence under the systems of plunder which they called fiscal arrangements, and in the secrecy of their frightful courts of justice.

It must be acknowledged that the benefits of freedom, so far as they have hitherto been enjoyed, were obtained by the extension of its privileges to a part only of the community; and that a government in which they are extended impartially to all is a desideratum still unrealized. But though every approach to this has an independent value, and in many cases more than an approach could not, in the existing state of general improvement, be made, the participation of all in these benefits is the ideally perfect conception of free government. In proportion as any, no matter who, are excluded from it, the interests of the excluded are left without the guarantee accorded to the rest, and they themselves have less scope and encouragement than they might otherwise have to that exertion of their energies for the good of themselves and of the community, to which the general prosperity is always proportioned.

Thus stands the case as regards present well-being; the good management of the affairs of the existing generation. If we now pass to the influence of the form of government upon character, we shall find the superiority of popular government over every other to be, if possible, still more decided and indisputable.

This question really depends upon a still more fundamental one, viz., which of two common types of character, for the general good of humanity, it is most desirable should predominate—the active, or the passive type; that which struggles against evils, or that which endures them: that which bends to circumstances, or that which endeavours to make circumstances bend to itself.

The commonplaces of moralists, and the general sympathies of mankind, are in favour of the passive type. Energetic characters may be admired, but the acquiescent and submissive are those which most men personally prefer. The passiveness of our neighbours increases our sense of security, and plays into the hands of our wilfulness. Passive characters, if we do not happen to need their activity, seem an obstruction the less in our own path. A contented character is not a dangerous rival. Yet nothing is more certain than that improvement in human affairs is wholly the work of the uncontented characters; and, moreover, that it is much easier for an active mind to acquire the virtues of patience than for a passive one to assume those of energy.

Of the three varieties of mental excellence, intellectual, practical, and moral, there never could be any doubt in regard to the first two which side had the advantage. All intellectual superiority in the fruit of active effort. Enterprise, the desire to keep moving, to be trying and accomplishing new things for our own benefit or that of others, is the parent even of speculative, and much more of practical, talent. The intellectual culture compatible with the other type is of that feeble and vague description which belongs to a mind that stops at amusement, or at simple contemplation. The test of real and vigorous thinking, the thinking which ascertains truths instead of dreaming dreams, is successful application to practice. Where that purpose does not exist, to give definiteness, precision, and an intelligible meaning to thought, it generates nothing better than the mystical metaphysics of the Pythagoreans or the Vedas. With respect to practical improvement, the case is still more evident. The character which improves human life is that which struggles with natural powers and tendencies, not that which gives way to them. The self-benefiting qualities are all on the side of the active and energetic character: and the habits and conduct which promote the advantage of each individual member of the community must be at least a part of those which conduce most in the end to the advancement of the community as a whole.

But on the point of moral preferability, there seems at first sight to be room for doubt. I am not referring to the religious feeling which has so generally existed in favour of the inactive character, as being more in harmony with the submission due to the divine will. Christianity as well as other religions has fostered this sentiment; but it is the prerogative of Christianity, as regards this and many other perversions, that it is able to throw them off. Abstractedly from religious considerations, a passive character, which yields to obstacles instead of striving to overcome them, may not indeed be very useful to others, no more than to itself, but it might be expected to be at least inoffensive. Contentment is always counted among the moral virtues. But it is a complete error to suppose that contentment is necessarily or naturally attendant on passivity of character; and useless it is, the moral consequences are mischievous. Where there exists a desire for advantages not possessed, the mind which does not potentially possess them by means of its own energies is apt to look with hatred and malice on those who do. The person bestirring himself with hopeful prospects to improve his circumstances is the one who feels goodwill towards others engaged in, or who have succeeded in, the same pursuit. And where the majority are so engaged, those who do not attain the object have had the tone given to their feelings by the general habit of the country, and ascribe their failure to want of effort or opportunity, or to their personal ill luck. But those who, while desiring what others possess, put no energy into striving for it, are either incessantly grumbling that fortune does not do for them what they do not attempt to do for themselves, or overflowing with envy and ill will towards those who possess what they would like to have. . . .

He who is continually measuring his energy against difficulties learns what are the difficulties insuperable to him, and what are those which, though he might overcome, the success is not worth the cost. He whose thoughts and activities are all needed for, and habitually employed in, practicable and useful enterprises, is the person of all others least likely to let his mind dwell with brooding discontent upon things either not worth attaining, or which are not so to him. Thus the active, self-helping character is not only intrinsically the best, but is the likeliest to acquire all that is really excellent or desirable in the opposite type.

Now there can be no kind of doubt that the passive type of character is favoured by the government of one or a few, and the active self-helping type by that of the Many. Irresponsible rulers need the quiescence of the ruled more than they need any activity but that which they can compel. Submissiveness to the prescriptions of men as necessities of nature is the lesson inculcated by all governments upon those who are wholly without participation in them. The will of superiors, and the law as the will of superiors, must be passively yielded to. But no men are mere instruments or materials in the hands of their rulers who have will or spirit or a spring of internal activity in the rest of their proceedings: and any manifestation of these qualities, instead of receiving encouragement from despots, has to get itself forgiven by them. Even when irresponsible rulers are not sufficiently conscious of danger from the mental activity of their subjects to be desirous of repressing it, the position itself is a repression. Endeavour is even more effectually restrained by the certainty of its impotence than by any positive discouragement. Between subjection to the will of others, and the virtues of self-help and self-government, there is a natural incompatibility. This is more or less complete, according as the bondage is strained or relaxed. Rulers differ very much in the length to which they carry the control of the free agency of their subjects, or the supression of it by managing their business for them. But the difference is in degree, not in principle; and the best despots often go the greatest lengths in chaining up the free agency of their subjects. A bad despot, when his own personal indulgences have been provided for, may sometimes be willing to let the people alone; but a good despot insists on doing them good, by making them do their own business in a better way than they themselves know of. The regulations which restricted to fixed processes all the leading branches of French manufacturers were the work of the great Colbert.

Very different is the state of the human faculties where a human being feels himself under no other external restraint than the necessities of nature, or mandates of society which he has his share in imposing, and which it is open to him, if he thinks them wrong, publicly to dissent from, and exert himself actively to get altered. No doubt, under a government partially popular, this freedom may be exercised even by those who are not partakers in the full privileges of citizenship. But it is a great additional stimulus to any one's self-help and self-reliance when he starts from even ground, and has not to feel that his success depends on the impression he can make upon the sentiments and dispositions of a body of whom he is not one. It is a great discouragement to an individual, and a still greater one to a class, to be left out of the constitution; to be reduced to plead from outside the door to the arbiters of their destiny, not taken into consultation within. The maximum of the invigorating effect of freedom upon the character is only obtained when the person acted on either is, or is looking forward to becoming, a citizen as fully privileged as any other. What is still more important than even this matter of feeling is the practical discipline which the character obtains from the occasional demand made upon the citizens to exercise, for a time and in their turn, some social function. It is not sufficiently considered how little there is in most men's ordinary life to give any largeness either to their conception or to their sentiments. Their work is a routine; not a labour of love, but of self-interest in the most elementary form, the satisfaction of daily wants; neither the thing done, nor the process of doing it, introduces the mind to thoughts or feelings extending beyond individuals; if instructive books are within their reach, there is no stimulus to read them; and in most cases the individual has no access to any person of cultivation much superior to his own. Giving him something to do for the public, supplies, in a measure, all these deficiencies. If circumstances allow the amount of public duty assigned him to be considerable, it makes him an educated man. Notwithstanding the defects of the social system and moral ideas of antiquity, the practice of the dicastery and the ecclesia raised the intellectual standard of an average Athenian citizen far beyond anything of which there is yet an example in any other mass of men, ancient or modern. The proofs of this are apparent in every page of our great historian of Greece; but we need scarcely look further than to the high quality of the addresses which their great orators deemed best calculated to act with effect on their understanding and will. A benefit of the same kind, though far less in degree, is produced on Englishmen of the lower middle class by their liability to be placed on juries and to serve parish offices; which, though it does not occur to so many, nor is so continuous nor introduces them to so great a variety of elevated considerations, as to admit of comparison with the public education which every citizen of Athens obtained from her democratic institutions, must make them nevertheless very different beings, in range of ideas and development of faculties, from those who have done nothing in their lives but drive a quill, or sell goods over a counter. Still more salutary is the moral part of the instruction afforded by the participation of the private citizen, if even rarely, in public function. He is called upon, while so engaged, to weigh interests not his own; to be guided, in case of conflicting claims, by another rule than his private partialities; to apply, at every turn, principles and maxims which have for their reason of existence the common good: and he usually finds associated with him in the same work minds more familiarised than his own with these ideas and operations, whose study it will be to supply reasons to his understanding, and stimulation to his feeling for the general interest. He is made to feel himself one of the public, and whatever is for their benefit to be for his benefit. Where this school of public spirit does not exist, scarcely any sense is entertained that private persons, in no eminent social situation, owe any duties to society, except to obey the laws and submit to the government. There is no unselfish sentiment of identification with the public. Every thought or feeling, either of interest or of duty, is absorbed in the individual and in the family. The man never thinks of any collective interest, of any objects to be pursued jointly with others, but only in competition with them, and in some measure at their expense. A neighbour, not being an ally or an associate, since he is never engaged in any common understanding for joint benefit, is therefore only a rival. Thus even private morality suffers, while public is actually extinct. Were this the universal and only possible state of things, the utmost aspirations of the lawgiver or the moralist could only stretch to make the bulk of the community a flock of sheep innocently nibbling the grass side by side.

From these accumulated considerations it is evident that the only government which can fully satisfy all the exigencies of the social state is one in which the whole people participate; that any participation, even in the smallest public function, is useful; that the participation should everywhere be as great as the general degree of improvement of the community will allow; and that nothing less can be ultimately desirable than the admission of all to a share in the sovereign power of the State. But since all cannot, in a community exceeding a single small town, participate personally in any but some very minor portions of the public business, it follows that the ideal type of a perfect government must be representative.

NEGATIVE

Representation and Suffrage

GAETANO MOSCA

1. Many doctrines that advocate liberty and equality, as the latter terms are still commonly understood—doctrines which the eighteenth century thought out, which the nineteenth perfected and tried to apply and which the twentieth will probably dispense

with or modify substantially—are summed up and given concrete form in the theory that views universal suffrage as the foundation of all sound government. It is commonly believed that the only free, equitable and legitimate government is a government that is based upon the will of the majority, the majority by its vote delegating its powers for a specified length of time to men who represent it. Down to a few generations ago—and even today in the eyes of many writers and statesmen—all flaws in representative government were attributed to incomplete or mistaken applications of the principles of representation and suffrage. . . .

A following so large, beliefs so widespread, are not to be discredited in a page or two. We shall not, therefore, attempt a systematic refutation of the theories on which universal suffrage is based. We shall simply refer to some of the main considerations that most seriously undermine the foundations on which universal suffrage as an intellectual edifice rests. We deem it sufficient for our purposes here to demonstrate that the assumption that the elected official is the mouthpiece of the majority of his electors is as a rule not consistent with the facts; and we believe that this can be proved by facts of ordinary experience and by certain practical observations that anyone can make on the manner in which elections are conducted.

What happens in other forms of government—namely, that an organized minority imposes its will on the disorganized majority—happens also and to perfection, whatever the appearances to the contrary, under the representative system. When we say that the voters "choose" their representative, we are using a language that is very inexact. The truth is that the representative *has himself elected* by the voters, and, if that phrase should seem too inflexible and too harsh to fit some cases, we might qualify it by saying that *his friends have him elected*. In elections, as in all other manifestations of social life, those who have the will and, especially, the moral, intellectual and material *means* to force their will upon others take the lead over the others and command them.

The political mandate has been likened to the power of attorney that is familiar in private law. But in private relationships, delegations of powers and capacities always presuppose that the principal has the broadest freedom in choosing his representative. Now in practice, in popular elections, that freedom of choice, though complete theoretically, necessarily becomes null, not to say ludicrous. If each voter gave his vote to the candidate of his heart, we may be sure that in almost all cases the only result would be a wide scattering of votes. When very many wills are involved, choice is determined by the most various criteria, almost all of them subjective, and if such wills were not coordinated and organized it would be virtually impossible for them to coincide in the spontaneous choice of one individual. If his vote is to have any efficacy at all, therefore, each voter is forced to limit his choice to a very narrow field, in other words to a choice among the two or three persons who have some chance of succeeding; and the only ones who have any chance of succeeding are those whose candidacies are championed by groups, by committees, by *organized minorities*. . . .

How do these organized minorities form about individual candidates or groups of candidates? As a rule they are based on considerations of property and taxation, on common material interests, on ties of family, class, religion, sect or political party. Whether their component personnels be good or bad, there can be no doubt that such committees—and the representatives who are now their tools, now their leaders or "bosses"—represent the organization of a considerable number of social values and forces. In practice, therefore, the representative system results not at all in government by the majority; it results in the participation of a certain number of social values in the guidance of the state, in the fact that many political forces which in an absolute state, a state ruled by a bureaucracy alone, would remain inert and without influence upon government become organized and so exert an influence on government.

2. In examining the relations between the representative system and juridical defense, a number of distinctions and observations have to be borne in mind.

The great majority of voters are passive, it is true, in the sense that they have not so much freedom to choose their representatives as a limited right to exercise an option among a number of candidates. Nevertheless, limited as it may be, that capacity has the effect of obliging candidates to try to win a weight of votes that will serve to tip the scales in their direction, so that they make every effort to flatter, wheedle and obtain the good will of the voters. In this way certain sentiments and passions of the "common herd" come to have their influence on the mental attitudes of the representatives themselves, and echoes of a widely disseminated opinion, or of any serious discontent, easily come to be heard in the highest spheres of government.

It may be objected that this influence of the majority of voters is necessarily confined to the broad lines of political policy and makes itself felt only on a very few topics of a very general character, and that within limits as narrow as that even in absolute governments the ruling classes are obliged to take account of mass sentiments. In fact the most despotic of governments has to proceed very cautiously when it comes to shocking the sentiments, convictions or prejudices of the majority of the governed, or to requiring of that majority pecuniary sacrifices to which they are not accustomed. But wariness about giving offense will be much greater when every single representative, whose vote may be useful or necessary to the executive branch of government, knows that the discontent of the masses may at almost any moment bring about the triumph of a rival. We are aware that this is a two-edged argument. The masses are not always any wiser in discerning and protecting their interests than their representatives are; and we are acquainted with regions where public discontent has created greater obstacles to desirable reforms than the mistakes of parliamentary representatives and ministries.

The representative system, furthermore, has widely different effects according as the molecular composition of the electoral body varies. If all the voters who have some influence, because of education or social position, are members of one or another of the organized minorities, and if only a mass of poor and ignorant citizens are left outside of them, it is impossible for the latter to exercise their right of option and control in any real or effective manner. In these circumstances, of the various organized minorities that are disputing the field, that one infallibly wins which spends most money or lies most persuasively. . . .

The real juridical safeguard in representative governments lies in the public discussion that takes place within representative assemblies. Into those assemblies the most disparate political forces and elements make their way, and the existence of a small independent minority is often enough to control the conduct of a large majority and, especially, to prevent the bureaucratic organization from becoming omnipotent. But when, beyond being organs of discussion and publicizing, assemblies come to concentrate all the prestige and power of legitimate authority in their own hands, as regularly happens in parliamentary governments, then in spite of the curb of public discussion the whole administrative and judiciary machine falls prey to the irresponsible and anonymous tyranny of those who win in the elections and speak in the name of the people, and we get one of the worst types of political organization that the real majority in a modern society can possibly be called upon to tolerate.

In governments that are based very largely on the representative principle the referendum is in some respects a fairly effective instrument. By it the mass of likes and dislikes, enthusiasms and angers, which, when they are truly widespread and truly general, constitute what may quite plausibly be called public opinion, is enabled to react against the conduct and enterprise of the governing minority. In a referendum it is a question not of making a choice, or an election, but of pronouncing a "yes" or a "no" upon a specific question. No single vote, therefore, is lost, and each single vote has its practical importance independently of any coordination or organization along lines of sect, party or committee. However, the democratic ideal of majority government is not realized even by the referendum. Governing is not altogether a matter of allowing or prohibiting modifications in constitutions or laws. It is quite as much a matter of managing the whole military, financial, judiciary and administrative machine, or of influencing those who manage it. Then again, even if the referendum does serve to limit the arbitrariness of the governing class, it is no less true that often it seriously hampers improvements in the political organism. Such improvements will always be more readily appreciated by a governing class, however selfish and corrupt it may be, than by the ill-informed majority of the governed. In many countries, for instance, if increases in taxes were to be submitted to referendum, they would always be rejected, even though they were of the most unqualified urgency and would be of the most obvious benefit to the public.

SYNTHESIS

The Dual Nature of Representation

CARL FRIEDRICH

Historically speaking, representative assemblies developed in most European countries in the course of the later Middle Ages as an important part of the medieval constitutional order. Very often the three "estates" were composed of nobility, clergy, and the merchants of the cities (the burgesses.) But the greatest variations existed in this respect. The most important of these assemblies is undoubtedly the English Parliament, where the higher nobility were joined with the higher clergy in the "Lords Spiritual and Temporal," while the knights together with the burgesses constituted the Commons. Thus the more important groups in the community—nowadays often referred to as "classes"—were represented and called together by the king through his "minister" for the purpose of securing their consent to extraordinary taxes or levies. This was necessary because the undeveloped state of central administrative systems and the absence of effective means of coercion . . . rendered the collection of such levies impossible without local co-operation. Quite naturally, these representatives when gathered together undertook to bargain for their consent to such grants of money; they presented complaints and petitions, which the crown had to heed in order to secure what it wanted. These, then, were not national representatives but agents of local powers acting under special instructions or mandates. This was true, however, only as long as they acted separately. When the king and the two houses of Parliament acted together, after having settled their differences and reached a compromise, they were taken to *represent* the whole body politic. More particularly, they were supposed to represent the entire body politic of the realm of England when acting as a high court, which was taken to be their most solemn function down to the seventeenth century. Historically, then, one cannot draw a hard and fast line between agents with definite instructions or mandates and representatives empowered to attend to a general task. An elected body may and

From Carl J. Friedrich, *Constitutional Government and Democracy,* revised edition, (excerpts from Chapters XIV-XVI), Ginn and Company, Boston, 1950.

usually will be both a set of agents from different interests, and a representative group determining the common interest. Therefore, . . . [with] Burke, a parliament is both: a deliberative assembly from *one* nation, with *one* interest, that of the whole, and a congress of ambassadors from different and hostile interests. . . .

How can we explain the fact that legislation came to be considered the peculiar province of representative, popularly elected bodies, when in fact medieval representatives had little or no concern with legislation? Because ever since the sixteenth century, legislation was believed to be the most striking manifestation of political and governmental power. Legislation entailed the making of rules binding upon the whole community. Bodin maintained that this power was the peculiar characteristic of a state. As we have seen before, the medieval notion of law as eternal custom, as something already there and merely to be discovered by learned men, was giving way to a realization that laws are man-made, that they are essentially decisions as to what ought to be rather than as to what is. The shift, of course, was merely one in view and emphasis. The High Court of Parliament had changed the law in the process of finding it, and so had the other courts of the realm. But the great Coke, before his identification with Parliament, insisted at times upon the "higher law" as a standard and criterion by which to evaluate parliamentary enactments. . . . He saw it as fixed and immutable, the peculiar and precious heritage of every Englishman, an embodiment of the principles upon which his life was built. This relation of general rules to religious, moral, and other principles was the other pillar upon which men's preoccupation with laws and legislation as a manifestation of governmental power rested. That human beings cannot be forced in matters of principle is the underlying idea. A specific act of government may be justified in terms of a specific emergency, but no general rule ever can be so justified. This leads to the important if elementary consideration that the making of a rule presupposes that there is a series of events which have certain aspects in common. In other words, there must be a "normal" situation. This means that time is available for deliberation to determine what had best be done regarding such a situation. Representative, deliberative bodies require time, obviously, and therefore legislation seems to be peculiarly fitted for such bodies. Some writers on the Continent have thereby been led into linking parliamentary deliberation to the romantic passion for everlasting conversation, a generalization which is as glittering as it is uninformed. For parliamentary deliberation is entirely focused upon and organized with a view toward action, the enactment of a general rule. The history and practice of parliamentary procedure proves this beyond doubt. But the enactment of such a general rule requires careful co-ordination of conflicting viewpoints. Really effective compromises must be reached. Such compromises are justified, because any considerable group of people in a given community possesses the capacity effectively to resist the enforcement of certain rules which they do not, or which they cannot, approve.

To put the foregoing analysis into a very abstract formula, one might say: the community requires recurrent integration. The failure to perceive this fact underlies the totalitarian contempt for elected representatives as valuable guides in the enactment of permanent legislation. The totalitarian emphasis upon the desirability of unity in a community does not solve the problems which arise from the diversity of actual interests. They assert that only a single leader, or a small elite, can achieve effective integration. They assert that when the conflict of norms in a given community becomes insoluble, when therefore the several groups have no common ground upon which to reach an effective compromise, the arbitrary superimposition of one possible solution is the only alternative to civil war or complete dissolution. Communists and Fascists both maintain that such was the case in recent times, and they both proceeded to impose their particular norms. Once one grants their premise—and one has to when *their* factions grow to any considerable size—he cannot escape from their conclusion. But this is so not because there is a disagreement on fundamentals, for such we have had all the time. It is so because these particular groups have adopted organized violence as a method of party warfare. Constitutionalism and democracy, if they are true to themselves, will outlaw such methods of party strife as private uniforms, police, and the rest. This outlawing was done in the British *Public Order Act* of 1936 . . . and also in a number of American states. Federal legislation may be desirable. If this is done, there is no need for denying the rights of citizenship, such as our civil liberties, to people whose views are antidemocratic. The provisions exempting Germans with certain antidemocratic views from the protection of the basic human rights of the new German Basic Law . . . appear much too broad from this standpoint; "abuse" of these rights "to attack the free, democratic basic order" seems much too vague a criterion for so dangerous a limitation on rights which the first article had declared to be "inviolable and inalienable." Compromise is, therefore, essential in making general rules; through argument and discussion the area of agreement is determined in the representative legislature. . . .

The underlying idea of all the various systems [of proportional representation] is to secure a representative assembly reflecting with more or less mathematical exactness the various divisions in the electorate. Why should such divisions be reflected? They should be "represented"! The voice of minorities should be heard! Justice requires that no votes be lost. . . . A man of the eminence of John Stuart Mill extolled the virtues of the scheme in his *Considerations on Representative Government* and called it one of "the very greatest improvements yet made in the theory and practice of government." Yet proportional representation shifts the basic meaning of representation. An important part of representation . . . is to represent the citizenry as a whole, not just the divisions among them. Representation means the exercise of the people's influence through a smaller number acting in their behalf. Proportional representation, on the other hand, looks upon the divisions in the electorate as the only entities to be represented; in the last analysis it looks upon the individual as the representable element or unit. . . .

. . . [L]et us assume for a moment that representation through a person elected by the majority of your fellow townsmen is "unjust" to some minority, and that this can be remedied by giving this minority a chance of combining with others constituting a similar minority elsewhere. If there were only one such minority, it would simply mean that there would be more men in parliament to criticize than before. This would mean less action, rather than different action. If there were many such minorities, so that no group any longer had a majority, it would mean complete inaction over long periods. In either case, is it not a question of competing claims? Why should the problem of what is just to a minority be given precedence over what is just to the majority? Admittedly the majority wants action. Such action is, through Proportional Representation, or P. R., being delayed or altogether prevented. What is the justice of that? It would appear that Mill, in his concern over the minority, had neglected the majority. Problems of justice are problems of adjustment between conflicting claims. The election of representatives therefore always involves the paring down of *some* claims; justice can only be achieved if these claims are equitably adjusted. Presumably the majority's claims are weightier than those of any minority. Representation is a broad thing; representatives are elected so that many may participate indirectly in the essential tasks. The majority participates through acting, the minority through discussion and criticism. If the majority fails to be represented adequately, because its representatives are unable to act, the injustice is just as great, or greater, than if the minority fails to be represented adequately, because its representatives cannot talk as much as they would like to. It is not a question of justice, then, but of more adequate representation of minorities. This may or may not be a desirable thing. But it should be considered on its merits. . . .

Unquestionably, Bagehot put his finger upon the central objection from a governmental standpoint. . . . In terms of the accepted focal interests of political science, it is more important that a majority system of elections oblige the voter to *decide* between two or more alternatives than that the constituency be compulsory.* The need of a decision is paramount when the representative body has over and above everything else the function of constituting either the executive or the government which is to hold office as long as the representative body is willing to support it. As everyone knows, such a system of parliamentary government makes the executive dependent upon and responsible to a majority in the representative assembly. For, if the assembly becomes divided into so many factions that there cannot be found a stable majority for the executive's support, all governmental activity becomes paralyzed. It is appalling to read with care the astounding documentation which Dr. Hermens has assembled to show how in country after country precisely this paralysis crept in. Eventually the people lost hope that effective action would ever be produced, and "parliamentarism" became a by-word for inefficiency and inaction. England resisted the lure of proportionalism. Sticking to

* *I.e.,* to Bagehot, the simplifying of alternatives in the single-member, geographical constituency of Britain and the United States outweighed the sacrifice of the unrepresented minorities—those who consistently voted for the losers.—Ed.

their traditions, most Englishmen, including the Labour party, rejected P. R., recognizing it as the most important function of the English Parliament to support the government. For a long time this function was obscured by the doctrine of a separation of powers, particularly since such a separation prevailed in the United States. Parliament was looked upon as a legislative assembly. But while the legislative function is quite important, it is not *as* important as the maintenance and functioning of the government itself. The influence of the whole electorate upon this executive management must become focalized into a few clear alternatives. For, as Lowell has so clearly shown, large numbers of people cannot decide between any but two or three very simple alternatives.

But what if the elected representatives do not have this function of constituting the executive? It is, after all, by no means a foregone conclusion that the function of the representative assembly should be a decision as to who shall govern. Not only in the United States, but in Switzerland and in prewar Germany, the main function of the representative assembly was legislation. Such legislation, particularly modern economic and social legislation, touches the everyday interests of all citizens, and the divisions of interest between them are fairly persistent. It cannot, for example, reasonably be expected that the employer and capitalist would be persuaded to hand all profits over to his workers, nor can we hope that the workers will readily yield to those who expect them to be satisfied with the joy of work, and be content with long hours at starvation wages. Legislation touching these and many similar issues between the various groups in the community must be framed as an acceptable compromise in which all relevant views are voiced with a vigor approximately comparable to their actual strength in the community. A representative assembly, then, whose primary function is the framing of such legislation, would greatly benefit from a well-thought-out system which would bring into it the various groups in the community in rough proportion at least to their strength. But there must still be an effective majority ready to support a fairly coherent policy. The difficulties in the way of achieving that purpose are great under the American presidential system even without any multiplication of parties such as proportionalism envisages and engenders.

. . . [T]he prevalent English and American opinion against

proportional representation is practically sound. There are special conditions which might mitigate this conclusion. But the proportional representation enthusiasts, who would argue from the relative success of proportionalism in some small countries that we should try it in Great Britain and the United States, goes wrong. Although in the United States the constitutional order is based upon a separation-of-powers scheme, the President as chief executive must be elected by a simple plurality. While this might act as a deterrent to the development of minor parties, certain religious, class, and race cleaves might, in the course of time, emerge and plague us by their intransigeant attitude. The appeal of P. R. lies in the promise it holds out for breaking up corrupt machines. There can be no question that P. R. starts out by doing this quite effectively. But after the machine politicians have caught their breath, they are quite skillful in "taking over" proportional representation. Since proportional representation in the long run strengthens, rather than weakens party, that is, machine, control, the bosses return with another rampart added to their fortress. As Newton D. Baker put it in a communication to the *Cleveland Plain Dealer* on July 25, 1935: "We have groups of all sorts and kinds, formed around religious, racial, language, social and other contentious distinctions. Proportional representation invites these groups to seek to harden and intensify their differences by bringing them into political action where they are irrelevant, if not disturbing. A wise election system would invite them to forget these distracting prejudices." . . .

Parliaments until recently have been the institutional core of modern representative government. At present the executive, particularly when representing a majority party, is forging ahead and is tending to become the heart of representation. . . . [All] elected bodies have in common representative and deliberative functions which, though related, are quite distinct, and hence should be considered separately. The Fascist Grand Council also had representative functions; in letting itself be bellowed at by Mussolini it represented the Italian people as perfectly as the Nazi Reichstag represented the German people, but its deliberative functions were nil.

Traditionally, legislation is considered the peculiar province of representative assemblies. . . . Representative assemblies are in fact referred to as *the* legislature, although it is always at once conceded that these assemblies do not have exclusive control over legislation nor are they concerned only with legislation. Nevertheless, legislation is traditionally looked upon as their primary function. Such a view is formal rather than political. Politically speaking, the function of making laws is nowadays at least as much carried on by the central bureaucracy, which drafts all important bills in England, France, and other European countries, and to an increasing extent in the United States. The political function of representative assemblies today is not so much the initiation of legislation as the carrying on of popular education and propaganda and the integration and co-ordination of conflicting interests and viewpoints. The representative must be a master in the art of compromise. Parliaments and parliamentarians appear as integrating agencies through which the policy of the government and the claims of the various interest groups are expounded to the larger public with a view to discovering a suitable balance. There can be little doubt that this educational function is highly significant. The average citizen, that is, you and I, needs to have the pros and cons of pending proposals dramatized for him. The clash of argument in representative groups helps this greatly. The drama of the filibustering senator, though often arousing indignation, helps the citizen to appreciate the implications and significance of new legislation. The consequences of the lack of such contact between the government and the citizen are very apparent in totalitarian regimes. A great many measures of the government, which may be intrinsically necessary, meet with sullen indifference if not with hostility from the people merely because they are not understood. Occasional rhetorical outbursts on the part of a few leaders are not sufficient.

Integration is not, however, automatic, but highly dependent upon the structure of thought and outlook, feeling and interest, of the electorate. Hence the pious formula that representatives are not bound by mandate, that they are subject only to their conscience and are supposed to serve the common weal, which is repeated in so many European constitutions, while significant as a norm, may lead to differentiating as well as to integrating results. As in mathematics, so in politics, differential and integral functions are interrelated. . . .

. . . [R]epresentation and responsibility are closely linked. Representatives of the people are intended to be responsible to those whom they represent; in turn such responsible conduct enhances the representative quality. In fact, it is not too much to say that systems of representation developed out of the need of insuring constitutional responsibility. More especially elections, by permitting a recurrent review of the actions of representatives at regular intervals, are supposed to be the most rational method of establishing responsible government. This review brought about the development of parties . . . they both differentiate and integrate. While trying to integrate as many voters as possible, they succeed in integrating perhaps half of them, the other half being integrated by a competing group of leaders. Such polarization of the electorate into two focal differentiations is characteristic of the majority system of representation, while the proportional system, as we have seen, produces multiple differentiation. . . .

SECTION II *The American Congress: Powers, Organization, Processes*

Chapter Two | SCOPE OF ACTION: The Dual Nature of Federalism

THE REACH OF MODERN LAW

*Wickard** v. *Filburn*
317 U.S. 111 (1942)

Mr. Justice Jackson delivered the opinion of the Court:

The appellee [Filburn] for many years past has owned and operated a small farm in Montgomery County, Ohio, maintaining a herd of dairy cattle, selling milk, raising poultry and eggs. It has been his practice to raise a small acreage of winter wheat, sown in the Fall and harvested in the following July; to sell a portion of the crop; to feed part to poultry and livestock on the farm, some of which is sold; to use some in making flour for home consumption; and to keep the rest for the following seeding. The intended disposition of the crop here involved has not been expressly stated.

In July of 1940, pursuant to the Agricultural Adjustment Act of 1938, as then amended, there were established for the appellee's

* Secretary of Agriculture.—Ed.

1941 crop of wheat acreage allotment of 11.1 acres and a normal yield of 20.1 bushels of wheat an acre. He was given notice of such allotment in July of 1940 before the Fall planting of his 1941 crop of wheat, and again in July of 1941, before it was harvested. He sowed, however, 23 acres, and harvested from his 11.9 acres of excess acreage 239 bushels, which under the terms of the Act as amended on May 26, 1941, constituted farm marketing excess, subject to a penalty of 49 cents a bushel, or $117.11 in all. The appellee has not paid the penalty and he has not postponed or avoided it by storing the excess under regulations of the Secretary of Agriculture, or by delivering it up to the Secretary. The Committee, therefore, refused him a marketing card, which was, under the terms of Regulations promulgated by the Secretary, necessary to protect a buyer from liability to the penalty and upon its protecting lien.

The general scheme of the Agricultural Adjustment Act of 1938 as related to wheat is to control the volume moving in interstate and foreign commerce in order to avoid surpluses and shortages and the consequent abnormally low or high wheat prices and obstructions to commerce. Within prescribed limits and by prescribed standards the Secretary of Agriculture is directed to ascertain and proclaim each year a normal acreage allotment for the next crop of wheat, which is then apportioned to the states and their counties, and is eventually broken up into allotments for individual farms. Loans and payments to wheat farmers are authorized in stated circumstances.

The Act provides further that whenever it appears that the total supply of wheat as of the beginning of any marketing year, beginning July 1, will exceed a normal year's domestic consumption and export by more than 35 per cent, the Secretary shall so proclaim not later than May 15 prior to the beginning of such marketing year; and that during the marketing year a compulsory national marketing quota shall be in effect with respect to the marketing of wheat. Between the issuance of the proclamation and June 10, the Secretary must, however, conduct a referendum of farmers who will be subject to the quota to determine whether they favor or oppose it; and if more than one-third of the farmers voting in the referendum do oppose, the Secretary must prior to the effective date of the quota by proclamation suspend its operation. . . .

It is urged that under the Commerce Clause of the Constitution, Article I Sec. 8, clause 3, Congress does not possess the power it has in this instance sought to exercise. The question would merit little consideration since our decision in United States v. Darby, [1947], . . . sustaining the federal power to regulate production of goods for commerce except for the fact that this Act extends federal regulation to production not intended in any part for commerce but wholly for consumption on the farm. The Act includes a definition of "market" and its derivatives so that as related to wheat in addition to its conventional meaning it also means to dispose of "by feeding (in any form) to poultry or livestock which, or the products of which, are sold, bartered, or exchanged, or to be so disposed of." Hence, marketing quotas not only embrace all that may be sold without penalty but also what may be consumed on the premises. Wheat produced on excess acreage is designated as "available for marketing" as so defined and the penalty is imposed thereon. Penalties do not depend upon whether any part of the wheat either within or without the quota is sold or intended to be sold. The sum of this is that the Federal Government fixes a quota including all that the farmer may harvest for sale or for his own farm needs, and declares that wheat produced on excess acreage may neither be disposed of nor used except upon payment of the penalty or except it is stored as required by the Act or delivered to the Secretary of Agriculture.

Appellee says that this is a regulation of production and consumption of wheat. Such activities are, he urges, beyond the reach of Congressional power under the Commerce Clause, since they are local in character, and their effects upon interstate commerce are at most "indirect." In answer the Government argues that the statute regulates neither production nor consumption, but only marketing; and, in the alternative, that if the Act does go beyond the regulation of marketing it is sustainable as a "necessary and proper" implementation of the power of Congress over interstate commerce.

The Government's concern lest the Act be held to be a regulation of production or consumption rather than of marketing is attributable to a few dicta and decisions of this Court which might be understood to lay it down that activities such as "production," "manufacturing," and "mining" are strictly "local" and, except in special circumstances which are not present here, cannot be regulated under the commerce power because their effects upon interstate commerce are, as matter of law, only "indirect." Even today, when this power has been held to have great latitude, there is no decision of this Court that such activities may be regulated where no part of the product is intended for interstate commerce or intermingled with the subjects thereof. We believe that a review of the course of decision under the Commerce Clause will make plain, however, that questions of the power of Congress are not to be decided by reference to any formula which would give controlling force to nomenclature such as "production" and "indirect" and foreclose consideration of the actual effects of the activity in question upon interstate commerce.

At the beginning Chief Justice Marshall described the federal commerce power with a breadth never yet exceeded. . . . He made emphatic the embracing and penetrating nature of this power by warning that effective restraints on its exercise must proceed from political rather than from judicial processes. . . .

For nearly a century, however, decisions of this Court under the Commerce Clause dealt rarely with questions of what Congress might do in the exercise of its granted power under the Clause and almost entirely with the permissibility of state activity which it was claimed discriminated against or burdened interstate commerce. During this period there was perhaps little occasion for the affirmative exercise of the commerce power, and the influence of the Clause on American life and law was a negative one, resulting almost wholly from its operation as a restraint upon the powers of the states. In discussion and decision the point of reference instead of being what was "necessary and proper" to the exercise by Congress of its granted power, was often some concept of sovereignty thought to be implicit in the status of statehood. Certain activities such as "production," "manufacturing," and "mining" were occasionally said to be within the province of state governments and beyond the power of Congress under the Commerce Clause.

It was not until 1887 with the enactment of the Interstate Commerce Act that the interstate commerce power began to exert positive influence in American law and life. This first important federal resort to the commerce power was followed in 1890 by the Sherman Anti-Trust Act and, thereafter, mainly after 1903, by many others. These statutes ushered in new phases of adjudication, which required the Court to approach the interpretation of the Commerce Clause in the light of an actual exercise by Congress of its power thereunder.

When it first dealt with this new legislation, the Court adhered to its earlier pronouncement, and allowed but little scope to the power of Congress. . . . These earlier pronouncements also played an important part in several of the five cases in which this Court later held that Acts of Congress under the Commerce Clause were in excess of its power.

Even while important opinions in this line of restrictive authority were being written, however, other cases called forth broader interpretations of the Commerce Clause destined to supersede the earlier ones, and to bring about a return to the principles first enunciated by Chief Justice Marshall in Gibbons v. Ogden. . . .

In the Shreveport Rates Cases [1914] . . . , the Court held that railroad rates of an admittedly intrastate character and fixed by authority of the state might, nevertheless, be revised by the Federal Government because of the economic effects which they had upon interstate commerce. The opinion of Mr. Justice Hughes found federal intervention constitutionally authorized because of "matters having such a close and substantial relation to intrastate traffic that the control is essential or appropriate to the security of that traffic, to the efficiency of the interstate service, and to the maintenance of the conditions under which interstate commerce may be conducted upon fair terms and without molestation or hindrance." . . .

The Court's recognition of the relevance of the economic effects in the application of the Commerce Clause exemplified by this statement has made the mechanical application of legal formulas no longer feasible. Once an economic measure of the reach of the power granted to Congress in the Commerce Clause is accepted, questions of federal power cannot be decided simply by finding the activity in question to be "production" nor can consideration of its economic effects be foreclosed by calling them "indirect." The present Chief Justice has said in summary of the present state of the law: "The commerce power is not confined in its exercise to the regulation of commerce among the states. It extends to those activities intrastate which so affect interstate commerce, or the exertion of the power of Congress over it, as to make regulation of them appropriate means to the attainment of a legitimate end, the effective execution of the granted power to regulate interstate commerce. . . . The power of Congress over interstate commerce is plenary and complete in itself, may be exercised to its utmost extent, and acknowledges no limitations other than are prescribed in the Constitution. . . . It follows that no form of state activity can constitutionally thwart the regulatory power granted by the Commerce Clause to Congress. Hence the reach of that power extends to those intrastate activities which in a substantial way interfere with or obstruct the exercise of the granted power." . . .

Whether the subject of the regulation in question was "production," "consumption," or "marketing" is, therefore, not material for purposes of deciding the question of federal power before us. That an activity is of local character may help in a doubtful case to determine whether Congress intended to reach it. The same consideration might help in determining whether in the absence of Congressional action it would be permissible for the state to exert its power on the subject matter, even though in so doing it to some degree affected interstate commerce. But even if appellee's activity be local and though it may not be regarded as commerce, it may still, whatever its nature, be reached by Congress if it exerts a substantial economic effect on interstate commerce and this irrespective of whether such effect is what might at some earlier time have been defined as "direct" or "indirect."

The parties have stipulated a summary of the economics of the wheat industry. Commerce among the states in wheat is large and important. Although wheat is raised in every state but one, production in most states is not equal to consumption. Sixteen states on average have had a surplus of wheat above their own requirements for feed, seed, and food. Thirty-two states and the District of Columbia, where production has been below consumption, have looked to these surplus-producing states for their supply as well as for wheat for export and carryover.

The wheat industry has been a problem industry for some years. Largely as a result of increased foreign production and import restrictions, annual exports of wheat and flour from the United States during the ten-year period ending in 1940 averaged less than 10 per cent of total production, while during the 1920's they averaged more than 25 per cent. The decline in the export trade has left a large surplus in production which in connection with an abnormally large supply of wheat and other grains in recent years caused congestion in a number of markets; tied up railroad cars; and caused elevators in some instances to turn away grains, and railroads to institute embargoes to prevent further congestion.

Many countries, both importing and exporting, have sought to modify the impact of the world market conditions on their own economy. Importing countries have taken measures to stimulate production and self-sufficiency. The four large exporting countries of Argentina, Australia, Canada, and the United States have all undertaken various programs for the relief of growers. Such measures have been designed in part at least to protect the domestic price received by producers. Such plans have generally evolved towards control by the central government.

In the absence of regulation the price of wheat in the United States would be much affected by world conditions. During 1941 producers who cooperated with the Agricultural Adjustment program received an average price on the farm of about $1.16 a bushel as compared with the world market price of 40 cents a bushel.

Differences in farming conditions, however, make these benefits mean different things to different wheat growers. There are several large areas of specialization in wheat, and the concentration on this crop reaches 27 per cent of the crop land, and the average harvest runs as high as 155 acres. Except for some use of wheat as stock feed and for seed, the practice is to sell the crop for cash. Wheat from such areas constitutes the bulk of the interstate commerce therein.

On the other hand, in some New England states less than one percent of the crop land is devoted to wheat, and the average harvest is less than five acres per farm. In 1940 the average percentage of the total wheat production that was sold in each state as measured by value ranged from 29 per cent thereof in Wisconsin to 90 per cent in Washington. Except in regions of large-scale production, wheat is usually grown in rotation with other crops; for a nurse crop for grass seeding; and as a cover crop to prevent soil erosion and leaching. Some is sold, some kept for seed, and a percentage of the total production much larger than in areas of specialization is consumed on the farm and grown for such purpose. Such farmers, while growing some wheat, may even find the balance of their interest on the consumer's side.

The effect of consumption of home-grown wheat on interstate commerce is due to the fact that it constitutes the most variable factor in the disappearance of the wheat crop. Consumption on the farm where grown appears to vary in an amount greater than 20 per cent of the average production. The total amount of wheat consumed as food varies but relatively little, and use as seed is relatively constant.

The maintenance by government regulation of a price for wheat undoubtedly can be accomplished as effectively by sustaining or increasing the demand as by limiting the supply. The effect of the statute before us is to restrict the amount which may be produced for market and the extent as well to which one may forestall resort to the market by producing to meet his own needs. That appellee's own contribution to the demand for wheat may be trivial by itself is not enough to remove him from the scope of federal regulation where, as here, his contribution, taken together with that of many others similarly situated, is far from trivial. . . .

It is well established by decisions of this Court that the power to regulate commerce includes the power to regulate the prices at which commodities in that commerce are dealt in and practices affecting such prices. One of the primary purposes of the Act in question was to increase the market price of wheat and to that end to limit the volume thereof that could affect the market. It can hardly be denied that a factor of such volume and variability as home-consumed wheat would have a substantial influence on price and market conditions. This may arise because being in marketable condition such wheat overhangs the market and if induced by rising prices tends to flow into the market and check price increases. But if we assume that it is never marketed, it supplies a need of the man who grew it which would otherwise be reflected by purchases in the open market. Home-grown wheat in this sense competes with wheat in commerce. The stimulation of commerce is a use of the regulatory function quite as definitely as prohibitions or restrictions thereon. This record leaves us in no doubt that Congress may properly have considered that wheat consumed on the farm where grown if wholly outside the scheme of regulation would have a substantial effect in defeating and obstructing its purpose to stimulate trade therein at increased prices.

It is said, however, that this Act, forcing some farmers into the market to buy what they could provide for themselves, is an unfair promotion of the markets and prices of specializing wheat growers. It is of the essence of regulation that it lays a restraining hand on the self-interest of the regulated and that advantages from the regulation commonly fall to others. The conflicts of economic interest between the regulated and those who advantage by it are wisely left under our system to resolution by the Congress under its more flexible and responsible legislative process. Such conflicts rarely lend themselves to judicial determination. And with the wisdom, workability, or fairness, of the plan of regulation we have nothing to do. . . .

Reversed *

THE PROBLEM OF MODERN LAW

Civil Rights Cases
109 U.S. 3 (1883)

Mr. Justice Bradley delivered the opinion of the Court:

It is obvious that the primary and important question in all the cases, is the constitutionality of the law; for if the law is unconstitutional, none of the prosecutions can stand. . . .

Are [Sections 1 and 2 of the Civil Rights Act] constitutional? The 1st section, which is the principal one, cannot be fairly understood without attending to the last clause, which qualifies the preceding part. The essence of the law is, not to declare broadly that all persons shall be entitled to the full and equal enjoyment of the accommodations, advantages, facilities and privileges of inns, public conveyances and theaters; but that such enjoyment shall not be subject to any conditions applicable only to citizens of a particular race or color, or who had been in a previous condition of servitude. In other words: it is the purpose of the law to declare that, in the enjoyment of the accommodations and privileges of inns, public conveyances, theaters and other places of public amusement, no distinction shall be made between citizens of different race or color, or between those who have and those who have not been slaves. Its effect is, to declare that, in all inns, public conveyances and places of amusement, colored citizens, whether for-

* The lower court had decided in favor of Filburn.—Ed.

merly slaves or not, and citizens of other races, shall have the same accommodations and privileges in all inns, public conveyances, and places of amusement as are enjoyed by white citizens; and vice versa. The 2d section makes it a penal offense in any person to deny to any citizen of any race or color, regardless of previous servitude, any of the accommodations or privileges mentioned in the 1st section.

Has Congress constitutional power to make such a law? Of course, no one will contend that the power to pass it was contained in the Constitution before the adoption of the last three Amendments. The power is sought, first, in the 14th Amendment, and the views and arguments of distinguished Senators, advanced whilst the law was under consideration, claiming authority to pass it by virtue of that Amendment, are the principal arguments adduced in favor of the power. We have carefully considered those arguments, as was due to the eminent ability of those who put them forward, and have felt, in all its force, the weight of authority which always invests a law that Congress deems itself competent to pass. But the responsibility of an independent judgment is now thrown upon this court; and we are bound to exercise it according to the best lights we have.

The 1st section of the 14th Amendment, which is the one relied on, after declaring who shall be citizens of the United States, and of the several States, is prohibitory in its character, and prohibitory upon the States. It declares that "No State shall make or enforce any law which shall abridge the privileges of immunities of citizens of the United States; nor shall any State deprive any person of life, liberty or property without due process of law; nor deny to any person within its jurisdiction the equal protection of the laws." It is state action of a particular character that is prohibited. Individual invasion of individual rights is not the subject-matter of the Amendment. It has a deeper and broader scope. It nullifies and makes void all state legislation, and state action of every kind, which impairs the privileges and immunities of citizens of the United States, or which injures them in life, liberty or property without due process of law, or which denies to any of them the equal protection of the laws. It not only does this, but, in order that the national will, thus declared, may not be a mere *brutum fulmen,* the last section of the Amendment invests Congress with power to enforce it by appropriate legislation. To enforce what? To enforce the prohibition. To adopt appropriate legislation for correcting the effects of such prohibited state laws and state Acts, and thus to render them effectually null, void and innocuous. This is the legislative power conferred upon Congress, and this is the whole of it. It does not invest Congress with power to legislate upon subjects which are within the domain of state legislation; but to provide modes of relief against state legislation or state action, of the kind referred to. It does not authorize Congress to create a code of municipal law for the regulation of private rights; but to provide modes of redress against the operation of state laws, and the action of state officers executive or judicial, when these are subversive of the fundamental rights specified in the Amendment. Positive rights and privileges are undoubtedly secured by the 14th Amendment; but they are secured by way of prohibition against state laws and state proceedings affecting those rights and privileges, and by power given to Congress to legislate for the purpose of carrying such prohibition into effect; and such legislation must, necessarily, be predicated upon such supposed state laws or state proceedings, and be directed to the correction of their operation and effect. . . .

An apt illustration of this distinction may be found in some of the provisions of the original Constitution. Take the subject of contracts, for example; the Constitution prohibited the States from passing any law impairing the obligation of contracts. This did not give to Congress power to provide laws for the general enforcement of contracts; nor power to invest the courts of the United States with jurisdiction over contracts, so as to enable parties to sue upon them in those courts. It did however give the power to provide remedies by which the impairment of contracts by state legislation might be counteracted and corrected; and this power was exercised. The remedy which Congress actually provided was that contained in the 25th section of the Judiciary Act of 1789 [1 Stat. at L., 85], giving to the Supreme Court of the United States jurisdiction by writ of error to review the final decisions of state courts whenever they should sustain the validity of a state statue or authority alleged to be repugnant to the Constitution or laws of the United States. By this means, if a state law was passed impairing the obligation of a contract, and the state tribunals sustained the validity of the law, the mischief could be corrected in this court. The legislation of Congress, and the proceedings provided for under it, were corrective in their character. No attempt was made to draw into the United States courts the litigation of contracts generally; and no such attempt would have been sustained. We do not say that the remedy provided was the only one that might have been provided in that case. Probably Congress had power to pass a law giving to the courts of the United States direct jurisdiction over contracts alleged to be impaired by a state law; and under the broad provisions of the Act of March 3, 1875, giving to the circuit courts jurisdiction of all cases arising under the Constitution and laws of the United States, it is possible that such jurisdiction now exists. But under that or any other law it must appear, as well by allegation as proof at the trial, that the Constitution had been violated by the action of the State Legislature. Some obnoxious state law, passed or that might be passed, is necessary to be assumed, in order to lay the foundation of any federal remedy in the case; and for the very sufficient reason, that the constitutional prohibition is against state laws impairing the obligation of contracts.

And so in the present case, until some state law has been passed or some state action through its officers or agents has been taken, adverse to the rights of citizens sought to be protected by the 14th Amendment, no legislation of the United States under said Amendment, nor any proceeding under such legislation, can be called into activity; for the prohibitions of the Amendment are against state laws and acts done under state authority. Of course, legislation may and should be provided in advance to meet the exigency when it arises; but it should be adapted to the mischief and wrong which the Amendment was intended to provide against; and that is, state laws, or state action of some kind, adverse to the rights of the citizen secured by the Amendment. Such legislation cannot properly cover the whole domain of rights appertaining to life, liberty and property, defining them and providing for their vindication. That would be to establish a code of municipal law regulative of all private rights between man and man in society. It would be to make Congress take the place of the State Legislatures and to supersede them. It is absurd to affirm that, because the rights of life, liberty and property, which include all civil rights that men have, are, by the Amendment, sought to be protected against invasion of the part of the State without due process of law, Congress may, therefore, provide due process of law for their vindication in every case; and that, because the denial by a State to any persons, of equal protection of the laws, is prohibited by the Amendment, therefore Congress may establish laws for their equal protection. In fine, the legislation which Congress is authorized to adopt in this behalf is not general legislation upon the rights of the citizen, but corrective legislation, that is, such as may be necessary and proper for counteracting such laws as the States may adopt or enforce, and which, by the Amendment, they are prohibited from making or enforcing, or such acts and proceedings as the States may commit or take, and which, by the Amendment, they are prohibited from committing or taking. It is not necessary for us to state, if we could, what legislation would be proper for Congress to adopt. It is sufficient for us to examine whether the law in question is of that character.

An inspection of the law shows that it makes no reference whatever to any supposed or apprehended violation of the 14th Amendment on the part of the States. It is not predicated on any such view. It proceeds *ex directo* to declare that certain acts committed by individuals shall be deemed offenses, and shall be prosecuted and punished by proceedings in the courts of the United States. It does not profess to be corrective of any constitutional wrong committed by the States; it does not make its operation to depend upon any such wrong committed. It applies to cases arising in States which have the justest laws respecting the personal rights of citizens, and whose authorities are ever ready to enforce such laws, as to those which arise in States that may have violated the prohibition of the Amendment. In other words, it steps into the domain of local jurisprudence, and lays down rules for the conduct of individuals in society towards each other, and imposes sanctions for the enforcement of those rules, without referring in any manner to any supposed action of the State or its authorities.

If this legislation is appropriate for enforcing the prohibitions of the Amendment, it is difficult to see where it is to stop. Why may not Congress with equal show of authority enact a code of laws for the enforcement and vindication of all rights of life, liberty and property? If it is supposable that the States may deprive persons of life, liberty and property without due process of law, and the Amendment itself does suppose this, why should not

Congress proceed at once to prescribe due process of law for the protection of every one of these fundamental rights, in every possible case, as well as to prescribe equal privileges in inns, public conveyances and theaters? The truth is, that the implication of a power to legislate in this manner is based upon the assumption that if the States are forbidden to legislate or act in a particular way on a particular subject, and power is conferred upon Congress to enforce the prohibition, this gives Congress power to legislate generally upon that subject, and not merely power to provide modes of redress against such state legislation or action. The assumption is certainly unsound. It is repugnant to the 10th Amendment of the Constitution, which declares that powers not delegated to the United States by the Constitution, nor prohibited by it to the States, are reserved to the States respectively or to the people. . . .

In this connection it is proper to state that civil rights, such as are guaranteed by the Constitution against state aggression, cannot be impaired by the wrongful acts of individuals, unsupported by state authority in the shape of laws, customs or judicial or executive proceedings. The wrongful act of an individual, unsupported by any such authority, is simply a private wrong, or a crime of that individual; an invasion of the rights of the injured party, it is true, whether they affect his person, his property or his reputation; but if not sanctioned in some way by the State, or not done under state authority, his rights remain in full force, and may presumably be vindicated by resort to the laws of the State for redress. An individual cannot deprive a man of his right to vote, to hold property, to buy and to sell, to sue in the courts or to be a witness or a juror; he may, by force or fraud, interfere with the enjoyment of the right in a particular case; he may commit an assault against the person, or commit murder, or use ruffian violence at the polls, or slander the good name of a fellow citizen; but, unless protected in these wrongful acts by some shield of state law or state authority he cannot destroy or injure the right; he will only render himself amenable to satisfaction or punishment; and amenable therefor to the laws of the State where the wrongful acts are committed. Hence, in all those cases where the Constitution seeks to protect the rights of the citizen against discriminative and unjust laws of the State by prohibiting such laws, it is not individual offenses, but abrogation and denial of rights, which it denounces, and for which it clothes the Congress with power to provide a remedy. This abrogation and denial of rights, for which the States alone were or could be responsible, was the seminal and fundamental wrong which was intended to be remedied. And the remedy to be provided must necessarily be predicated upon that wrong. It must assume that in the cases provided for, the evil or wrong actually committed rests upon some state law or state authority for its excuse or perpetration. . . .

On the whole we are of opinion, that no countenance of authority for the passage of the law in question can be found in either the 13th or 14th Amendment of the Constitution; and no other ground of authority for its passage being suggested, it must necessarily be declared void, at least so far as its operation in the several States is concerned. . . .

Mr. Justice Harlan dissenting:

The opinion in these cases proceeds, it seems to me, upon grounds entirely too narrow and artificial. I cannot resist the conclusion that the substance and spirit of the recent Amendments of the Constitution have been sacrificed by a subtle and ingenious verbal criticism. "It is not the words of the law but the internal sense of it that makes the law; the letter of the law is the body; the sense and reason of the law is the soul." Constitutional provisions, adopted in the interest of liberty, and for the purpose of securing, through national legislation, if need be, rights inhering in a state of freedom, and belonging to American citizenship, have been so construed as to defeat the ends the people desired to accomplish, which they attempted to accomplish, and which they supposed they had accomplished by changes in their fundamental law. By this I do not mean that the determination of these cases should have been materially controlled by considerations of mere expediency or policy. I mean only, in this form, to express an earnest conviction that the court has departed from the familiar rule requiring, in the interpretation of constitutional provisions, that full effect be given to the intent with which they were adopted.

The purpose of the 1st section of the Act of Congress of March 1, 1875, was to prevent race discrimination in respect of the accommodations and facilities of inns, public conveyances and places of public amusement. It does not assume to define the general conditions and limitations under which inns, public conveyances and places of public amusement may be conducted, but only declares that such conditions and limitations, whatever they may be, shall not be applied so as to work a discrimination solely because of race, color or previous condition of servitude. The 2d section provides a penalty against any one denying, or aiding or inciting the denial, to any citizen, of that equality of right given by the 1st section, except for reasons by law applicable to citizens of every race or color and regardless of any previous condition of servitude.

There seems to be no substantial difference between my brethren and myself as to the purpose of Congress; for, they say that the essence of the law is, not to declare broadly that all persons shall be entitled to the full and equal enjoyment of the accommodations, advantages, facilities and privileges of inns, public conveyances and theaters; but that such enjoyment shall not be subject to conditions applicable only to citizens of a particular race of color, or who had been in a previous condition of servitude. The effect of the statute, the court says, is, that colored citizens, whether formerly slaves or not, and citizens of other races, shall have the same accommodations and privileges in all inns, public conveyances and places of amusement as are enjoyed by white persons; and vice versa.

The court adjudges, I think erroneously, that Congress is without power. . . .

The assumption that this Amendment consists wholly of prohibitions upon state laws and state proceedings in hostility to its provisions, is unauthorized by its language. The first clause of the 1st section—"All persons born or naturalized in the United States, and subject to the jurisdiction thereof, are citizens of the United States, and of the State wherein they reside"—is of a distinctly affirmative character. In its application to the colored race, previously liberated, it created and granted, as well citizenship of the United States, as citizenship of the State in which they respectively resided. It introduced all of that race, whose ancestors had been imported and sold as slaves, at once, into the political community known as the "People of the United States." They became, instantly, citizens of the United States, and of their respective States. Further, they were brought, by this supreme act of the Nation, within the direct operation of that provision of the Constitution which declares that "The citizens of each State shall be entitled to all privileges and immunities of citizens in the several States." Art. 4, sec. 2.

The citizenship thus acquired, by that race, in virtue of an affirmative grant from the Nation, may be protected, not alone by the judicial branch of the government, but by congressional legislation of a primary direct character; this, because the power of Congress is not restricted to the enforcement of prohibitions upon state laws of state action. It is, in terms distinct and positive, to enforce "the provisions of this article" of Amendment; not simply those of a prohibitive character, but the provisions—all of the provisions—affirmative and prohibitive, of the Amendment. It is, therefore, a grave misconception to suppose that the 5th section of the Amendment has reference exclusively to express prohibitions upon state laws or state action. If any right was created by that Amendment, the grant of power, through appropriate legislation, to enforce its provisions, authorizes Congress, by means of legislation, operating throughout the entire Union, to guard, secure and protect that right.

It is, therefore, an essential inquiry what, if any, right, privilege or immunity was given, by the Nation to colored persons when they were made citizens of the State in which they reside? Did the constitutional grant of state citizenship to that race, of its own force, invest them with any rights, privileges and immunities whatever? That they became entitled, upon the adoption of the 14th Amendment, "to all privileges and immunities of citizens in the several States," within the meaning of section 2 of article 4 of the Constitution, no one, I suppose will for a moment question. What are the privileges and immunities to which, by that clause of the Constitution they became entitled? To this it may be answered, generally, upon the authority of the adjudged cases, that they are those which are fundamental in citizenship in a free republican government, such as are "common to the citizens in the latter States under their constitutions and laws by virtue of their being citizens." Of that provision it has been said with the approval of this court, that no other one in the Constitution has tended so strongly to constitute the citizens of the United States one people. . . .

My brethren say, that when a man has emerged from slavery, and by the aid of beneficent legislation has shaken off the inseparable concomitants of that state, there must be some stage in the progress of his elevation when he takes the rank of a mere citizen, and ceases to be the special favorite of the laws, and when his rights as a citizen, or a man, are to be protected in the ordinary modes by which other men's rights are protected. It is, I submit, scarcely just to say that the colored race has been the special favorite of the laws. The Statute of 1875, now adjudged to be unconstitutional, is for the benefit of citizens of every race and color. What the Nation, through Congress, has sought to accomplish in reference to that race, is—what had already been done in every State of the Union for the White race—to secure and protect rights belonging to them as freemen and citizens; nothing more. It was not deemed enough "to help the feeble up, but to support him after." The one underlying purpose of congressional legislation has been to enable the black race to take the rank of mere citizens. The difficulty has been to compel a recognition of the legal rights of the black race to take the rank of citizens and to secure the enjoyment of privileges belonging, under the law, to them as a component part of the people for whose welfare and happiness government is ordained. At every step, in this direction, the Nation has been confronted with class tyranny, which a contemporary English historian says is, of all tyrannies, the most intolerable, "For it is ubiquitous in its operation, and weighs, perhaps, most heavily on those whose obscurity or distance would withdraw them from the notice of a single despot." Today, it is the colored race which is denied, by corporations and individuals wielding public authority, rights fundamental in their freedom and citizenship. At some future time, it may be that some other race will fall under the ban of race discrimination. If the constitutional Amendments be enforced, according to the intent with which, as I conceive, they were adopted, there cannot be in this Republic, any class of human beings in practical subjection to another class, with power in the latter to dole out to the former just such privileges as they may choose to grant. The supreme law of the land has decreed that no authority shall be exercised in this country upon the basis of discrimination, in respect of civil rights, against freemen and citizens because of their race, color or previous condition of servitude. To that decree—for the due enforcement of which, by appropriate legislation, Congress has been invested with express power—every one must bow, whatever may have been, or whatever now are, his individual views as to the wisdom or policy, either of the recent changes in the fundamental law, or of the legislation which has been enacted to give them effect.

For the reasons stated I feel constrained to withhold my assent to the opinion of the court.

CAN CITIZENSHIP BE NATIONALIZED?

To Secure These Rights

PRESIDENT'S COMMITTEE ON CIVIL RIGHTS

The Constitution, as it came from the Philadelphia Convention in 1787, granted to Congress no express power to enact civil rights legislation of any kind. Moreover, the first ten Amendments, which make up our Bill of Rights, far from granting any positive powers to the federal government, serve as express limitations upon it. The Thirteenth, Fourteenth, and Fifteenth Amendments added to the Constitution immediately following the close of the Civil War do expressly authorize Congress to pass laws in certain civil rights areas. But the areas are of limited extent and are not clearly defined. Thus, there is nothing in the Constitution which in so many words authorizes the national government to protect the civil rights of the American people on a comprehensive basis. . . .

There are [however] several specific constitutional bases upon which a federal civil rights program can be built. Some have been recognized and approved by the courts. Others have the support of leading students of the American constitutional system. Some are beyond dispute; others are frankly controversial. Collectively, however, they provide an encouraging basis for action. The President and Congress must determine the wisdom of a broader civil rights program at the policy level. They should be advised that such a program, carefully framed, will meet the test of constitutionality.

The several specific constitutional bases for federal action in the civil rights field brought to our attention follow. Those numbered from one through eight have either been specifically approved by

From *The Report of the President's Committee on Civil Rights* (p. 90 ff.), United States Government Printing Office, Washington, 1947.

the Supreme Court or seem to be clearly valid. Those numbered from nine through eleven are more controversial and will be discussed at greater length.

1. *Power to protect the right to vote.*—The extent of federal power to protect the suffrage varies, depending on the type of election (state or national), the type of interference (whether it affects the voting procedure, or is based on race or sex) and the source of interference (state and local officers or private persons). Among the specific sources of federal power are: Article I, Section 4, which permits federal protection of the procedure for voting in federal elections against interference from any source; the Fourteenth Amendment which supports protection against state interference with equality of opportunity to vote in any election; the Fifteenth Amendment which supports action against state interference because of race or color with the right to vote in any election; and the Nineteenth Amendment, which supports action against state interference based on sex with the right to vote in any election.

2. *Power to protect the right to freedom from slavery and involuntary servitude.*—This power derives from the Thirteenth Amendment: "Neither slavery nor involuntary servitude, except as a punishment for crime whereof the party shall have been duly convicted, shall exist within the United States, or any place subject to their jurisdiction." This permits legislation designed to protect against action of private persons or state or local officials.

3. *Power to protect rights to fair legal process, to free speech and assembly, and to equal protection of the laws.*—This power, derived from the "due process," "equal protection" and "privileges or immunities" clauses of the Fourteenth Amendment, cannot be readily summarized, except for the fact that, under Supreme Court rulings, it protects only against interferences by agencies of state or local government. In a wide variety of specific situations —such as cases involving the validity of ordinances licensing the distribution of handbills, the adequacy of representation by counsel, or the validity of state laws or administrative action claimed to discriminate against minorities—The Supreme Court has delineated areas of activity protected by these constitutional provisions. Congress is expressly authorized to enact legislation to implement this power, and has passed some statutes for this purpose.

4. *The war power.*—Under Section 8 of Article I of the Consti-

tution Congress has extensive power to regulate the armed forces and to legislate concerning the national defense and security. Congress may thus legislate with respect to treatment of minority groups in the services, with respect to interference with members of the services, and with respect to construction or operation of military and naval installations. Related is the congressional power to assure distribution of veterans' benefits on an equal basis.

5. *Power to regulate activities which relate to interstate commerce.*—Congress has exercised its broad power to regulate interstate commerce, derived from Article I, Section 8 of the Constitution, to institute reforms in many fields. Outstanding examples are the Fair Labor Standards Act, which fixes maximum hours and minimum wages in work relating to interstate commerce, the National Labor Relations Act, which regulates labor-management relations affecting interstate commerce, and the Federal Safety Appliance Act, which specifies safety standards for interstate transportation. The commerce power could be the basis for fair employment legislation relating to activities affecting interstate commerce, and for laws prohibiting discriminatory practices by interstate carriers.

6. *The taxing and spending powers.*—Also derived from Article I, Section 8, these are among the most extensive congressional powers, and have been repeatedly used to effectuate federal programs. An outstanding example is the Social Security program. Federal grants-in-aid have almost always been conditioned on compliance with congressionally declared standards, as have exemptions from taxation. Congress has power to impose similarly appropriate conditions in spending or taxing programs which affect civil rights problems. Another facet of these powers permits Congress to require persons who enter into contracts with the federal government, or supply the government with goods or services to conform with national policy. For example, in the Walsh-Healey Act, Congress has made compliance with minimum wage and maximum hour standards a condition of performance of federal supply contracts.

7. *The postal power.*—Under its plenary power over the postal system (stemming from Article I, Section 8) Congress has acted to protect use of the mails against certain undesirable purposes. This power is, of course, subject to the constitutional limits on

congressional power to impair free speech. Within those limits, however, there may be room for certain types of legislation—such as the exclusion of anonymous hate group literature from the mails.

8. *Power over the District of Columbia and the Territories.*—Under Article I, Section 8 and Article IV, Section 3, Congress has full power of government over the District of Columbia and the various territories. It may thus pass any legislation proper for complete protection of the civil rights of all persons residing in those areas.

9. *Power derived from the Constitution as a whole to protect the rights essential to national citizens in a democratic nation.*

No such power is expressly granted to Congress in the Constitution. It has long been asserted that the basic rights falling into this category, such as freedom of speech and press or the right of assembly, exist at the state level and depend upon state action for their protection against interference by private persons. However, the Supreme Court long ago suggested that such rights have a national significance as exercised in connection with the national political process, and that they may be protected by national legislation. . . .

As recently as 1940, the Fifth Circuit Court of Appeals in the case of *Powe* v. *United States,* . . . in a dictum said:

> Because the federal government is a republican one in which the will of the people ought to prevail, and because that will ought to be expressive of an informed public opinion, the freedom of speaking and printing on subjects relating to that government, its elections, its laws, its operations and its officers is vital to it.

And the court said that Congress has power under the Constitution to protect freedom of discussion, so defined, against all threats.

Unfortunately, these dicta have not been directly tested in practice. It is impossible to say how far the courts may be willing to go in recognizing the existence of specific rights at the national level, or in approving the power of Congress to protect these rights as necessary to a democratic nation. But the basis seems to be a valid one and it might support national civil rights legislation of considerable significance.

10. *Power derived from the treaty clause in Article II, Section*

2 of the Constitution, to protect civil rights which acquire a treaty status.

In its decision in *Missouri* v. *Holland* in 1920, the Supreme Court ruled that Congress may enact statutes to carry out treaty obligations, even where, in the absence of a treaty, it has no other power to pass such a statute. This doctrine has an obvious importance as a possible basis for civil rights legislation.

The United Nations Charter, approved by the United States Senate as a treaty, makes several references to human rights. Articles 55 and 56 are of particular importance. . . .

A strong argument can be made under the precedent of *Missouri* v. *Holland* that Congress can take "separate action" to achieve the purposes set forth in Article 55 by passing legislation designed to secure "respect for, and observance of, human rights and fundamental freedoms for all without distinction as to race, sex, language, or religion." . . .

The Human Rights Commission of the United Nations is at present working on a detailed international bill of rights designed to give more specific meaning to the general principle announced in Article 55 of the Charter. If this document is accepted by the United States as a member state, an even stronger basis for congressional action under the treaty power may be established.*

11. *Power derived from the "republican form of government" clause in Article IV, Section 4 of the Constitution, to protect rights essential to state and local citizens in a democracy.*

This clause reads "The United States shall guarantee to every State in this Union a republican form of government. . . ." This phraseology is admittedly vague, and has had relatively little interpretation by the Supreme Court. But other vague clauses of the Constitution, such as the commerce clause or the due process of law clauses, have lent themselves to broad interpretation. It is possible that guaranteeing "a republican form of government" includes the power to protect essential civil rights against interference by public officers or private persons.

In view of this analysis of the Constitution, both as to its broad character and its more specific clauses, the Committee believes that federal legislation in support of civil liberty is legitimate and well within the scope of the Constitution. . . .

* Fear of such an eventuality led to the Bricker Amendment movement.—Ed.

Chapter Three

INTERNAL ORGANIZATION AND PROCESSES: Debating Society or Power Arena?

GOVERNMENT BY COMMITTEE

The Imperious Authority of the Standing Committees

WOODROW WILSON

The leaders of the House are the chairmen of the principal Standing Committees. Indeed, to be exactly accurate, the House has as many leaders as there are subjects of legislation; for there are as many Standing Committees as there are leading classes of legislation, and in the consideration of every topic of business the House is guided by a special leader in the person of the chairman of the Standing Committee, charged with the superintendence of measures of the particular class to which that topic belongs. It is this multiplicity of leaders, this many-headed leadership, which makes the organization of the House too complex to afford uninformed people and unskilled observers any easy clue to its

From Woodrow Wilson, *Congressional Government* (pp. 58-81), Meridian edition.

methods of rule. For the chairmen of the Standing Committees do not constitute a cooperative body like a ministry. They do not consult and concur in the adoption of homogeneous and mutually helpful measures; there is no thought of acting in concert. Each Committee goes its own way at its own pace. It is impossible to discover any unity or method in the disconnected and therefore unsystematic, confused, and desultory action of the House, or any common purpose in the measures which its Committees from time to time recommend.

And it is not only to the unanalytic thought of the common observer who looks at the House from the outside that its doings seem helter-skelter, and without comprehensible rule; it is not at once easy to understand them when they are scrutinized in their daily headway through open session by one who is inside the House. The newly-elected member, entering its doors for the first time, and with no more knowledge of its rules and customs than the more intelligent of his constituents possess, always experiences great difficulty in adjusting his preconceived ideas of congressional life to the strange and unlooked-for conditions by which he finds himself surrounded after he has been sworn in and has become a part of the great legislative machine. Indeed there are generally many things connected with his career in Washington to disgust and dispirit, if not to aggrieve, the new member. In the first place, his local reputation does not follow him to the federal capital. Possibly the members from his own State know him, and receive him into full fellowship; but no one else knows him, except as an adherent of this or that party, or as a new-comer from this or that State. He finds his station insignificant, and his identity indistinct. But this social humiliation which he experiences in circles in which to be a congressman does not of itself confer distinction, because it is only to be one among many, is probably not to be compared with the chagrin and disappointment which come in company with the inevitable discovery that he is equally without weight or title to consideration in the House itself. No man, when chosen to the membership of a body possessing great powers and exalted prerogatives, likes to find his activity repressed, and himself suppressed, by imperative rules and precedents which seem to have been framed for the deliberate purpose of making usefulness unattainable by individual members. Yet such the new member finds the rules and precedents of the House to be. It matters not to him, because it is not apparent on the face of things, that those rules and precedents have grown, not out of set purpose to curtail the privileges of new members as such, but out of the plain necessities of business; it remains the fact that he suffers under their curb, and it is not until "custom hath made it in him a property of easiness" that he submits to them with anything like good grace. . . .

Often the new member goes to Washington as the representative of a particular line of policy, having been elected, it may be, as an advocate of free trade, or as a champion of protection; and it is naturally his first care upon entering on his duties to seek immediate opportunity for the expression of his views and immediate means of giving them definite shape and thrusting them upon the attention of Congress. His disappointment is, therefore, very keen when he finds both opportunity and means denied him. He can introduce his bill; but that is all he can do, and he must do that at a particular time and in a particular manner. This he is likely to learn through rude experience, if he be not cautious to inquire beforehand the details of practice. He is likely to make a rash start, upon the supposition that Congress observes the ordinary rules of parliamentary practice to which he has become accustomed in the debating clubs familiar to his youth, and in the mass-meetings known to his later experience. His bill is doubtless ready for presentation early in the session, and some day, taking advantage of a pause in the proceedings, when there seems to be no business before the House, he rises to read it and move its adoption. But he finds getting the floor an arduous and precarious undertaking. There are certain to be others who want it as well as he; and his indignation is stirred by the fact that the Speaker does not so much as turn towards him, though he must have heard his call, but recognizes some one else readily and as a matter of course. If he be obstreperous and persistent in his cries of "Mr. Speaker," he may get that great functionary's attention for a moment,—only to be told, however, that he is out of order, and that his bill can be introduced at that stage only by unanimous consent: immediately there are mechanically-uttered but emphatic exclamations of objection, and he is forced to sit down confused and disgusted. He has, without knowing it, obtruded himself in the way of the "regular order of business," and been run over in consequence, without being quite clear as to how the accident occurred. . . .

. . . [I]f he supposes, as he naturally will, that after his bill has been sent up to be read by the clerk he may say a few words in its behalf, and in that belief sets out upon his long-considered remarks, he will be knocked down by the rules as surely as he was on the first occasion when he gained the floor for a brief moment. The rap of Mr. Speaker's gavel is sharp, immediate, and peremptory. He is curtly informed that no debate is in order; the bill can only be referred to the appropriate Committee.

This is, indeed, disheartening; it is his first lesson in committee government, and the master's rod smarts; but the sooner he learns the prerogatives and powers of the Standing Committees the sooner will he penetrate the mysteries of the rules and avoid the pain of further contact with their thorny side. The privileges of the Standing Committees are the beginning and the end of the rules. Both the House of Representatives and the Senate conduct their business by what may figuratively, but not inaccurately, be called an odd device of *disintegration*. The House virtually both deliberates and legislates in small sections. Time would fail it to discuss all the bills brought in, for they every session number thousands; and it is to be doubted whether, even if time allowed, the ordinary processes of debate and amendment would suffice to sift the chaff from the wheat in the bushels of bills every week piled upon the clerk's desk. Accordingly, no futile attempt is made to do anything of the kind. The work is parceled out, most of it to the forty-seven* Standing Committees which constitute the regular organization of the House, some of it to select committees appointed for special and temporary purposes. Each of the almost numberless bills that come pouring in on Mondays is "read a first and second time,"—simply perfunctorily read, that is, by its title, by the clerk, and passed by silent assent through its first formal courses, for the purpose of bringing it to the proper stage for commitment,—and referred without debate to the appropriate Standing Committee. Practically, no bill escapes commitment—save, of course, bills introduced by committees, and a few which may now and then be crowded through under a suspension of the rules, granted by a two-thirds vote—though the exact disposition to be made of a bill is not always determined easily and as

* At present twenty, with several additional *ad hoc* committees.—Ed.

a matter of course. Besides the great Committee of Ways and Means and the equally great Committee on Appropriations, there are Standing Committees on Banking and Currency . . . on the Judiciary, . . . on Agriculture, . . . and on a score of other branches of legislative concern; but careful and differential as is the topical division of the subjects of legislation which is represented in the titles of these Committees, it is not always evident to which Committee each particular bill should go. Many bills affect subjects which may be regarded as lying as properly within the jurisdiction of one as of another of the Committees; for no hard and fast lines separate the various classes of business which the Committees are commissioned to take in charge. Their jurisdictions overlap at many points, and it must frequently happen that bills are ready which cover just this common ground. Over the commitment of such bills sharp and interesting skirmishes often take place. There is active competition for them, the ordinary, quiet routine of matter-of-course reference being interrupted by rival motions seeking to give very different directions to the disposition to be made of them. . . .

The fate of bills committeed is generally not uncertain. As a rule, a bill committeed is a bill doomed. When it goes from the clerk's desk to a committee-room it crosses a parliamentary bridge of sighs to dim dungeons of silence whence it will never return. The means and time of its death are unknown, but its friends never see it again. Of course no Standing Committee is privileged to take upon itself the full powers of the House it represents, and formally and decisively reject a bill referred to it; its disapproval, if it disapproves, must be reported to the House in the form of a recommendation that the bill "do not pass." But it is easy, and therefore common, to let the session pass without making any report at all upon bills deemed objectionable or unimportant, and to substitute for reports upon them a few bills of the Committee's own drafting; so that thousands of bills expire with the expiration of each Congress, not having been rejected, but having been simply neglected. There was not time to report upon them.

Of course it goes without saying that the practical effect of this Committee organization of the House is to consign to each of the Standing Committees the entire direction of legislation upon those subjects which properly come to its consideration. As to those subjects it is entitled to the initiative, and all legislative action with regard to them is under its overruling guidance. It gives shape and course to the determinations of the House. In one respect, however, its initiative is limited. Even a Standing Committee cannot report a bill whose subject matter has not been referred to it by the House, "by the rules or otherwise;" it cannot volunteer advice on questions upon which its advice has not been asked. But this is not a serious, not even an operative, limitation upon its functions of suggestion and leadership for it is a very simple matter to get referred to it any subject it wishes to introduce to the attention of the House. Its chairman, or one of its leading members, frames a bill covering the point upon which the Committee wishes to suggest legislation; bring it in, in his capacity as a private member, on Monday, when the call of States is made; has it referred to his Committee; and thus secures an opportunity for the making of the desired report.

It is by this imperious authority of the Standing Committees that the new member is stayed and thwarted whenever he seeks to take an active part in the business of the House. Turn which way he may, some privilege of the Committees stands in his path. The rules are so framed as to put all business under their management; and one of the discoveries which the new member is sure to make, albeit after many trying experiences and sobering adventures and as his first session draws towards its close, is, that under their sway freedom of debate finds no place of allowance, and that his long-delayed speech must remain unspoken. For even a long congressional session is too short to afford time for a full consideration of all the reports of . . . [all the] Committees, and debate upon them must be rigidly cut short, if not altogether excluded, if any considerable part of the necessary business is to be gotten through with before adjournment. There are some subjects to which the House must always give prompt attention; . . . therefore the Committee of Ways and Means and the Committee on Appropriations are clothed with extraordinary privileges; and revenue and supply bills may be reported, and will ordinarily be considered, at any time. . . . The rest must take their turns in fixed order as they are called on by the Speaker, contenting themselves with such crumbs of time as fall from the tables of the four Committees of highest prerogative. . . .

. . . The House is conscious that time presses. It knows that, hurry as it may, it will hardly get through with one eighth of the business laid out for the session, and that to pause for lengthy debate is to allow the arrears to accumulate. Besides, most of the members are individually anxious to expedite action on every pending measure, because each member of the House is a member of one or more of the Standing Committees, and is quite naturally desirous that the bills prepared by his Committees, and in which he is, of course, specially interested by reason of the particular attention which he has been compelled to give them, should reach a hearing and a vote as soon as possible. It must, therefore, invariably happen that the Committee holding the floor at any particular time is the Committee whose proposals the majority wish to dispose of as summarily as circumstances will allow, in order that the rest of the [other] unprivileged Committees to which the majority belong may gain the earlier and the fairer chance of a hearing. A reporting Committee, besides, is generally as glad to be pushed as the majority are to push it. It probably has several bills matured, and wishes to see them disposed of before its brief hours of opportunity are passed and gone. . . .

These are the customs which baffle and perplex and astound the new member. In these precedents and usages, when at length he comes to understand them, the novice spies out the explanation of the fact, once so confounding and seemingly inexplicable, that when he leaped to his feet to claim the floor other members who rose after him were coolly and unfeelingly preferred before him by the Speaker. Of course it is plain enough now that Mr. Speaker knew beforehand to whom the representative of the reporting Committee had agreed to yield the floor; and it was no use for any one else to cry out for recognition. Whoever wished to speak should, if possible, have made some arrangement with the Committee before the business came to a hearing, and should have taken care to notify Mr. Speaker that he was to be granted the floor for a few moments.

Unquestionably this, besides being a very interesting, is a very novel and significant method of restricting debate and expediting legislative action,—a method of very serious import, and obviously fraught with far-reaching constitutional effects. The practices of debate which prevail in its legislative assembly are manifestly of the utmost importance to a self-governing people; for that legislation which is not thoroughly discussed by the legislating body is practically done in a corner. It is impossible for Congress itself to do wisely what it does so hurriedly; and the constituencies cannot understand what Congress does not itself stop to consider. . . .

. . . [T]he debates of Congress cannot, under our present system, have that serious purpose of search into the merits of policies and that definite and determinate party—or, if you will, partisan—aim without which they can never be effective for the instruction of public opinion, or the cleansing of political action. The chief of these reasons, because the parent of all the rest, is that there are in Congress no authoritative leaders who are the recognized spokesman of their parties. Power is nowhere concentrated; it is rather deliberately and of set policy scattered amongst many small chiefs. It is divided up, as it were, into forty-seven seigniories, in each of which a Standing Committee is the court-baron and its chairman lord-proprietor. These petty barons, some of them not a little powerful, but none of them within reach of the full powers of rule, may at will exercise an almost despotic sway within their own shires, and may sometimes threaten to convulse even the realm itself; but both their mutual jealousies and their brief and restricted opportunities forbid their combining, and each is very far from the office of common leader.

I know that to some this scheme of distributed power and disintegrated rule seems a very excellent device whereby we are enable to escape a dangerous "one-man power" and an untoward concentration of functions; and it is very easy to see and appreciate the considerations which make this view of committee government so popular. It is based upon a very proper and salutary fear of *irresponsible* power; and those who most resolutely maintain it always fight from the position that all leadership in legislation is hard to restrain in proportion to its size and to the strength of its prerogatives, and that to divide it is to make it manageable. They aver, besides, that the less a man has to do—that is to say, the more he is confined to single departments and to definite details—the more intelligent and thorough will his work be. They like the Committees, therefore, just because they are many and weak, being quite willing to abide their being despotic within their narrow spheres.

It seems evident, however, when the question is looked at from another standpoint, that, as a matter of fact and experience, the more power is divided the more irresponsible it becomes. . . .

In a word, the national parties do not act in Congress under the restraint of a sense of immediate responsibility. Responsibility is spread thin; and no vote or debate can gather it. It rests not so much upon parties as upon individuals; and it rests upon individuals in no such way as would make it either just or efficacious to visit upon them the iniquity of any legislative act. Looking at government from a practical and business-like, rather than from a theoretical and abstractly-ethical point of view,—treating the business of government as a business,—it seems to be unquestionably and in a high degree desirable that all legislation should distinctly represent the action of parties as parties. I know that it has been proposed by enthusiastic, but not too practical, reformers to do away with parties by some legerdemain of governmental reconstruction, accompanied and supplemented by some rehabilitation, devoutly to be wished, of the virtues least commonly controlling in fallen human nature; but it seems to me that it would be more difficult and less desirable than these amiable persons suppose to conduct a government of the many by means of any other device than party organization, and that the great need is, not to get rid of parties, but to find and use some expedient by which they can be managed and made amenable from day to day to public opinion. . . .

. . . [T]here is within Congress no *visible,* and therefore no *controllable* party organization. The only bond of cohesion is the caucus, which occasionally whips a party together for cooperative action against the time for casting its vote upon some critical question. There is always a majority and a minority, indeed, but the legislation of a session does not represent the policy of either; it is simply an aggregate of the bills recommended by Committees composed of members from both sides of the House, and it is known to be usually, not the work of the majority men upon the Committees, but compromise conclusions bearing some shade or tinge of each of the variously-colored opinions and wishes of the committeemen of both parties.

It is plainly the representation of both parties on the Committees that make party responsibility indistinct and organized party action almost impossible. If the Committees were composed entirely of members of the majority, and were thus constituted representatives of the party in power, the whole course of congressional proceedings would unquestionably take on a very different aspect. There would then certainly be a compact opposition to face the organized majority. Committee reports would be taken to represent the views of the party in power, and, instead of the scattered, unconcerted opposition, without plan or leaders, which now sometimes subjects the propositions of the Committees to vexatious hindrances and delays, there would spring up debate under skillful masters of opposition, who could drill their partisans for effective warfare and give shape and meaning to the purposes of the minority. But of course there can be no such definite division of forces so long as the efficient machinery of legislation is in the hands of both parties at once; so long as the parties are mingled and harnessed together in a common organization.

THE POTENCY OF PROCEDURAL RULES

Senate Rules and the Civil Rights Bill: A Case Study

HOWARD E. SHUMAN

The rules of the Senate of the United States are only 40 in number and comprise only 49 of the 832 pages of the *Senate Manual.* Yet, when literally invoked they can bring Senate business to a standstill. They are most often ignored or circumvented by unanimous consent in order that the Senate may operate conveniently as a deliberative and parliamentary body. To pass legislation when they are invoked is a formidable enterprise.

Just as the law is said to be no better than the procedures by which it is carried out, so the substance of legislation is shaped and modified by the procedures that may be required under the Senate rules, or by the mere threat to invoke those procedures, for they are compelling. The procedures preceding and surrounding the passage of the first civil rights bill in over 80 years illumine and illustrate the effect of the rules on the substance of legislation as have few other legislative controversies in recent years.

The Senate rules are the product of sectionalism. They were designed to prevent action unacceptable to a sectional minority. Among the more important specific rules with this design are: sections 2 and 3 of Rule XXII—the filibuster rule; section 1f of Rule

From Howard E. Shuman, *The American Political Science Review* (December 1957, pp. 955-975), American Political Science Association.

XXII, which makes a tabling motion not debatable and which, therefore, acts as a "negative" form of majority cloture for, if successful, it can stop talk and kill a bill or amendment without a vote on the merits;[1] Rule XXVI, which requires that all reports and motions to discharge a committee of a bill must lie over one legislative day—in practice this can mean several weeks if the Senate recesses from day to day rather than adjourns; Rule XL which requires one (legislative) day's notice to suspend the rules; Rule VII, which requires that a petition to discharge a committee be filed in the so-called morning hour, except by unanimous consent; and the same Rule VII which when literally followed requires the reading of the Journal in full, the presentation of messages from the President and reports and communications from executive departments, and numerous other time-consuming procedures in the morning hour, and so may preclude the opportunity for discharge petitions to be reached, for at the close of that hour the Senate must proceed to the unfinished or pending business; and two unwritten rules, first, of seniority, and second, the rule of recognition under which the chair recognizes either the Majority or Minority Leader as against other Senators who are seeking recognition. This can prevent a Senator from making a timely motion or point of order to which the leadership is opposed and so helps give the leadership command of the parliamentary situation.

How these rules affected the course of the civil rights debate and the strategy of both sides in the 1956 and 1957 sessions is now to be shown.

I. THE ABORTIVE CIVIL RIGHTS BILL OF 1956

With only a few days of the 84th Congress remaining in July, 1956, the House of Representatives, by a margin of 279 to 126, passed H.R. 627, a bill substantially the same as H.R. 6127 of the 85th Congress, part of which is now the law of the land. A small band composed of Senators Hennings, Douglas, and Lehman and finally supported by Senators Langer, Ives, and Bender, attempted to gain Senate action on the bill when it came from the House. This move was made notwithstanding the determined opposition of both Majority and Minority Leaders which, in the end, proved crushing.

[1] The Senate has no similar form of "majority" cloture which could end debate and bring a vote on the substance of a bill or an amendment.

Senator Douglas was guarding the Senate floor as the House passed the bill, and left his seat to go to the House chamber to escort H.R. 627 through the long corridor from the Speaker's to the Vice President's desk. As he was walking to the House he was passed, unknowing, by a messenger carrying the bill to the Senate. With Senator Douglas outside the Senate chamber and with Senator Hill of Alabama in the chair, the bill, with jet-age speed, was read a first and second time and referred to the Senate Judiciary Committee where its Senate counterparts had languished for two years.

This action took place by unanimous consent and so by-passed the specific provisions of Rule XIV, which require three readings of the bill prior to passage, "Which [readings] shall be on three different days," but state that bills from the House of Representatives ". . . shall be read once, and may be read twice, on the same day, if not objected to, for reference. . . ."

An attempt was then made under Rule XXVI, section 2, to file a petition to discharge the Judiciary Committee from the further consideration of H.R. 627. Except by unanimous consent the petition must be introduced in the morning hour.

On the same calendar day the bill came from the House a unanimous consent request to file the petition was blocked by a motion of the Majority Leader to recess overnight. At the beginning of the next day's session, in what would ordinarily have been the morning hour, the Senator from Georgia, Mr. George, ruled that the petition could not be filed, except by unanimous consent, for the Senate had recessed the previous evening and, in fact, had not adjourned since the evening of July 13, *i.e.*, 10 days previously. Although the date was then July 24, the legislative day was July 16, and thus technically there was no morning hour for the routine business of filing bills, reports, petitions, etc. Individual Senators then objected to further unanimous consent requests to file the petition. The Senate recessed that day and did not adjourn overnight until July 26, the evening before adjournment *sine die*. In the meantime a motion by Senator Douglas to adjourn for five minutes, in order to bring a new legislative day and a morning hour, was defeated by the crushing vote of 76 to 6.

In the morning hour on the last day of the session, the discharge petition was finally filed. But a discharge petition, under section 2 of Rule XXVI, must lie over one further "legislative" day. If consideration of the petition is not reached or is not concluded in the morning hour or before 2 o'clock on the next "legislative" day, it goes to the calendar. Then the motion to proceed to its consideration and the motion on passage of the petition are both subject to unlimited debate, unless cloture is applied to each. Such action, even if successful, would only result in placing the bill itself on the calendar, where it in turn must lie for another "legislative" day. The motion to proceed to its consideration and the motion on final passage are also both subject to unlimited debate, unless cloture is applied. Thus the filing of the petition came too late to bring action in the 84th Congress. Even if commenced at the beginning of a session, and even if [67] * votes were obtainable for cloture on each of the four occasions when they are potentially necessary, the process of discharging a committee can be drawn out over several weeks, and even months, if the rules of the Senate are literally invoked.

Although this attempt was abortive the experience was useful to the civil rights proponents in 1957. It brought a familiarity with the rules of the Senate which can only be gained from step-by-step proceedings under them; from it they concluded that action must begin very early in the session if it were to be successful; they saw that the route of discharging a committee meant meeting countless roadblocks, which could only be stormed and surmounted by determined efforts and with overwhelming bi-partisan support; and they concluded that a fight to change Rule XXII was essential because the inadequacy of cloture had either killed previous civil rights bills or brought their death by the mere threat of a filibuster.[2]

II. THE FIGHT TO CHANGE RULE XXII

The effort to change Rule XXII was made at the opening of the 85th Congress in January 1957. In the past Rule XXII has been the gravedigger in the Senate graveyard for civil rights bills. Section 2 of Rule XXII requires [67] affirmative votes to limit debate and section 3 provides that on a motion to proceed to the consideration of a change in the rules there can be no limit on debate of

* At time article was written, this figure was 64.—Ed.

[2] Since 1917, or for 40 years, cloture has been successful on only four of twenty-two attempts and never on a civil rights bill. Sixty-four votes have been forthcoming only three times, all in the period 1917 to 1927. Thus, no cloture motion has successfully prevailed in the last 30 years.

any kind. The rules of the Senate have carried over from Congress to Congress and changes in them have been made only after a unanimous consent agreement has been reached narrowly limiting the language and amendments which could come before the Senate.

Because of section 3, the only chance of success seemed to lie in a move at the beginning of a Congress that the Senate proceed to adopt new rules, relying on Article I, Section 5 of the Constitution which provides that ". . . each House may determine the rules of its proceedings." Such a motion was made in 1953 and was defeated by a vote of 70 to 21. Its opponents argued then that a civil rights bill would be passed, and that the rules should be changed only by ordinary processes of piecemeal amendment.

In 1957 the vote to table the motion to proceed to the consideration of new rules was carried, 55 to 38. Three absentees, Senators Neely and Wiley, and Javits, who had not yet taken his seat, opposed tabling and so brought to 41 the total who favored adopting new rules. Thus a shift of seven votes, plus a Vice President's favorable vote or ruling, was all that was now required to change Rule XXII. This was a major gain over 1953, for these 41 votes were obtained over the concerted objections of the leadership of both parties.

The size of the vote and its near success caught Southern Senators on the horns of a dilemma. They knew that any actual and organized use of the filibuster would ultimately bring an end to Rule XXII, and they also knew that if they did not use the filibuster Congress would most likely pass a civil rights bill. The fight to change Rule XXII thereby produced a climate in which not only a meaningful bill could pass but, it can be persuasively argued, a bill much stronger than that which was actually passed. The arguments and the parliamentary strategy involved in the Rule XXII fight were therefore crucial.

The opponents of the change relied basically on a single argument, namely, that the Senate was a continuing body, and as two-thirds of its members carry over from Congress to Congress, its rules should therefore also carry over from Congress to Congress as they have in the past.

The proponents argued that whatever the Senate had done in the past it had explicit constitutional power to adopt its rules at the beginning of a new Congress. Unlike their course in 1953, when the attempt to adopt new rules was hastily devised, the proponents did not meet the continuing body argument head on, but argued instead that it was immaterial whether the Senate was a continuing body or not. Acceptance of the continuing body argument did not deny to a majority of the Senate the right to adopt its own rules. Proponents also argued that proceedings on all bills and resolutions, as well as on treaties, begin again in a new Congress; that the Senate is newly organized and new committees are appointed; and that the newly elected one-third, even though only one-third, could alter the party alignment and thus provide a new majority and a new mandate which it had the right to carry out.

A second argument by the opponents, less used but probably more telling than the first, was that until the adoption of new rules the Senate would be in a parliamentary "jungle." Senator Russell combined with this argument a threat to proceed to rewrite each of the 40 rules of the Senate.

In rejoinder the proponents argued that the House of Representatives entered and left the parliamentary "jungle" in a very few minutes at each new Congress. They proposed that until the rules were adopted the Senate should proceed under general parliamentary rules including the motion for the previous question under which debate could be shut off by a simple majority. The proponents also relied on the precedents of the Senate to support the contention that majority cloture could be applied, for it was shown that the previous question rule was a part of the Senate rules from 1789 to 1806 and was used to bring debate to a close on several occasions.

The potential parliamentary moves were extremely involved, but basically the proponents sought to gain a ruling from the Vice President that their motion to proceed to the immediate consideration of the adoption of new rules was in order. This was their strongest position but, in the end, it was not gained.

It was their strongest position for a variety of reasons. To succeed, strong bi-partisan support was needed. The Democratic Party, by its nature, was split on the issue and could not provide a majority of votes. This was true even though the Democrats have traditionally supplied more votes on procedural issues in support of civil rights, and occasionally more on substantive civil rights issues, than the Republicans. In 1953, of the 21 votes for the adoption of new rules, 15 were Democratic. Only 5 Republicans and Wayne Morse, then an independent, voted for the change. That year Vice President Barkley let it be known that he would rule such a motion in order. But he had no opportunity to do so for Senator Taft gained the floor and gave immediate and prearranged notice that he would move to table the motion and thus shut off argument after a short debate. In 1957 with a Republican Vice President and with Republican votes needed to win, it was obvious that the strongest position would follow from a favorable ruling by the Vice President, and on the vote to uphold or overturn his ruling. The Democrats could provide no more than half of their numbers in support of such a favorable ruling. But the Republicans could provide, potentially, almost all of their votes if the issue were one of supporting their own Vice President.

In 1953 it mattered little whether the motion to proceed to the adoption of new rules were tabled, or whether a point of order were made and a ruling sought, for there would still have been a limit to the number of potential Democratic votes on this issue in support of a Democratic Vice President. The Republicans were obviously under no political pressure to support the ruling of a Democratic Vice President who was to leave office in a very few days.

In 1957 it was a different matter. Whether the vote came on a motion to table or on an appeal from the ruling of the Chair was critically important. If a Republican Vice President now ruled favorably, he would no doubt be supported by more than a majority of his own party which, combined with the Democratic support, could provide the winning margin. The proponent group knew that they would make gains over 1953 however the Vice President ruled, but if he ruled for them there was an opportunity for spectacular gains and perhaps a victory.

The strategy was therefore devised that the mover of the motion to proceed to the consideration of new rules for the Senate should also couple with his motion a parliamentary request for a ruling from the Chair that the motion was in order. If this was not done a motion to table would no doubt be made, thereby cutting off debate and bringing an immediate vote. The proponents of a change in Rule XXII not only had more to gain from a ruling from the Chair but also felt that time for debate, which could educate and arouse public opinion, was necessary to the success of the effort. A steering committee representing those who favored adoption of the new rules therefore met with the Vice President to advise him of their proposed course of action. They did not seek nor did they receive the Vice President's opinion as to the merits of their proposal.

They were advised, however, that the Majority Leader had informed the Vice President that immediately following the motion to proceed to the consideration of new rules he would seek recognition for the purpose of tabling that motion. The Vice President then gave his opinion that under the precedents of the Senate a point of order could not be coupled with the substantive motion, and that under the unwritten rule of recognition he must recognize the Majority Leader as against some other Senator seeking the floor. This meant, of course, that once the motion was made the Majority Leader would be recognized to move to table that motion and thereby shut off debate before any other Senator, including the mover of the motion, could raise a point of order.

The unwritten rule of recognition thus brought the vote on the issue of Rule XXII on the least advantageous grounds for the proponents of new rules and an end to the filibuster. It was, however, very ironic that the proponents of unlimited debate should immediately move to shut off debate on the question of changing Senate Rule XXII which, in effect, provides for unlimited debate. Recognition of this anomaly led to a unanimous consent agreement which fixed a limited time for debate on the tabling motion. When the motion to proceed to the consideration of new rules was made, consequently, and was sent to the desk and read by the clerk, the Majority Leader sought and gained recognition. He proposed to table the motion which, but for the unanimous consent agreement, would have cut off debate immediately; as it was, debate was limited and the issue came to a vote as had been planned.

In the course of these events the Vice President gave it as his informal opinion, though not as a formal ruling, (1) that a majority of the Senate could adopt new rules at the beginning of a new Congress if it wished; (2) that Section 3 of Rule XXII was unconstitutional for it allowed a previous Senate to bind a majority of a future Senate;[3] and (3) that until such time as the Senate either adopted new rules or by some action, such as the tabling motion, acquiesced in the old rules, the Senate would proceed under its previous rules except for those which could deny a majority of the Senate the right or opportunity to adopt new ones, or, in short, sections 2 and 3 of Rule XXII.

Thus, the unwritten rule of recognition and the use of the tabling motion as a negative form of majority cloture, not available to the proponents of a motion, bill, or amendment, were decisive parliamentary weapons in the fight over Rule XXII and the filibuster.

Although the fight was lost it nevertheless brought several clear gains to the proponents of the civil rights bill and of majority rule, apart from the dilemma of the Southern Senators over their future use of the filibuster. First, rhetorically, it foreshadowed the end of the effectiveness of the argument that the Senate is a continuing body with necessarily continuing rules. The debate showed it to be irrelevant as well as circuitous to argue that the rules carry over because the Senate is a continuing body, and that the Senate is a continuing body because the rules carry over. Second, substantively, the episode brought clear bi-partisan gains over 1953; the Democratic vote increased from 15 to 21, and the Republican from 5 to 17. While the press was predicting an overwhelming defeat for the 1957 effort those close to the scene estimated quite accurately that approximately 40 would support the motion to proceed to the adoption of new rules. Third, tactically, this fight gave a political urgency to civil rights legislation which it might not otherwise have had, and improved immeasurably the chances for a meaningful bill.

III. FILIBUSTER BY COMMITTEE

H.R. 6127 passed the House on June 18, 1957. In the Senate its companion bill, as well as some 15 other civil rights bills, still had not been acted on by the Judiciary Committee.

[3] It has been asked why, if the Vice President believed section 3 was unconstitutional, Senators did not press the issue later in the session. The answer is that the Vice President's position was that it was unconstitutional to the extent that it bound one Senate by the actions of a previous Senate. However, if the new Senate agreed to be bound, *i.e.*, acquiesced in the old rules as it did when the tabling motion was successful, section 3 would remain in effect throughout the 85th Congress.

This inaction followed precedent. In the 83d Congress four civil rights bills were reported from the Subcommittee on Constitutional Rights to the full Judiciary Committee, where they died. In the 84th Congress, the Constitutional Rights Subcommittee reported three bills on February 23, 1956 and a fourth bill on March 4, 1956, to the full Judiciary Committee; but they too died following 10 days of hearings by the full committee spread over the 11-week period from April 24 to July 13. In the 85th Congress, after every legitimate attempt by Senator Hennings and his colleagues to gain action on the bills, not one was reported to the Senate during the entire session. A chronology of the efforts to report a bill to the Senate will show how filibuster by committee takes place.

A number of civil rights bills were introduced during the first days of the session. On January 22, Senator Hennings moved in committee that February 18 be set as the deadline for ending hearings on them and that a vote on the legislation and the reporting of a bill to the Senate should not be delayed beyond one further week. This motion was not acted on.

Four days later, on January 26, the 14 bills by then in committee were referred to the Constitutional Rights Subcommittee.

On January 30 Senator Hennings, the chairman, presented an omnibus bill to the subcommittee and moved that it be reported to the full committee. The motion was defeated.

The subcommittee then agreed to hold hearings and Senator Hennings moved that these should begin on February 12 and be limited to two weeks, after which the subcommittee should act on the bills immediately. This motion was defeated.

Hearings by the subcommittee did begin on February 14 and ended after three weeks on March 5. On March 19, the subcommittee approved S. 83 and reported it, along with majority and minority views, to the full committee.

On March 21, Senator Hennings introduced S. 1658; its language was identical with that of H.R. 6127.

On April 1, in the full committee, Senator Hennings moved that the Judiciary Committee dispose of civil rights legislation by April 15. He was unable to obtain a vote on this motion.

On April 8, Senator Hennings intended to renew his motion, but there was no meeting of the committee owing to the absence of a quorum.

On April 15, Senator Hennings moved that S. 83 be voted on by May 6. The committee took no action.

On May 13, at the next meeting, Senator Hennings desired to move that the committee meet every morning and all day, when the rules of the Senate permitted, and in the evenings if necessary, so that a vote on the bill could be taken by May 16. He was unable to obtain recognition to make this motion.

On June 3, the committee added the sweeping "jury trial" amendment to the bill.

On June 10 and June 17, Senator Hennings was unable to gain recognition during committee meetings.

On June 18 the House passed H.R. 6127 and it was sent to the Senate.

How was it possible for the Judiciary Committee, which contained only a minority of Southern Senators, to delay action on civil rights for such a lengthy period of time? Under Section 134 (c) of the Legislative Reorganization Act, "No standing committee of the Senate . . . shall sit, without special leave, while the Senate . . . is in session." Under Section 133 (a) of the same Act, each standing committee is required to fix a regular day on which to meet. The regular meeting day of the Senate Judiciary Committee is Monday. While the Senate is often in recess on other days of the week, it is invariably in session on Monday, because that day is set for the call of the calendar of unobjected-to bills, and because the Constitution provides that neither House may adjourn for more than three days without the consent of the other. Consequently, when the hour of 12 noon arrives or when, as in the latter stages of the session the Senate meets at an earlier hour, any member of the Judiciary Committee may make a point of order that the Committee may no longer sit. This was done, and was one means of postponing action.

In addition, by the chairman's power to recognize an opponent first, and by his power to hold off a vote on a motion until such a member has concluded his remarks on it, it was easy for the chairman either to prevent a motion from being offered or to prevent action on a specific bill during the Committee's normal two-hour meeting. Further, the unwritten rule of seniority has generally placed a Southern Senator in the chair when the Democratic Party controls Congress. While Rule XXIV reads that ". . . the Senate, unless otherwise ordered, shall proceed by ballot to appoint severally the chairman of each committee . . .", this rule was not enforced either when Senator Eastland was first appointed chairman, on the death of Senator Kilgore, or at the beginning of the 85th Congress when he was reappointed. There was neither a ballot nor a motion to "order otherwise." Finally, on several Mondays it was impossible to muster a quorum.

IV. PLACING H.R. 6127 ON THE SENATE CALENDAR

Faced with this situation, a small group of pro-civil-rights Democratic Senators met a few days prior to the passage of H.R. 6127 by the House of Representatives, to determine on a course of action when that bill arrived in the Senate.

Several possibilities were canvassed. These included: (1) moving to send H.R. 6127 to the Judiciary Committee with instructions to report it to the Senate on a specific date; (2) allowing H.R. 6127 to go to Committee but moving to discharge the Judiciary Committee from further consideration either of that bill or of one of several of the Senate bills; (3) moving to suspend the rules under Rule XL in order to place H.R. 6127 on the calendar; and (4) moving to place the bill on the calendar under Rule XIV.

After consultation with the Senate Parliamentarian the group ruled out the first possibility, of sending the bill to committee with instructions to report it to the Senate on a day certain. Such instructions may be added to a motion to refer or to commit only when the bill itself has been motioned up and is actually before the Senate. Before the bill could come before the Senate it had first to be placed on the calendar, and then to be motioned up. Such a motion is subject to unlimited debate unless cloture is applied. This procedure was therefore evidentally impossible, notwithstanding later statements by Senator Morse who, in justifying his opposition to placing the bill directly on the calendar, asserted that instructions to report the bill on a day certain could have been added after the second reading.

Similarly, as we have already seen, the method of discharging a committee is lengthy, and was probably impossible for legislation as controversial as a civil rights bill. More specifically, the steps involved in this procedure include:

1. Filing a discharge petition during the morning hour.
2. A successful motion to adjourn so that a new legislative day may arrive.

3. Reaching the petition during the morning hour, in which case it would go to the foot of the calendar if debate were not concluded in two hours; or, if it was not reached in the morning hour, motioning it up at a later stage.
4. Moving to proceed to consideration of the petition, after it has reached the calendar, and after one legislative day has elapsed (which requires an intervening adjournment), when such a motion becomes in order.
5. Securing a vote on this motion, which is debatable and requires either unanimous consent or cloture and [67] affirmative votes to bring the debate to an end. Passage of this procedural motion requires only a simple majority.
6. Securing a vote on the next motion, to agree to the petition to discharge the committee. This motion too is debatable and requires cloture.
7. Placing the bill, now discharged from committee, at the foot of the Rule VIII calendar, which follows automatically if the previous steps are successful. It must remain there for another legislative day, which requires another successful motion to adjourn in order to reach a new legislative day.
8. Moving to proceed to consideration of the bill and securing a vote on this motion, which is by now in order, is debatable, requires cloture to end debate, and a simple majority for passage.
9. Moving to agree to the bill and securing a vote on it, after all amendments have been dealt with; this again is debatable and requires cloture.

In the face of determined opposition, and without the help of the party leadership, the procedures outlined here would take a minimum of five to eight weeks even if there were [67] votes in support of action at every stage, which was by no means certain. The group therefore determined that the route of discharging the Judiciary Committee was impractical; indeed, that the votes and physical endurance necessary to break four successive potential filibusters made it impossible.

Suspending the rules of the Senate in order to place the House-passed bill on the calendar was also considered. This procedure is no near cousin of the method of moving to suspend the rules and pass the bill, which is a short-cut frequently used in the House of Representatives and common in state legislatures, where with the backing of the party leadership and a disciplined two-thirds vote at hand an opposition minority can be steam-rollered. In the Senate version it has the advantage merely of reducing from four to three the number of potential filibusters and cloture motions to be met.[4] On the other hand, in comparison with the discharge procedure, it has two immediate drawbacks. First, because the tradition that all matters, unless by unanimous consent, should go to a committee before floor action is rightly very strong, suspension of the rules is open to the charge of by-passing the committee; the discharge procedure at least makes a gesture of giving the committee a chance to act. Second, because the suspension procedure has been so rarely used, it is open also to the charge of novelty in procedure—an unorthodox means of gaining an unorthodox end. The steering group of civil rights senators therefore discarded this alternative, and in fact concluded that if a choice had to be made between the two, the discharge route was preferable.

Finally, the possibility of placing the House-passed bill on the calendar under Rule XIV was canvassed. The relevant parts of Rule XIV read as follows:

> No bill or joint resolution shall be committed or amended until it shall have been twice read, after which it *may* be referred to a committee;

[4] The steps involved in suspending the rules in order to place the bill on the calendar run as follows: (1) When the bill arrives from the House, either a motion that it be laid before the Senate, or a wait until the presiding officer laid it before the Senate in order to object to the second reading of the bill on the same day. (2) Simultaneously giving notice of an intention to move to suspend the rules, and reading or placing in the *Record* the terms of the motion. (3) Gaining an adjournment to bring a new legislative day. (4) On the new legislative day and after the reading of the Journal, either calling up the motion to suspend the rules, or waiting until the presiding officer laid the bill before the Senate for a second reading. At this time, and prior to the customary referral to committee, gaining recognition to prevent such a reference by calling up the motion to suspend the rules. Since no motion to proceed to the consideration of that motion would be necessary, one potential filibuster is avoided at this point. (5) Securing a vote on the motion to suspend the rules, which is debatable and would require cloture to stop a filibuster. An affirmative two-thirds vote of those present and voting on this motion would send the bill to the calendar. (6) From this stage on the procedure is the same as with the discharge method—an adjournment to bring a new legislative day, when a motion to proceed to the consideration of the bill would be in order; a vote on this motion, which is debatable and would require cloture; disposition of amendments and a vote on final passage, which again is debatable and would require cloture.

bills and joint resolutions introduced on leave, and bills and joint resolutions from the House of Representatives, shall be read once, and may be read twice, on the same day, if not objected to, for reference, but shall not be considered on that day nor debated, except for reference, unless by unanimous consent. (Section 3, emphasis added.)

Every bill and joint resolution reported from a committee, not having previously been read, shall be read once, and twice, if not objected to, on the same day, and placed on the Calendar in the order in which the same may be reported; and every bill and joint resolution introduced on leave, *and every bill and joint resolution of the House of Representatives which shall have received a first and second reading without being referred to a committee, shall, if objection be made to further proceeding thereon, be placed on the Calendar.* (Section 4, emphasis added.)

Although infrequently used, this seemed to be a relatively simple and direct method of placing the House-passed bill on the calendar. If it could be attacked for by-passing the committee, it was nevertheless a well settled part of the rules of the Senate; and compared with many rules, its meaning appeared to be crystal clear. On that count it was therefore preferable to suspending the rules. And although perhaps less orthodox than discharging the committee, it reduced the potential number of filibusters in finally passing the bill from four to two. It was decided, therefore, that this method had the best, and perhaps the only, chance of success.

On June 14, following press reports that a group of Republican senators, including their leadership, were also considering using Rule XIV to place the bill on the calendar, a group of 15 Democratic liberals issued a statement in which they (1) urged the Judiciary Committee to report out a bill promptly, (2) stated that, while they preferred to act on a Senate bill, if a Senate bill were not reported they would join and cooperate with any other senator or groups of senators on either side of the aisle who wished to place the House bill on the calendar under Rule XIV, (3) gave formal notice of their intention to do so to the leadership and whips on both sides of the aisle, to the Parliamentarian, and to all other Senators, and (4) gave notice that they would not give unanimous consent to any motion to refer the House-passed bill to committee and formally requested that they be notified before the bill was laid before the Senate or referred, so that they might be in their places to ask certain parliamentary questions or to make certain motions. This last request grew out of the experience of 1956, when the House-passed bill was referred to committee while interested Senators were not on the floor. A further important reason for giving notice was that bills from the House as well as bills introduced in the Senate are ordinarily, for the convenience of all, read perfunctorily, not actually laid down by the presiding officer, and automatically referred to committee. Even when a bill is actually laid before the Senate, this can be done at any time and while the floor is unguarded, for under section 7 of Rule VII,

> The Presiding Officer may at any time lay, and it shall be in order at any time for a Senator to move to lay, before the Senate, any bill or other matter sent to the Senate by the President or the House of Representatives, and any question pending at that time shall be suspended for this purpose. Any motion so made shall be determined without debate.

Thus with a senator who opposed civil rights in the chair, another senator could move to, or the chair without a motion could, lay the House bill before the Senate and have it referred before another senator could gain recognition to object.

Certain precautionary steps were therefore taken. The first was to try to make certain that a senator in sympathy with the move to place the bill on the calendar, or the Vice President, would be in the chair when the bill arrived at the desk. Teams of senators were organized to guard the floor at all times. Arrangements were made with House members to notify key senators of the step-by-step actions on the bill in the House. Further, it was publicly pointed out that when the bill arrived the Senate would be in executive session considering the Atomic Energy Treaty, and hence that the bill would remain in limbo at the desk until the Senate moved back into legislative session. As the Senate can move back and forth from legislative to executive session by a simple unanimous consent request, attention was called to this fact so that senators would not lower their guard and stay off the floor during executive sessions under the mistaken impression that no action on the bill could be taken. Sheets of instructions were issued to the Democratic senators in sympathy with the move, in which parliamentary details were outlined; these instructed them to object to any attempt to read the bill a second time or to refer it, and to call for a quorum when in doubt. As a result, the rights of individual senators were protected as they had not been in

1956. Agreements were entered into at almost every stage for a specific time when action would take place and motions would be made, so that the rights of each senator could be asserted.

H.R. 6127 was laid before the Senate on June 19. It was read a first time, after which Senator Russell asked unanimous consent that it be read a second time on that day. Objections were heard from Senators Knowland and Douglas.

At this time Senator Russell argued that Rule XXV took precedence over Rule XIV. He claimed that following the procedures under Rule XIV would ". . . throw out the window the laws, the rules, and the Constitution in order to get at 'these infernal southerners' in a hurry." His major argument rested on the premise that the changes made in the rules by the Legislative Reorganization Act of 1946 superseded other rules with which they were inconsistent. In his view the language of Rule XXV, which enumerates the subject matter over which specific committees have jurisdiction, was in conflict with Rule XIV and therefore took precedence over that rule. He quoted Section 101 (a) of the Reorganization Act which reads, in part, ". . . such rules shall supersede other rules only to the extent that they are inconsistent therewith," and Section (k) of Rule XXV which reads:

> Committee on the Judiciary, to consist of fifteen Senators, to which *shall be referred* all proposed legislation, messages, petitions, memorials, and other matters relating to the following subjects. (Emphasis added.)

A list of subjects then follows, including "civil liberties." Senator Russell urged specifically that the phrase "shall be referred" is mandatory and superseded sections 3 and 4 of Rule XIV.

The proponents of the move argued that nothing could be clearer than the language of Rule XIV; that Rule XXV was not mandatory concerning referral but merely a specification of the subject matter over which each committee had jurisdiction; that the history of the Legislative Reorganization Act showed this to be true; that there were numerous examples of House bills going directly to the calendar both by precedent and under Rule XIV; and that the phrase "shall be referred," should not now be construed as mandatory when it had not been so on hundreds of other occasions.[5]

[5] There were only a few examples of a bill going to the calendar under Rule XIV prior to 1946. Since then procedures under this rule were followed once on May 3, 1948 when Senator Downey of California objected after second

Development of the argument brought out examples of House-passed bills which were automatically placed on the Senate calendar when a Senate companion bill was already on the Senate calendar, and examples of a House-passed bill placed on the calendar prior to the Senate bill being placed there, when it was known that a Senate bill would soon be reported. Further, although this point was not made on the floor, it is well known that, especially on the last day of a session, numerous House-passed bills are motioned up on the floor of the Senate when there are no Senate companion bills. There have even been examples of the bill clerk officially referring a bill to a committee and entering that referral in the Journal, only to find that the House bill is motioned up and passed in the last few hours before adjournment. In such cases the Journal has been corrected after the fact to show that the bill was sent to the calendar, in order to be there legitimately when motioned up. These examples added considerable weight to the argument that the phrase "shall be referred" in Rule XXV was by no means mandatory. Since these bills were sent to the calendar by a private decision of the Vice President or his agent, it was argued that what one man could do *in camera* under the precedents a majority of the Senate could do openly under the provisions of a specific rule.

On June 20, Senator Knowland objected to the "further proceeding thereon" immediately after H.R. 6127 was read a second time. Senator Russell raised the point of order that Rule XXV took precedence; and debate on this point, which is not debatable except at the pleasure of the Chair, took place for several hours. One problem concerning the use of Rule XIV bothered some Senators, namely, that a "single" Senator, by objection, could prevent a bill going to committee. The proponents of the move argued that while such a case might theoretically arise, there would no doubt, on an issue of such importance as a civil rights bill, be a point of order, such as Senator Russell raised; and that a majority of the Senate would, in fact, decide whether the bill should go to the calendar or to the committee.

Senator Case of New Jersey was particularly concerned about

---

reading to further proceedings on the Tidelands Oil bill, which then went directly to the calendar. Immediately following that action and on the same day Senator Fulbright attempted to do the same thing to the oleomargarine tax repeal bill. . . .

a single Senator's objection sending the bill to the calendar, and felt that greater support for the move could be obtained if some method were found to decide the issue more directly by majority vote. He proposed that, after the second reading, a motion rather than an objection should be made, to send the bill to the calendar. He had numerous discussions with the Vice President on this point and prepared a detailed memorandum outlining his views. The Vice President's opinion on the Russell point of order reflects, to a considerable extent, these original views of Senator Case.

The leaders of the liberal Democratic group, while sympathizing with Senator Case's position, believed that if a specific motion were made to place the bill on the calendar following the second reading, rather than an objection by a single Senator under Rule XIV, such a motion would be debatable and hence would require [67] affirmative votes and cloture to end debate. If this were true then the attempt to place the bill on the calendar could not succeed.

This point was overcome by the opinion of the Vice President, who stated (1) that Rule XXV did not require a mandatory referral to committee; (2) that if objection were made under Rule XIV and no point of order were raised the bill would go directly to the calendar; but (3) that if a point of order were raised the effect of it would be to put the substantive question, "Shall the bill be referred," in which case the issue would be decided by a majority vote. A filibuster at this stage was precluded when the Vice President went on to state that a motion to table could lie against the point of order. A simple majority, therefore, could end debate by moving to table the point of order. No such tabling motion was made, but the fact that it could be made allowed the Senate to vote on the substantive issue, "Shall the bill be referred?" The vote was 35 to sustain Senator Russell's point of order and 45 who opposed; and the bill went to the calendar.

Major Results of the Maneuver. There were at least three major, and perhaps historic, results of this action. In the first place it was probably the only method by which a civil rights bill could have been placed in a position to come before the Senate. Without it the civil rights bill would no doubt have languished again in the Senate Judiciary Committee until the end of the Congress. This procedural move was a major and essential step towards the final passage of the bill.

Secondly, for the first important occasion since 1938, the coalition of Southern Democrats and conservative Republicans was shattered. The *quid pro quo* of that coalition has long been that Southern Democrats would provide enough votes to defeat liberal social and economic legislation while the conservative Republicans provided the votes to defeat civil rights moves. Now, for the first time, a coalition of Northern Republicans and liberal Northern Democrats had acted together on a procedural issue of further the progress of a civil rights bill. This was all the more significant for, in the past, the conservative Republicans had furnished their votes in support of the South mainly on procedural rather than substantive issues, such as the 1949 appeal from the decision of the chair and amendment to Rule XXII which made it even more difficult than before, to shut off debate. They provided just enough votes or absentees so that cloture could not be applied to previous civil rights bills. They opposed and defeated the 1953 and 1957 attempts to adopt new rules of the Senate at the beginning of a new Congress. In that way the Republicans hoped to avoid the charge of opposing civil rights, for they professed their willingness to support, at least in part, the bills themselves on which, in almost every case, they prevented action. This was playing both sides of an issue and, because procedural niceties are little understood by the public and even more difficult to explain, they avoided condemnation for opposing civil rights which was the real effect of their actions.

In place of this coalition two new coalitions emerged. One was the Knowland-Douglas Axis, as Senator Russell referred to it, on the civil rights issue. This coalition is probably limited to civil rights and was more the result of public opinion, of the Republican gains in the Negro districts in 1956, possibly of the personal Presidential ambitions of individual Senators, and of the effective filibuster by committee, than the basis for any agreement or tacit arrangement for mutual support on other issues.

The other coalition was a revival of cooperation between the Southern and Western Democrats together with the remaining hard core of the Republican right wing. In many respects this coalition was not new for it had operated for years on such economic issues common to both areas as legislation on sugar cane and sugar beets, rivers and harbors and reclamation projects, the wool tariff, the silver subsidy, aid to the Western mining industry, and similar matters. As the course of the civil rights debate continued, this combination became dominant and civil rights, apparently, was added as a part of the bargain.

A third and most important effect of the vote was that for the first time in many years the Senate asserted a disciplinary jurisdiction over on of its committees. In theory, at least, committees of the Senate should be the servants of the Senate as a whole. Notoriously, in practice this has not been so. Examples include the unwillingness of the Senate to deal with the excesses of investigating committees; the tacit arrangement whereby the leadership, committee chairmen, and those Senators who are within or who are seeking admittance to the "inner circle" join to provide 52 to 55 votes to defeat motions and amendments on the floor when offered by individual Senators who are not members of the committee; and the unwritten rule of the Senate leadership that it supports the substance of committee action without regard to opposition by what may be even a majority of the party. In this respect, placing the civil rights bill on the calendar was unique and precedent setting. Although committees will no doubt continue to operate substantially as they have in the past, the possibility or threat of similar action may well serve to allow action by the full Senate on controversial bills of great importance for which there is overwhelming support and which otherwise would die in a committee stacked against them.

V. THE DEBATE ON H.R. 6127

Although the vote to take up the bill was 71 to 18, the new Southern-Western coalition proved powerful enough to effect major changes in the bill itself. They forced the delection of Section III of the bill and they added a jury trial amendment to the voting section which, as it passed the Senate, would have made the bill least effective in those areas of the Deep South where it was most needed.

Apart from the coalition, two other major factors operated towards weakening the bill. The first was the press conference statement of the President on Section III, saying that it was not his intention that the Attorney General should have the power to initiate civil rights suits under that Section and the 14th Amendment. The second was the fact that the press centered its coverage almost wholly on the contest—the strategy and maneuverings in connection with the bill—and avoided, almost completely, the moral and substantive grounds for supporting it in the first place. For example, Senator Douglas placed in the Record a detailed legal brief on the jury trial amendment and contempt proceedings, showing that no "right" to trial by jury was being denied by the provisions of the bill. This was ignored by the press. County-by-county figures on Negro registration in the South were also detailed, as were the various subtle methods by which Negroes are denied the franchise; and these too were largely, although not entirely, ignored. Further, Senator Javits and others made lengthy and even brilliant rebuttals of the attack on Section III of the bill which were little reported and went almost unnoticed even by such papers as the *Washington Post* and the *New York Times.*

On three further occasions after the bill was taken up the rules of the Senate, together with other internal and external factors, affected the substance of the bill materially. These include the abortive attempt on the part of the Knowland-Douglas forces to modify Section III when it was clear, following the President's press conference, that it would otherwise be stricken; the various revisions of the jury-trial amendment; and the successful use of the unanimous consent device to bring a third reading and deny the possibility of further amendmends at the late stages in the debate.

Striking Out Section III. Once the bill was before the Senate, Senators Anderson and Aiken moved to strike out Section III. This section would have permitted the Attorney General to seek injunctive remedies under the equal rights provisions of the 14th Amendment in cases affecting the use of schools, busses, public parks, etc., either on his own initiative, or at the request of an aggrieved party, or at the request of local public authorities which, in practice, would generally have meant school boards. Despite repeated claims to the contrary during the course of debate, the bill gave him no power to issue court orders or to decide how fast school integration must proceed. The remedies sought were milder in form, though easier, it was hoped, to obtain, than the criminal penalties now available against those who deny rights guaranteed under the Constitution; they were to supplement, not supplant, these penalties. The Little Rock, Arkansas case has since shown something of the potential effectiveness of the injunctive remedies. But the Attorney General was able to act in that case only because the original court order was sought by the Little Rock School Board, and because the court then invited him to intervene. Section III would have given the Attorney General the right to take the initiative.

When it was clear, after the President's press conference, that Section III would be deleted, the Knowland-Douglas forces sought to reach agreement on some substitute which could gain majority support. The Knowland position was that such an amendment should allow the Attorney General to intervene only when he was requested to do so by the local school boards or officials. The Douglas group's position was that the amendment should enable the Attorney General to intervene in these cases and also when an aggrieved party sought his intervention. Both versions abandoned the provision for the Attorney General to initiate action on his own and without specific request.

The parliamentary situation was that the amendment to strike out Section III could only be decided after perfecting amendments to the section in its original form had been offered and voted on. Under the rules even though the motion to strike out was offered first its priority for purposes of voting was last. The Knowland forces were unable to agree to the Douglas amendment, largely because they felt they could not push beyond the President's position; but the two groups tried to work out a strategy whereby they would fall back step by step, attempting to pick up strength as they did so. They decided that Senator Knowland should first offer his amendment, and that Senator Douglas would then move to substitute his own amendment for it. In this way they hoped that the liberal Democrats and other supporters of the stronger position could vote for the Douglas motion and when defeated, as they no doubt would have been, they could join the Knowland position as the next defensive move.

Because of the rules and precedents of the Senate this strategy had eventually to be abandoned. The supporters of the Douglas position were willing to fall back a step at a time, but could not agree to support a weaker provision when it was presented against a stronger position. They could vote for the Douglas motion as against the Knowland motion. They could vote for the Douglas or the Knowland motion as against the Anderson-Aiken motion to strike out Section III. They could not vote for the Douglas or the Knowland motion if either were to lie against Section III.

The parliamentary situation made it impossible to carry out their strategy. Once the Douglas motion was defeated there was no way in which the Knowland motion could be made to lie against the Anderson motion to strike Section III. The issue would have been between the Knowland motion and Section III, in which case the liberal Democrats and some Republicans would have felt compelled to vote against the Knowland motion. This was true because of the precedent that a motion to strike is only voted on after the perfecting amendments to the basic provisions of a section have been disposed of. Efforts to substitute a weaker provision for the existing Section III were therefore abandoned at this stage. It was decided to let the vote come on the Anderson motion to strike, and to offer a revised Section III at a later stage, preferably following a victory on some substantive issue.

The Moving Target. Yet another example of the effect of the rules of the Senate on the substance of legislation may be seen in the successive revisions of the jury trial amendment. It is a cardinal principle of most parliamentary procedures that once a motion is offered it belongs to the full body and not to the mover. The parliamentary body determines what action should be taken, *i.e.,* to amend, commit, refer, etc. This is not true of the Senate of the United States. An amendment, even after it is offered, belongs to the mover of the amendment and until such time as the yeas and nays have been ordered, he may amend it, revise it, or change it as he sees fit. In this fashion the jury trial amendment was changed almost from day to day, not by any vote of the Senate but by offering or acceptance of revisions on the part of its mover, Senator O'Mahoney. As Senator Douglas said on the floor, the opponents of the jury trial amendment were "shooting at a moving target." The initial point at issue was the definition of the criminal contempts to which a jury trial would be made applicable—an exceedingly intricate technical question.

The first version met strenuous objection. The distinction it drew between civil and criminal contempt was whether or not questions of fact were at issue. As any good defense lawyer could raise a question of fact, the effect of this version was to allow a jury trial in all contempt cases.

The second version attempted to distinguish between civil and criminal contempt on the basis of whether or not the act committed was a crime. The traditional distinction between the two types of contempt, often hard to draw in practice, turns on whether the action of the courts for the purpose of compelling compliance with a previous court order, or for the purpose of punishment for failure to carry out the order. Thus in a voting case, a local registrar could be held in contempt for failing to carry out the court's order, but so long as he could remove that contempt by compliance with the order it would be civil contempt. Once the day for election had arrived and passed, and the defendant was no longer able to remove his contempt by compliance, then the contempt would be criminal, for the court could send him to jail or impose a fine only for the purpose of punishment. Since almost all obstructive actions connected with voting in federal elections are criminal, the effect of the second version was to grant a jury trial in contempt cases arising from interferences with voting.

In the third version of the O'Mahoney amendment the orthodox distinction was finally drawn between civil and criminal contempt. In an attempt to gain more widespread support for it, however, the amendment was broadened to apply not only to voting cases but to all contempt actions under federal law. At least 40 other statutes were affected, but primarily this revision was aimed at gaining labor support, particularly from the Railroad Brotherhoods and the United Mine Workers who were sensitive about past abuses of labor injunctions and who, in turn, influenced a number of key votes in the Senate. This provision was a most radical departure from existing procedures. Like the second version, it was merely accepted on the floor by Senator O'Mahoney, and no vote was taken on the question of substituting it for the previous version.

At this stage the question of passage of a jury trial amendment was touch and go. Those opposed to it still appeared to be in the majority. Finally, a fourth version was offered to meet the complaints over the absence of Negroes from Southern juries, and so to pick up a few more votes. Federal law sets certain standards for service on Federal juries, but also provides that no one may serve on a federal jury who is incompetent to serve on the grand or petit jury under the laws of his state. As one must be a voter or qualified elector in Texas, Arkansas, Mississippi, South Carolina, and the Parish of New Orleans in order to be eligible to serve on a local grand or petit jury, and as Negroes are largely excluded from voting in these states, this means that by law Negroes are also excluded from federal jury service there. The fourth version, offered by Senator Church, repealed the provisions of the United States Code which excluded those from federal jury service who could not meet state qualifications. The effect of this final version was to provide the margin of strength to pass the jury trial amendment. However, as Negroes are excluded from jury service in other Southern states, in practice and by other means, it is doubtful that this change will have much practical effect.

The right to revise and modify an amendment at the will of its sponsor played a large part in attaching a jury trial amendment to the bill, for had the vote come on the first, second, or possibly the third version, it appears fairly certain that the amendment would have been defeated; and that, once defeated, the forces favoring it could not have recovered enough strength to pass even a greatly modified new amendment.

Unanimous Consent. The final instance in which parliamentary practice affected the substance of the bill occurred following the jury trial amendment vote and prior to the vote on the remaining amendments. Senator Russell referred to it in a speech on August 30, after the bill had passed, in which he justified and explained the failure of Southern Senators to filibuster the bill and took great credit for watering it down. He had this to say on the floor:

> When we had arrived at this particular stage of the proceedings in the Senate I happened to learn that a determined effort would be made to revive some of the provisions of Part III that had been stricken from the bill. The new amendment appeared harmless on its face, but if it had been adopted it would have placed the stamp of congressional approval on the erroneous, if not infamous, decision of the Supreme Court requiring the mixing of the children in the public schools without regard to the wishes of the parents of either race. We, therefore, quickly closed the bill to amendments in order to assure that none of the victories that we had gained would be snatched from us.

What happened was that a bi-partisan group determined to try to revive a part of the Section III previously stricken. Before they could offer their amendment a unanimous consent agreement was reached, at a time when there was general commotion on the floor, limiting further proceedings to those amendments which had already been offered and printed and confining the time for debate to 30 minutes on each amendment. Senator Douglas was within minutes of offering the revised Section III amendment and was prevented from doing so by Senator Johnson's unanimous consent request which was made and agreed to at a time of confusion when his request could not be heard in the chamber. Apparently a gentlemen's agreement had also been reached that all further amendments would be voted down by voice vote and without a roll call.

VI. THE FILIBUSTER: A PAPER TIGER?

One final point should be made concerning the effect of the rules of the Senate on the substance of the civil rights bill. A number of highly competent journalists who were not close to the debate, or who have since been misled by the interpretations placed on it by some, have asserted that the absence of a filibuster at any stage in the proceedings on the floor represented a willingness on the part of the Southern opponents to accommodate themselves at least to the voting rights provisions of the bill. A closer view leads to the opposite conclusion, that the passage of the bill represents no compromise or accommodation on the part of the Deep South Senators at all. Rather, the failure to filibuster may be regarded as a carefully calculated decision to avoid consequences which would have been worse, from the Southern point of view, than those of the bill as it passed the Senate.

Throughout the debate, and preceding the votes on Section III and the jury trial amendment, the threat of a filibuster was used to gain support for both these amendments. Senator Russell has since frankly admitted what many on the inside felt sure of at the time, namely, that the South would not filibuster and that the threat of doing so was more effective than the reality would have been. Notwithstanding the arguments made earlier in the year, that no meaningful civil rights bill could be passed unless Rule XXII was changed, the filibuster, after the Rule XXII fight and after the bill was placed on the calendar became a paper tiger. In retrospect it seems clear that the Southerners did not dare to use it because they feared the results would be the loss of Rule XXII and the passage of a much stronger bill than was passed. They were sufficiently convinced that a filibuster would so outrage the country and the Senate that they had more to lose than to gain by its use. This accounts for the severe condemnation of

Senator Thurmond by his Southern colleagues following his 24-hour "talkathon."

The Southern group decided, instead, to attempt to filibuster the bill to death in committee. In this they were successful; they could have kept it throttled there indefinitely. However, as a result of the great increase in votes for a change in Rule XXII and the vote to place the bill on the calendar, they knew they could not successfully transfer that filibuster to the floor. In Senator Russell's words:

> In years gone by, it has been a great source of pride to me that our group was able to defeat bills of this nature when they were forced to the consideration of the Senate. In the case of H.R. 6127 we were from the outset faced with greater odds than ever before. . . .
>
> There was not a man among us who was not willing to speak against this iniquitous bill until he dropped in his tracks. We would have done so, but for the conviction, growing out of our knowledge of the Senate and the experience of many years in this body, that a filibuster was certain to make a bad bill infinitely worse. . . .
>
> Our group held numerous meetings and the wisdom of launching a filibuster was often discussed. All members of the group were living with the problem from day to day, defending the things dearest to our heart while under heavy fire. At no time did any member of our group declare in any of our meetings that it was his belief that a filibuster was advisable, much less that one could be successfully waged. The contrary view was expressed on innumerable occasions. . . .

They therefore decided to avoid a filibuster while using the threat of it to gain their points. They decided also to keep debate relevant, and with one or two very glaring exceptions this was done. With the wholehearted support of Senator Johnson, the Democratic leader, they then pressed for the two basic amendments which, from their point of view, would gain the least offensive result. In this, too, they were successful. They took this course not from any desire for accommodation or willingness to compromise but because a different course would, from the Southern position, "make a bad bill infinitely worse."

Although the filibuster was not used, the existence of Rule XXII made it still possible for Senator Russell to claim that:

> . . . the fact that we were able to confine the Federal activities to the field of voting and keep the withering hand of the Federal Government out of our schools and social order is to me, as I look back over the years, the sweetest victory of my 25 years as a Senator from the State of Georgia.

Because of the filibuster rule, the unwillingness of some professed supporters of civil rights to see that the South dared not filibuster at this time, the consequent surrender to the mere threat of its use, and the skillful tactics of Senators Russell and Johnson, the bill as passed by the Senate was largely a victory for the forces of segregation. As civil rights proponents saw it, all their sweat and struggle to overcome the parliamentary obstacles had led to a bill which, except for a few minor gains, was almost form without substance. They took what consolation they could in watching the House revise it enough to make it a modest forward step.

THE IMPORTANCE OF BEING OLDER

The Seniority System in Congress

GEORGE GOODWIN

The seniority system ordinarily rates no more than two or three pages in books devoted to Congress. There is likely to be a brief description and a weighing of the arguments, pro and con, followed generally by the conclusion that the system is a poor one; occasionally an author will defend it stoutly. Regardless of the conclusions, the analyses are rarely thorough. This article attempts to fill a gap in the literature on Congress by describing and analyzing various aspects of its seniority system.

It is well to remember at the outset that very few human institutions ignore seniority entirely. Champ Clark, in his autobiography, noted that it is observed in all the affairs of life:

> No sane man would for one moment think of making a graduate from West Point a full general, or one from Annapolis an admiral, or one from any university or college chief of a great newspaper, magazine or business house. A priest or a preacher who has just taken orders is not immediately made a bishop, archbishop or cardinal. In every walk of life "men must tarry at Jericho till their beards are grown."

Yet, as George Galloway states, "in no other place, perhaps, does seniority or length of service carry so much weight as it does in the Congress of the United States." It is more than a means of choosing committee chairmen; it is a means of assigning members to committees, of choosing subcommittee chairmen and confer-

From George Goodwin, Jr., *The American Political Science Review* (June 1959, pp. 412-436), The American Political Science Association, Washington.

ence committee members. It affects the deference shown legislators on the floor, the assignment of office space, even invitations to dinners. In short, "it is a spirit pervading the total behavior of Congress." Its significance for constituencies was expressed by Senator Byrd, who, when he was persuaded to run again for his seat, explained that "seniority of service and committee rank have importance over and above the capabilities of the members." The system seems absolute in the assignment of office space, and nearly absolute in the choice of committee chairmen. Yet in other areas, it is often bypassed to a surprising degree. Our concern here is seniority as it relates to the standing committees of Congress.

I. WORKING RULES

As might be expected, seniority is not mentioned in the House or Senate rules, although it has drastically changed their effect. Senate Rule XXIV states simply, "in the appointment of standing committees, the Senate, unless otherwise ordered, shall proceed by ballot to appoint severally the chairmen of each committee, and then by one ballot, the other members necessary to complete the same." House Rule X reads, in part, "at the commencement of each Congress, the House shall elect as chairman of each standing committee one of the members thereof. . . . All vacancies in the standing committees of the House shall be filled by election by the House."

A distinction should be made between Congressional and committee seniority. Taking the former first, senators are ranked according to the length of uninterrupted service, dating in most cases from the opening day of the Congress to which they are elected. If they are elected or appointed to fill an unexpired term, different provisions prevail. The appointee starts accumulating seniority on the date on which a governor certifies his appointment. If a special election has been held, however, seniority commences on the day on which the new senator takes the oath of office, if the Senate is in session; or if it is not in session, then on the day after the election. Those entering on the same day are listed alphabetically, with the same rank number. House procedure is similar, except that greater credit is given for non-consecutive service. Those with three non-consecutive terms are ranked above those with two consecutive terms, for example. Congressional seniority is followed on social occasions, in the allocation of office space, and in making assignments to committees.

Committee seniority is established by consecutive service on a given committee. If two or more members go on a committee at the same time, note is taken of previous political experience, preference being given to former senators, to former representatives and finally to former governors. If previous political experience is equal, they are likely to be ranked alphabetically; in the House they may draw lots.[1]

When the committee party ratio changes because of a change in the party ratio of the house, members of the minority party with the least seniority may thereby lose their committee assignments. Otherwise the right to remain on a committee and to move up the ladder is generally unquestioned. A study of the committee assignments of Senate party bolters since 1925 shows only two examples of removal from a committee regardless of seniority (Frazier in 1925 and More in 1953) and four examples of members remaining on their committees but losing seniority (Ladd, Brookhart, Frazier and LaFollette in 1925). In all other cases, including those of 1948 when Senator Eastland supported the Dixiecrats and Senator Taylor ran on the Progressive ticket, no retaliatory committee action was taken.

If a ranking member leaves a vacancy because of transfer to another committee or retirement from Congress, all his fellow party members on the committee who were beneath him move up in rank. The career of Representative Sabath, to cite a case, gives a unique illustration of what can be accomplished by transfer, if it is combined with longevity. He entered Congress in 1907, transferred to the Rules Committee in 1929, after 22 years of service, became its chairman in 1939 after another ten years, and remained the ranking Democrat on the Committee for 13 more years.

A member who is defeated or who fails to run, and later returns to Congress again, loses his congressional and his committee seniority. He is likely, however, to receive more important com-

[1] So John M. Vorys of Ohio lost the draw to Robert B. Chiperfield of Illinois in 1939 when both were assigned as Republican freshmen to the House Foreign Affairs Committee. Twenty years later, when Vorys retired, though he had been for most of that period the Republican mainstay on the Committee, he was still only second ranking minority member—Chiperfield's district was as safe as his, and the seniority order once established was not disturbed.

mittee assignments than the average freshman. Alben Barkley, for example, after a tour of duty as Vice-President, was reassigned to his former committees, Finance and Foreign Relations.

In short, to become a chairman, a legislator must remain continuously on a given committee longer than any other fellow party member, and be of the majority party. It is not uncommon to find men on a given committee of higher House and Senate rank than the committee chairman. This is partly a matter of luck and partly a feeling on the part of some that it is better to be second or third on an important committee than chairman of a minor one. In the 85th Congress, for example, fourteen Democratic senators who were not chairmen had seen greater service in the upper house than Senator Hennings, the Rules Committee chairman, and sixty-one Democratic representatives who were not chairmen had seen greater service in the lower house than Congressman Burleson, chairman of the Committee on House Administration. But other members will stay with an early assignment, preferring to be bigger fish in smaller ponds.

Although they have no power to determine who shall be committee chairmen, party committees-on-committees in the House and Senate make important decisions on initial committee assignments and transfers from one committee to another. There is great variety in these committees, as can be seen from Table I, which describes the situation prevailing in the 85th Congress (1957-1958). House committee-on-committee members are chosen in a way that would seem to make them less subject to party leadership control than Senate members; however, there is no doubt that the House party leaders can influence the appointment of these members when they find it advisable.

In working out the "giant jig saw puzzle" of committee assignments certain limitations are generally observed by these committees-on-committees. They must, of course, be guided by the number of vacancies and by the number of applications for transfer. Care is taken to attain geographical distribution, if not balance.[2] Attention is paid to group desires[3] and to the experience

[2] In the Senate, for example, there may not be two senators of the same party from the same state on any committee, a practice that is convenient on other grounds, since it eliminates what otherwise might be a source of intrastate jurisdictional disputes between the two senators.

[3] Farm state representatives dominate the agriculture committees, for example, and only lawyers are seated on the judiciary committees.

and training of individual legislators. And balance among the various factions of the party is sought. Beyond these more or less objective factors, being in the good graces of the party leader is certainly important in getting on a major committee.

The House Republican Floor Leader presides over his party's committee-on-committee, and, while Speaker (or, in the 80th and 83rd Congresses, Floor Leader) Rayburn does not preside, "his presence is felt in the deliberations." Important positions are most likely to go to those who display party regularity or, at least, support for the party leader, as the following ditty tells:

> I love Speaker Rayburn, his heart is so warm,
> And if I love him he'll do me no harm.
> So I shan't sass the Speaker one least little bitty,
> And then I'll wind up on a major committee.

TABLE I. *Committees-on-Committees in the 85th Congress*

	Senate Democrats	Senate Republicans	House Democrats	House Republicans
No. of Members	15	23	15	38
How Chosen	By Floor Leader (Johnson); called Steering Committee	By Conference Chairman (Saltonstall) with Conference approval	Democratic members of Ways & Means, *ex officiis*, who are chosen by Democratic Caucus	Each State Republican delegation chooses one member, with as many votes as state has Republican Congressmen
Chairman	Floor Leader (Johnson)	(Bricker) designated by Conference Chairman	Ranking Democrat on Ways & Means (Cooper, followed in '58 by Mills)	Floor Leader (Martin)

This party control, which is expected in the more tightly knit House, is also found, though perhaps to a lesser degree, among the Senate Democrats. The so-called "Johnson Rule," initiated in 1953 when the present Democratic majority leader came into power, allows for departures from seniority in making appointments and, in so doing, leaves room for the application of less automatic criteria. According to the rule, no Senate Democrat is entitled to a second top committee assignment until every party member, no matter how junior, has one top position.

For all the committees-on-committees "it is handy to have the seniority system to pull them out of a dilemma"; but seniority has not been a controlling factor in the making of initial appointments and transfer, except among the Senate Republicans. Until the 86th Congress this group, however, placed the utmost emprasis on making the appointment process entirely automatic. Seniority was carefully measured, previous government service weighed and, if all else failed, the alphabet was resorted to in order to solve the committee assignment problem on an impersonal basis. In 1959, the Senate Republicans moved far in the direction of the "Johnson Rule," after considerable discussion in the Policy Committee and the Committee on Committees.

In making initial appointments and transfers there is room for choice and for favoritism, but there is almost no room for this in choosing committee chairmen. Becoming a chairman is a matter of party luck and of individual endurance. Once a member becomes a committee chairman, nothing but a change of party control or removal from the Congress is at all likely to force a change.[4] Chairmen have great powers. They subdivide the work of the committees, arrange the agenda and the work schedule, control the staff, preside over committee meetings, manage floor debate, and dominate conference committee proceedings, to mention only their more obvious activities.

Seniority also plays a part in the appointment of conference committee members and subcommittee chairmen. It is difficult to generalize about the former, because there is great variety in practice: but if the legislation involved is important, the chairmen of the committees which handled the bill originally, the ranking minority members and other senior members, will in all likelihood make up the conference committee.

Subcommittee chairmen are generally the senior members of the majority party on a given committee. In the 85th Congress, for example, every senior member had his own subcommittee on 12 of the 34 committees (three had no standing subcommittees at

[4] The voluntary abdication, early in 1959, of Senator Theodore F. Green of Rhode Island, then well into his nineties, as chairman of the Foreign Relations Committee, in order to make room for J. William Fulbright of Arkansas in that post, was a startling exception widely hailed as a tribute to Johnson's persuasive powers. Thoms S. Gordon of the House Foreign Affairs Committee relinquished his chairmanship during the 85th Congress on account of ill health.

all). On 19 committees, one or more of the senior members of the majority party was passed over in favor of a junior. In most cases a reason for this variance from seniority was obvious. The member, for example, may have been a party leader or the chairman of another committee. Yet in a number of instances there was no evident "automatic" reason for ignoring seniority. (One can guess at the reason why House Education and Labor Chairman Barden of North Carolina passed over Representative Adam Clayton Powell in favor of more junior members.)

II. HISTORICAL DEVELOPMENT

Historians of the House and Senate are not entirely clear as to when the seniority system, as we now know it, developed. This is not surprising, since it is a custom enforced by opinion, rather than by written rules. Seniority undoubtedly evolved first in the Senate, for this body was reluctant to give its presiding officer, the Vice President, the appointment power. He was thrust upon them by the Constitution, not chosen by the senators, and was not treated as a member of the Senate. Appointment power was vested in the president *pro tem* and in the majority leader, from time to time; but apparently the seniority system became firmly established with the development of standing rather than select committees, and with the crisis of the Mexican War. Since then, although there is no definitive listing, at least five departures from the seniority rule in choosing or displacing committee chairmen apparently have occurred in the Senate. In 1859 Stephen A. Douglas was denied the chairmanship of the Committee on Territories; in 1871 Charles Sumner, the chairmanship of the Committee on Interstate Commerce; in 1913 Benjamin R. Tillman, the chairmanship of the Appropriations Committee; in 1924 Albert Cummins, the chairmanship of the Agriculture Committee; and in 1925 Edwin F. Ladd, the Committee on Public Lands.

In the House the power of making committee appointments evidently gravitated early to the Speaker, who, unlike the Vice-President, was a member and the choice of his peers. It remained there until the revolt against Speaker Cannon in 1910 and 1911, when the seniority system took full hold. Even prior to this, however, seniority was a factor to be taken carefully into consideration. In carrying out the complex task of making committee assignments, the Speaker inevitably sought to regularize his work.

One study, for example, notes that seniority prevailed in four-fifths of Cannon's appointments during the 58th through the 61st Congresses.

In 1910, insurgent Republicans, working with Democrats, managed to take away many of the Speaker's powers, including the appointment of committee members and chairmen. Congressman Norris proposed that this power to given to a newly constituted Rules Committee which would represent the entire country and every interest in the country, and which would not include the Speaker. The Democrats, however, would not go along, and the system as we know it today developed instead.

Norris felt that "committee assignments were the rawhide used to promote party subserviency and to crush any spirit of independence." He was willing to take any lessening of the Speaker's powers on which he could reach agreement with the House Democrats, but he regretted the fact that he could not get support for his proposed committee on committees. Still unrepentant, he wrote in 1944, "If we had adopted this rule, as I originally proposed it and as agreed to by all the Insurgents, the seniority rule would not be here to trouble us now."

III. THE PROS AND CONS OF SENIORITY

The debate over the seniority system generally centers on the choice of committee chairmen. The favorable arguments stress the harmony which results from the system, the emphasis which it places on experience, and the lack of any more suitable alternative. The unfavorable arguments stress the effect of the system on party responsibility and Presidential leadership, the lack of any dependable relation between seniority and qualified leadership, and the fact that the committee leaders in Congress are by no means representative of many of the dominant interests either in the party or in the nation.

The most telling argument of the proponents of seniority is that the system promotes legislative harmony. It prevents hurt feelings on the part of those passed over in the struggle for appointment, and incidentally, it keeps pressure groups out of this struggle. As a result, it helps to create a more cooperative atmosphere, both in the legislative body as a whole, and on the various committees. Committees can act as more of a unit, and in a more nonpartisan manner. Roland Young makes this point in this fashion:

> The adjustment of rival claims must precede the adjustment of major conflicts without being permitted to divert attention for long from the larger task at hand. Some harmony within the legislature—including agreement on the location of internal authority—must exist before the legislature can itself promote harmony between conflicting groups.

Senator Barkley spoke in similar terms, when he opposed the Morse-Lehman attempt to prevent Senator Eastland from becoming Judiciary Chairman in 1956:

> The element of favoritism would come into play, and there would be log-rolling and electioneering for the votes of the committee members by those who wanted to be committee chairmen . . . Jealousies, ambitions, and all the frailties of human nature would crop out in the electioneering methods of men who wanted to be chairmen of committees.

Another argument of the proponents is that the system produces experienced chairmen—experienced both in the subject matter of the committee on which they have served so long, and in legislative procedure. They may also be better acquainted with the officials at working levels in the executive branch with whom they have to deal than the more transient department heads, who come and go with changes of Presidents. Robert Luce suggests that "though not the only factor in deciding merit, experience is the most important factor."

Finally, the proponents argue that the system is better than the alternatives, which range all the way from the even more arbitrary automatic proposals once made that the chairman be the member of the committee from the most Northern state, to one in which the President is responsible for the appointments. They take the essentially conservative position that there is no reason to change from a system that is working satisfactorily to a system about which the results are largely unknown. Some wonder if the system has not turned out to be a "rather handy scapegoat for Congressional inertia."

People on both sides of the fence tend to agree that when and if Americans turn toward party responsibility, "seniority will be an early casualty." The proponents of seniority, as one might expect, emphasize the harmonizing, rather than the issue-defining role of political parties, while the most outspoken critics of seniority favor responsible parties. They emphasize the diffusion of leadership among the 36 standing committees of Congress,[5] and the fact that there is no adequate way of integrating their various programs. In fact, they hold, the people most likely to become chairmen, the people from one-party constituencies, are the ones most likely to be out of tune with the party's program:

A chairmanship, after all, is the position of a quarterback on a football team. It should not be given to someone who refuses to be part of the team or who might even carry the ball across the wrong goal line.

The system, the critics argue, is no guarantee that chairmen will be well qualified. A hardy constitution and the ability to get re-elected in the home district do not necessarily fit a man to preside over committee meetings or to defend committee reports on the floor. If the system puts so much emphasis on experience, why, they ask, is a man who leaves to take an administrative post, but who returns later to Congress, given little or no credit for his previous experience? There have been examples, also, of chairmen who were too senile to be effective. When Senator Capper became chairman of the Agriculture Committee he could neither make himself understood, nor understand others. "The seniority principle is followed mainly because the seniors are pleased with themselves and see no sufficient reason for consigning their powers to others."[6]

Finally, the critics suggest that the system produces a large number of chairmen who are representative of only one element of the party, and that, generally, a minority element. They represent "stagnant" districts made safe by restrictions on voting, by a one-party monopoly, by the ascendency of a major interest group, or by an effective rural or urban political machine. Thus, the leaders of Congress, produced by the seniority system, are almost guaranteed to oppose the President, regardless of party, and a new non-constitutional dimension is added to our constitutional system of separation of powers.

[5] Two new standing committees were created by the 86th Congress, bringing the total to 36. These are the Senate Committee on Astronautical and Space Sciences and the House Committee on Science and Astronautics.

[6] This was phrased differently to the author by Senator Saltonstall, as follows, "The longer I stay in Washington, the more sympathetic I become with the system."

IV. SOME EFFECTS OF THE SENIORITY SYSTEM

Although it is impossible to prove the correctness of many of these appraisals of the seniority system, some can be analyzed statistically. Charges have been made, for example, that chairmen are approaching senility, that certain sections enjoy a disproportionate share of the chairmanships, that chairmen come from districts which are socially and politically stagnant, and that they vote against their party and the President a great percentage of the time.

The statistics concerning seniority in this section cover the years 1947 through 1958. This period from the 80th through the 85th Congress is a logical one to take for analysis, for the committee pattern has remained essentially unchanged since 1947 when the Legislative Reorganization Act cut the total number of committees from 80 to 34. The period includes two Republican Congresses (80th and 83rd) and four Democratic Congresses. There were a total of 60 Democratic and 30 Republican chairmen in the Senate; 76 Democratic and 38 Republican chairmen in the House of Representatives, counting each chairmanship for each Congress separately; altogether, 114 individuals occupied these 34 places during the time covered.

It is certainly true that chairmen are older than their colleagues, although perhaps not as markedly so as is commonly believed. The spread, greater in the House than in the Senate, averages 11 years in the former and six in the latter. Table II shows the age distribution of all chairmen at the commencement of each of the six Congresses studied. A greater percentage of Senate chairmen have been in their fifties than in any other ten-year period, while a greater percentage of House chairmen have been in their sixties. The youngest chairmen in the period studied were Representative Velde (42) and Senator McCarthy (43), both in the Republican 83rd Congress. The oldest chairmen, both Democrats, were Representative Doughton (87) in the 82nd Congress and Senator Green (89) at the commencement of the 85th Congress.

It is also true that the South provides a large percentage of the chairmen when the Democrats are in control, as the Middle West does when the Republicans are in control. . . . [Table III] Taking both parties together each of the four regions has had a reasonably equal number of chairmen, except for the West, which has produced few House chairmen. However, over half the Democratic chairmen from the House and the Senate have come from the South, and over half the Republican chairmen from the Midwest.

There are a number of ways of attempting, very roughly, to identify the more "stagnant" states to see if they tend to produce the greatest percentage of chairmen. Presumably, in our urban-industrial society, rural states and states with low total personal income should fall into this category. Furthermore, in this two-party country, one-party states and states with low voter turnout should also fall into this category.

TABLE II. *Age Distribution of House and Senate Committee Chairmen*

	House		Senate	
Age Range	Number	Per Cent	Number	Per Cent
40-49	9	8	6	7
50-59	32	28	29	32
60-69	43	38	28	31
70-79	24	21	20	22
80-89	6	5	7	8
	114	100	90	100

TABLE III. *Percentage Distribution of Committee Chairmen by Geographical Regions*

	Senate			House		
	Democrats and Republicans	Dems.	Reps.	Democrats and Republicans	Dems.	Reps.
East	20	12	37	22	17	31
Midwest	19	2	53	33	17	66
South	36	53	0	41	62	0
West	25	33	10	4	4	3
	100	100	100	100	100	100

Table IV relates the degree of urbanism of the states, grouped in quartiles, to the percentages of committee chairmen from the states so grouped, during the period under study. The Senate, particularly under Democratic control, has drawn its chairmen from the more rural states. The 24 least urban states have had 67 per cent of the Democratic and 40 per cent of the Republican chairmen. In sharp contrast, the House chairmen have tended to come from more urban states, but with a similar differential between the two parties. The 24 most urban states have produced 79 per cent of the Republican and 43 per cent of the Democratic chairmen. The House results are very different, however, when the analysis is made by congressional districts instead of states.[7]

Another test of the social and economic characteristics of the states which have produced chairmen is found in Table V. The states are divided into quartiles according to total personal income for 1956. In the Senate, in line with the general criticism of seniority, 65 per cent of the chairmen of both parties have come from the 24 states with the lowest incomes. In the House, on the other hand, more than half of the chairmen have come from the 12 states with the highest income.

Turning to more clearly political classifications, Table VI divides the states into those with one-party (10), with modified one-party (12), and with two-party systems (26). Almost exactly half of the House and Senate chairmen have come from two-party states, the remaining half being divided fairly evenly between one-party and modified one-party states. There are marked party differences, however, the most obvious being the fact that a greater percentage of Republicans come from two-party states. This is particularly noticeable in the House.[8]

A final test to see if chairmen tend to come from the more "stagnant" states, as is so often claimed, is to divide the states into quartiles according to the percentage of the adult population

[7] This perhaps more meaningful approach is to divide the 435 Congressional districts as nearly as possible into four quartiles. According to this breakdown, made for the 85th Congress only, the 109 most urban districts produced 21 per cent of the House chairmen, and 108 next most urban produced 5 per cent, the 110 next most urban 16 per cent, and the 108 least urban 58 per cent. See *Congressional Quarterly,* 1956, p. 790, for raw data.

[8] Another way to look at party strength is to determine what percentage of the members of Congress come from safe districts (districts which give them 60 per cent or more of the 2-party vote), fighting districts (districts which gave them between 55 and 59.9 per cent of their vote) and doubtful districts (those which gave them less than 55 per cent of their vote in the most recent election). Data for the 85th Congress show, as might be expected, that there are more safe House than Senate districts. Seventy-one per cent of House chairmen or ranking minority members have come from safe districts, while the comparable figure for the Senate is 44 per cent. More Democrats than Republicans have come from safe districts.

TABLE IV. *Percentage Distribution of Chairmen from States Grouped According to Degree of Urbanism*

	Senate			House		
	Democrats and Republicans	Dems.	Reps.	Democrats and Republicans	Dems.	Reps.
1st Quartile	11	5	23	46	31	76
2d Quartile	31	28	37	9	12	3
3d Quartile	25	28	17	21	21	21
4th Quartile	33	39	23	24	36	0
	100	100	100	100	100	100

TABLE V. *Percentage Distribution of Chairmen from States Grouped by Total Personal Income**

	Senate			House		
	Democrats and Republicans	Dems.	Reps.	Democrats and Republicans	Dems.	Reps.
1st Quartile	17	5	40	53	41	80
2d Quartile	18	27	0	37	51	7
3d Quartile	40	48	23	10	8	13
4th Quartile	25	21	37	0	0	0
	100	100	100	100	100	100

*Department of Commerce, *Survey of Current Business*, August, 1957, p. 8. Less recent total income figures make relatively little difference in the grouping of the states into quartiles so that it seems justifiable to use the 1956 figures for the entire period. The first quartile includes states which had between 2.16 and 11.96 per cent of the total national income, the second quartile between 1.23 and 2.15 per cent, the third between .51 and 1.22 per cent and the 4th between .18 and 50 per cent.

voting in the 1956 election, and relate this classification to the distribution of chairmen. The results are presented in Table VII. Because of the difficulty of obtaining data for previous elections, and the considerable variations in turnout over the years, this analysis was made for the 85th Congress only. A fairly even division among the four quartiles appears when both parties are combined, but a marked difference shows up again between the two parties. A considerable majority of Democratic House and Senate chairmen come from the 12 states with the lowest voter participation, nearly all of them southern.

TABLE VI. *Percentage Distribution of Chairmen from States Grouped by Their Party Systems*

	Senate			House		
	Democrats and Republicans	Dems.	Reps.	Democrats and Republicans	Dems.	Reps.
1-Party	33	47	7	21	32	0
Modified 1-Party	17	5	40	28	33	18
2-Party	50	48	53	51	35	82
	100	100	100	100	100	100

TABLE VII. *Percentage Distribution of Chairmen and Ranking Republican Committee Members from States Grouped according to Voting Percentage of Population, 85th Congress*

	House			Senate		
	Democrats and Republicans	Dems.	Reps.	Democrats and Republicans	Dems.	Reps.
1st Quartile	20	20	20	24	11	37
2d Quartile	17	13	20	16	5	26
3d Quartile	33	7	60	31	26	37
4th Quartile	30	60	0	29	58	0
	100	100	100	100	100	100

Now, turning to voting records, Figure 1 charts the chairmen's performance in voting with the rest of their party. A "party unity" score is used, which indicates the percentage of times that a member votes in agreement with a majority of his party when a majority of the other party votes in opposition. The graphs compare the average party unity scores of the chairmen, of all members, and of the floor leader of the majority party in the Senate and House. They also make these comparisons within the Democratic and Republican parties. When a party is not in control of a given Congress, the score of the ranking minority members of the committees is given. The chairmen's score is not far out of line with the average party member's score. It averages 3 per cent below in the Senate and 6 per cent below in the House. In the Republican-controlled 80th and 83rd Congresses, the House chairmen ac-

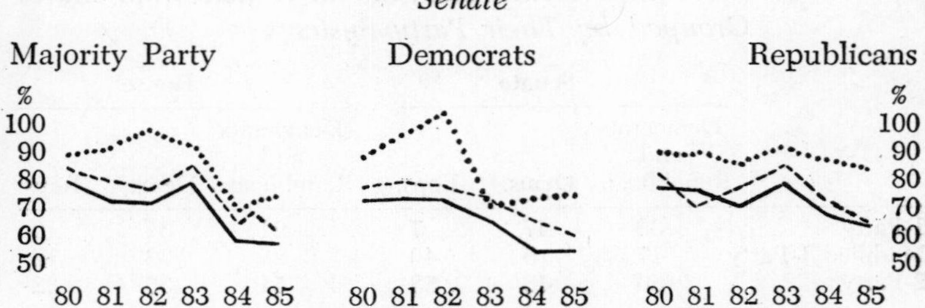

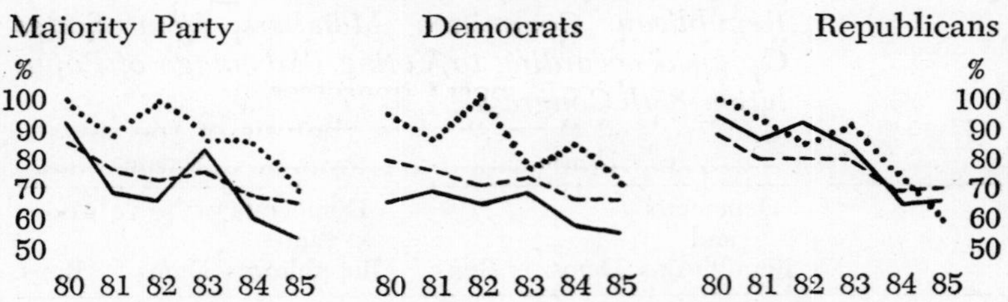

Fig. 1. Party Unity Score for Chairmen (or Ranking Minority Members) Compared with Score for Party Members and for Floor Leader, 80th-85th Congresses.*

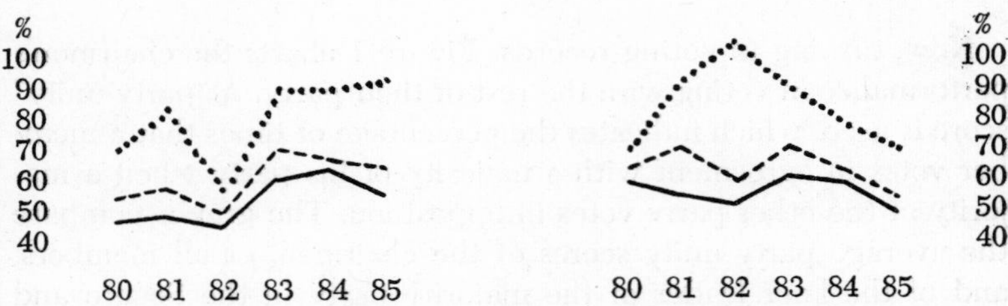

Fig. 2. Presidential Support by Members of the President's Party.*

Key ——— Chairmen's (or ranking members') presidential support score

------- Presidential support average of all members of President's party

. . . . . Presidential support score for President's floor leaders

* Data for these charts are taken from the appropriate volumes of *Congressional Quarterly*.

tually had a party unity score higher than the member's average.

The usual view is that the chairmen's party unity score would be higher if these key Congressional leaders were chosen by the party leaders, as is the practice in a majority of state legislatures. Yet even under the seniority rule, the average is not so much lower than the score of the party leader as is commonly supposed. The chairmen's average is 16 per cent lower than that of the party leader in the House and 12 per cent lower in the Senate.[9] The Congressional floor leaders, however, often have relatively low party unit scores. Party leaders, for example, voted on an average of 8 per cent below the highest individual party unity score in the House and 10 per cent below in the Senate. Well over half the chairmen are close to the top in party unity. Their average, however, is pulled down by the party mavericks who by seniority win one or two chairmanships in most Congresses.

Voting records also lend themselves to analysis of the degree of support that party chairmen, or ranking minority members, have accorded their President. Figure 2 compares the support given the President by the chairmen or ranking committee members of his party, by all the members of his party and by his party leaders in the House and Senate.[10] The chairmen's, or ranking members' score is not far below the average party member's score. It averages 4 per cent below in the House and 5 per cent in the Senate. The House chairmen's, or ranking member's, score averages 24 per cent below that of the floor leader, while the gap in the Senate is 21 per cent.

In conclusion, a comparison should be made between the seniority system as it operates in the House and as it operates in the Senate, as well as a comparison of its operation under Democrats and Republicans. Turning first to its operation in the two houses, the analysis above shows some interesting similarities. The House and the Senate are about equally likely to get Southern committee chairmen, and voting participation in the states furnishing

9 This quite obviously does not give the full measure of a chairman's relationship to his party's stand. He can do a great deal in his committee to keep things he does not like from coming to a vote on the floor.

10 During the 80th Congress there was a Democratic President and a Republican Congress; during the 81st and 82d both President and Congress were Democratic; during the 83d both President and Congress were Republican, and during the 84th and 85th there was a Republican President and a Democratic Congress.

chairmen and ranking Republican committee members in the 1956 election showed a remarkably similar pattern. Further, there is a close similarity in the House and Senate party system patterns with 50 per cent of the Senate and 51 per cent of the House chairmen being chosen from two-party states.

However, House chairmen come from more urban states (46 per cent from the most urban quartile while only 11 per cent of the Senate chairmen came from these states) and from states with higher total personal incomes (with 53 per cent from the first quartile compared to 17 per cent for the Senate). It is tempting to hazard a guess, therefore, that House chairmen, with a generally more urban-industrial background, should tend to be more closely aligned with their party and with a President of their party. The statistics presented on the voting records of chairmen fail to show this conclusively, however.[11] House chairmen and ranking members voted on an average 2.8 per cent more with their President than did Senate chairmen (60.8 per cent compared to 58.0 per cent for the Senate), but Senate chairmen voted, on the average, .7 per cent more with their party than did House chairmen (79.2 per cent compared to 78.5 per cent).

More marked differences show up in the backgrounds of the chairmen as between the two parties than as between the House and Senate chairmen; and a prediction of probable voting behavior based on these backgrounds is borne out. Democratic chairmen come from states which are more Southern and more rural, which have lower incomes, which tend more strongly to one-partyism and which have a lower voter turnout. It might be expected, consequently, that a greater percentage of Democratic chairmen would be out of line with their party and their President. In the period studied Senate Republican committee leaders supported their President 22.0 per cent more often than Democratic committee leaders supported theirs (70.7 per cent as compared to 48.7 per cent). They also showed slightly greater party unity than the Democrats (77.8 per cent as compared to 76.3 per cent). In the House, Republican presidential support was only 1.0 per cent greater than Democratic presidential support (61.3 per cent as compared to 60.3 per cent), and Republican party support was

[11] It must be remembered that much of the information concerning House Chairmen applies to the entire states from which they come, and not to the specific congressional districts which may be atypical of the states.

3.0 per cent greater than the party support of Democratic leaders.

This statistical analysis does not make as clear a case against seniority as many of the critics of the system seem to claim. Chairmen are older on the average than their colleagues, and yet with luck a number of younger men are singled out for chairmanships. The districts which produce chairmen are not as stagnant as is often suggested, and the degree of party unity and presidential support among chairmen is not as low as many believe. The picture, however, is far from the ideal held by the proponents of majority rule. . . .

CLUBHOUSE CABAL

The Making of a Senator

WILLIAM S. WHITE

The old definition of the Senate as "the most exclusive club in the world" is no longer altogether applicable, as perhaps it never was. It *is*, however, both a club and a club within a club. By the newly arrived and by some of the others the privileges are only carefully and sparingly used. To the senior members—and sometimes they are senior only in terms of power and high acceptability—privilege is inexhaustible and can be pressed to almost any limit. I have seen one member, say a Lehman of New York, confined by niggling and almost brutal Senate action to the most literal inhibitions of the least important of all the rules. And again I have seen a vital Senate roll call held off by all sorts of openly dawdling time-killing for hours, in spite of the fact that supposedly it is not possible to interrupt a roll call once it is in motion, for the simple purpose of seeing that a delayed aircraft has opportunity to land at Washington Airport so that a motorcycle escort can bring, say a Humphrey of Minnesota in to be recorded.

Lehman was, of course, a member of the Outer Club, which is composed of all the Senate. But Humphrey is, in part by the mysterious operation of acceptability-by-association, in or very close to the Inner Club. The inequality indicated here has nothing to do with political belief or activity; both Lehman and Humphrey are liberal Democrats and both have records of distinction. Humphrey simply got along better. . . .

. . . As a reform Mayor of Minneapolis he had become the hero of a liberal movement indigenous to the upper Middle West and as a delegate to the 1948 Democratic National Convention in Philadelphia he was shortly to become one of the heroes of the liberal movement nationally.

At that convention, the Democratic party appeared even to its oldest and most loyal partisan leaders to be in very poor shape for the Presidential contest shortly to come.

It had, two years before, lost Congress to the Republicans for the first time in half a generation and less recently it had lost its greatest modern leader, Franklin Roosevelt. The then President, Mr. Truman, had not by that time been recognized for the major contributions to history that he had made, as he is now fully recognized for these and the other contributions that later he made. No political estimate was more general than the estimate that the Democrats were very likely to lose the 1948 elections and that such a loss would become a moral certainty if the convention further inflamed a Democratic South-North division over civil rights.

All was accordingly arranged among the party leaders, in both factions, to deal softly in the platform with this highly sensitive issue. The platform committee duly brought out a carefully diluted document. Humphrey, a member of the committee and then only an aspirant to the Senate, would have none of this. He took to the convention floor, where it could not and did not lose, an appeal for a civil rights plank far more acceptable to the North than to the South.

Many will recall what followed: the angry march out into the rain of some of the Deep Southern delegations, the enfevered scene on the convention floor which even the most faithful considered a sure prelude to Democratic disaster in the following November. It did not, to be sure, turn out that way: Mr. Truman won after all and the Democrats regained Congress.

The point now, however, was that Humphrey, even before reaching the Institution in that November, . . . had broken the most underlying of all the unwritten rules. He had rejected the greatest political *raison d'être* of the Institution, the function of political compromise, and in the process he had made rude gestures toward those who were shortly to be his powerful Senatorial elders.

The road lay lonely and hostile before him, in consequence, when he appeared in the Senate to take the oath of office. The Outer Club was open to him only in the sense that all who belong to the Institution most belong to it. The Inner Club, at this point, lay immeasurably beyond any reckoning of hope for him.

What then, in the pursuit of this particular case history in the making of a Senator, saved Humphrey—or, more specifically, what was it that from this beginning made him a good Senator after all? Primarily there was the fact that though he had beyond doubt outraged the essential Doctrine of the Concurrent Majority these things, at least, *could* be said of him: His intolerable activities at Philadelphia had in any case occurred before he had been schooled in the Institution. Thus it could be urged in his behalf, by those who wished to give him a chance, that his had been an unconscious rather than a willful heresy. And it had to be admitted that his issue, however painfully he had insisted upon drawing it, was not a merely trifling or truly un-Senatorial one. (The Senate's instinctive memory could not wholly dismiss the fact that something akin to young Mr. Humphrey's issue in fact had been quite prominent in its affairs in another century, in the time of Webster and Calhoun.)

Finally, to a body of old men Humphrey was quite young and there was a certain tendency to forgive error in the young.

More important than all these considerations, however, his slow ascent to grace was the clear, but far from simple, fact that he had in him so many *latently* Senatorial qualities.

Not long had he been around before it became evident that, notwithstanding his regrettable past, he had a tactile sense of the moods and the habits and the mind of the place. Where another newcomer of the class of '48, Kefauver of Tennessee, seemed somehow usually to do the wrong thing at the right time, Humphrey seemed progressively to do things right. Where, for example, Kefauver suffered from a sad-eyed ebullience of highly personal effort that however worthy was notably disparte—from investigating crime to supporting some unlikely project like Atlantic Union—Humphrey unerringly set his purposes to be in harmony with the forms and spirit of the place.

He did not at all abandon his liberal designs (though as to civil rights the unyielding facts of life in the Senate forced him to move upon a zigzag course). He largely confined himself, however, to such suitably traditional liberal issues as higher farm subsidies and more generous labor laws. But he pursued these in complete awareness that in this body the best of motives will languish away unless one is able to marshall for them at best the support and at worst the fairly benevolent neutrality of at least some of the true Senate types.

Having recognized the nature of the problem Humphrey went about finding the human means with which to meet it. Unhurriedly—easy does it—and more or less naturally he fell into the habit of forgathering with the Democratic leader, Senator Johnson of Texas, and through Johnson there shortly developed a line of communication, however strained at first, with the other Southerners. With these Humphrey kept up a running and good-humored private debate, in the Senate lounges and on private occasions.

As he came really to know them, and particularly the able Senatorial politician who is Johnson, he began to suspect that there was, even on such matters as civil rights, less of blood-in-the-nostrils to their approach than he had supposed. And they came to suspect the same thing about him.

Slowly, by this means, Humphrey began to be taken into the informal and decisive deliberations of the Democratic hierarchs, if only as a spokesman among these centrists of a liberal view that did not characterize either his party there or the Institution itself. To be brought one way or another into this sort of deliberation is indispensable to becoming a good Senator, for such recognition foreshadows recognition for assignment to the committees from which one draws the greater part of his power in the Senate.

It is, however, a recognition that does not and will not come to those who fail to seek it or, seeking it, lack the peculiarly perceptive touch first to solicit perquisite without seeming to hunger for it and second to exercise perquisite without seeming to abuse it. (Abuse of perquisite is left to the long-established in the Senate; and in their case it is deemed no longer abuse but only the free exercise of what are regarded as the inherent and inalienable powers of the seniors in the Inner Club.)

Indeed, Humphrey had found, and now he illustrated, one of the ultimate truths of the Senate. This is that one *cannot* forever refuse there to make any compromise at all and remain a good, or effective, member. The art of high negotiation is an absolutely necessary part of Senatorial equipment. For the Institution, as it was at its beginning, is something more than a parliamentary body engaged upon parliamentary work. It is likewise an assemblage of diplomatists, in which each State in a sense sends Ambassadors to the Federal Republic, and the function of Ambassadors is not to reach proud, violent disagreement; it is, of course, to find acceptable agreement.

To accomplish this and yet not to let down one's principles, one's side, one's State—this is the unique achievement of a good Senate man. Because this is the highest requisite, it follows that this is no place for the man who has *only* principle; for every genuine political fanatic is simply awash with principle as he understands the term.

Humphrey, in short, as will all others new to the Senate, had found, and quite honestly found, that the career he had prefaced by scorning at the Philadelphia Convention the concept of necessary compromise would proceed in the Senate only to the degree that he accepted the inevitability, and even the desirability, of just that concept. The vehement heretic of yesterday had now embraced, perforce and indeed happily as his understanding grew, the Doctrine According to the Senate.

The tolerance of dissent—to a degree practiced in no other parliamentary body—that is characteristic of the place had now enabled Humphrey to find his home. In the process there had been a mutual erosion of views—his earlier views had to some extent been altered by the conservative views at which he had chipped. And those views had been somewhat altered by his.

By the year 1956 this circumstance had been interpreted by some of his more advanced liberal friends as a surrender to "reaction." And these, who had exulted when he took the lead on civil rights at Philadelphia, now began to fall away from him. It cannot readily be denied, however, that the more moderate Humphrey of the late fifties had, in consequence of all that had happened to him, put himself in infinitely better position to bring the Senate to adopt *some* bill in that area.

Because he was no longer looked at doubtfully by the Senate types (for an important illustration of this point) he was able in the Eighty-fourth Congress to bring off, by a *unanimous* Senate vote, one of the most cherished objectives alike of the liberals and of the true conservatives. This was the establishment, over the initial opposition of the Eisenhower Administration itself, of an independent commission to review the operations of the Government's loyalty security program. A man not so acceptable simply could not conceivably have done this, however fine might have been his bill.

Thus, the making of a good Senator involves several intangibles: A credible emanation of ultimate good faith in what he is about, one of the main criteria of good faith being the absence of petty exhibitionism. An understanding acceptance of the requirement of compromise, and therefore a willingness to abide dissent. A concentration upon the coherent and important and an avoidance of the diffuse and doubtful. A deep skill in sensing what may and may not be done. A gift if not for friendship at least for amicable association with other minds and with the interests of others.

And then, of purely human qualities there are yet more. The really good Senator must be a man of such sensitivity, a sensitivity not expressed by mere softness, as to be able to perceive those odd surges of feeling that mysteriously move among men generally, sometimes informing and sometimes obscuring the true meaning of issues before the Senate. He need not be particularly skilled in every kind of human relationship but this instinct of high discrimination is indispenable. It is, sometimes, the only quality that stands athwart hysterical action.

Then he must have a considerable essential ardor for life, an *élan vital* that is constant if not necessarily intense, to survive in a trying and hazardous way of life. This was the sort of quality that enabled Mr. Truman, an old Senate man, to go doggedly forward in 1948, refusing to be discouraged, while associates on his very campaign train were quite certain that he was finished. It was the quality that permitted Senator Taft, dying a rushing death from cancer, to go on working to the end, accomplishing in the weeks of his last illness more than he had accomplished before.

SECTION III *The Political Process in Congress*

Chapter Four

PARTY IN CONGRESS: Responsibility Achieved or Emergent?

THE WORKINGS OF PARTY DISCIPLINE

Party Membership in Congress

CLARENCE E. BERDAHL

If . . . the respective party organizations in Congress are almost completely independent of the national party organizations, and, still more, that the respective party organizations in House and Senate are almost completely independent of one another, the problem of party membership, in its relation to party organization and methods in Congress, clearly deserves special attention. It is in Congress that national platforms, declarations, and promises are presumably translated into legislation; it is therefore highly important to notice once more, and particularly in that congressional area, how the two-party system works and to what extent it is a system with or without meaning.

Although the operations of the congressional caucus in our early history, for the purpose of presidential nomination, are well

From Clarence Berdahl, *The American Political Science Review* (1949, pp. 309-21, 492-509, 721-35), American Political Science Association, Washington.

known, it is not quite so clear when party organization was established and the party caucus began to function in a formal sense for the purposes of legislative organization and program. Some would date that development rather late, but it seems much more probable that it was well under way for both parties and both houses by the time of the Jefferson administration. Whatever the exact date for its beginning, the use of the party caucus or conference obviously carries with it at once certain implications with respect to party membership—a Federalist caucus was for Federalists and for Federalists only, a Republican caucus is for Republicans and for Republicans only, a Democratic caucus for Democrats and for Democrats only. This implies, further, that there are certain criteria or rules by which a member's Federalism, Republicanism, Democracy, or other party affiliations may be determined in case of doubt.

Such rules, in any formal sense, were apparently non-existent until about 1909, and may have been supposed to be unnecessary, since members of Congress were chosen under party labels and might therefore be presumed to have had their party beliefs and attachments and activities already sufficiently passed upon and certified. Even to this day, the Republicans apparently have no formal rules with respect to party membership in either house, and such rules as they have of a permanent nature governing the party caucus provide in only the barest outline for a scheme of party organization; for the most part, they determine points of organization and procedure by *ad hoc* resolutions, which resolutions naturally reflect the practices and traditions of the past. This appears also to be the case with the Senate Democrats, though the House Democrats, on the other hand, have long recognized the desirability of a somewhat more formal organization, and in 1909 adopted a set of caucus rules, which have since remained virtually unchanged and which included (and still include) the following with respect to membership: "1. All Democratic members of the House of Representatives shall be prima facie members of the Democratic caucus. 2. Any member of the Democratic caucus of the House of Representatives failing to abide by the rules governing the same shall thereby automatically cease to be a member of the caucus."

With or without rules, however, cases arose of members in either house who wore no regular party label at all, members who wore the party label but wore it very lightly, members who wore more than one party label at the same time, members who changed their party label during the course of their service in Congress, members who bolted and even actively opposed the decisions of the party whose label they wore. There have been cases, in other words, of members whose formal party affiliation was in doubt and had somehow to be determined; there have been many more cases of members whose *bona fide* adherence to and loyal support of the party was subject to serious challenge and had somehow to be determined. Such party affiliation has had to be determined, primarily because of the custom of apportioning committee assignments among the different parties roughly in accordance with party strength, followed by the problem of the actual assignments to the various committees within that agreed proportion. It goes without saying that only Republicans can reasonably expect assignment within the Republican quota, and Democrats within the Democratic quota. The problem is to find who are the Republicans or the Democrats, and in case of doubt, what are the respective criteria of Republicanism and of Democracy.

I. REPUBLICAN PARTY

In general, the Republicans (and their predecessors) seem to have had the greater difficulty. The touchy slavery question brought on, as one might expect, an early test of party loyalty. In 1849, a Whig House caucus, composed of "all Whigs proper, or Whigs *quasi*, then in the city," met for the purpose of organizing the 31st Congress, and, in an atmosphere from which "a calm, collected, and unanimous expression of feeling was expected, as from a band of brothers assembling for a common purpose, to present a common front against a common enemy." Following the election of caucus officers, however, Robert Toombs of Georgia, that Southern firebrand but then a good Whig, exploded the caucus calm by introducing the resolution: "Resolved, That Congress ought not to pass any law prohibiting slavery in the territories of California or New Mexico, nor any law abolishing slavery in the District of Columbia." There was some vigorous debate on the merits of the resolution, but the general Whig position was probably best stated by Duer (N.Y.), who said that it was "well known that the Whigs differed on the subject of slavery, as they did on many other things as to which they had not agreed to act together, and as a national party they did not expect to coerce individuals to think alike on such exciting questions." The Toombs effort to commit the Whig party to a definite position was therefore voted neither up nor down, but was postponed by an overwhelming majority, with only eight votes in opposition; whereupon Toombs and five others left the caucus and apparently even bolted the caucus nominee for Speaker (Robert G. Winthrop). There is no record of any Whig punishment of Toombs and his followers for this disruption of the party calm, but it seems altogether probable that the occasion marked the end of Toombs' association with the party.

The impeachment of President Johnson was a question on which Republican doctrine and Republican loyalty were tested. Thus, in 1866, at a Republican joint House and Senate caucus, Henry J. Raymond was attacked as a Johnson man by several members, including Thaddeus Stevens, who said that he did not believe in the idea of Johnson Republicans and could not consent to let Johnson men into a Republican caucus. "But," he said, "if I had good, reliable evidence of the heartfelt repentance of Mr. Raymond, I would take him in on probation" . . . which left the matter to Raymond's own conscience—"if he honestly believed himself to be a member of that [Union or Republican] party, he could remain; if not, he could withdraw." A further attempt to throw Raymond out was defeated by the close vote of 36-38, and altogether the proceedings were a severe lesson to him and others not to play fast and loose with Johnsonism. . . .

Following the election of 1872, the Republican Senate caucus, on December 5, 1872, upheld its Committee on Committees in refusing to give any committee assignments at all to eight Liberal Republican senators (Trumbull, Sumner, Schurz, Tipton, Rice, Fenton, West, and Hamilton), and in that way read them out of the party. In this case the Democrats did the unusually generous thing of offering most of these men committee places from their own meager allotments as the minority party, even at the cost of sacrificing some regular Democrats. In that way, for example, Schurz was given the only Democratic (and, of course, the last) place on the Committee on Foreign Relations, and Trumbull a similar place on Privileges and Elections; while Tipton, Rice, and Hamilton were given the last places on committees (Public Lands,

Indian Affairs, and Pensions, respectively), with a regular Democrat in the place just ahead. This was done in spite of emphatic declarations by these Liberal Republican senators that they would not consider themselves Democrats and would not be bound by the caucus of either party, but would act independently and in accordance with their own best judgment on every question.

The independent movement of the 1880's and 1890's, which brought into Congress a miscellaneous group of Greenbackers, Farmers' Alliance men, Populists, and just plain Independents, provided many problems for both of the older parties, but again particularly for the Republicans, who during most of the time were nominally in control, but found their control threatened by these men of loose party conscience. The House elected in 1880, for example, was exceedingly close (147 Republicans, 136 Democrats, 9 Greenbackers, 1 Independent), with five of the nine Greenbackers classified as Republicans, only three of them, however, willing to participate in the Republican caucus on House organization. In 1887, when the Republicans were the minority, not one of the six Independents, including two who were "catalogued as Republicans," attended the Republican House caucus. Whether these Independents would have been welcomed had they attended, is not made clear, although it seems quite probable that they were, in fact, being cultivated. . . .

Following the Republican convention of 1896, with its dramatic bolt of the convention, platform, and ticket by several Silver senators and representatives, led by Senator Teller, the Republican Senate leaders finally decided, nevertheless, to send the bolters notices of the caucus scheduled for December 8, 1896, thus virtually inviting them to continue their association with the Republican party. Those Silver Republicans who were silver in priciple but had not opposed the election of McKinley were present at that caucus, but those who had bolted McKinley stayed away and probably saved the party considerable embarrassment.

In 1901, Senator Wellington (Maryland), who had been elected to the Senate as a Republican, but who had supported Bryan in 1900 on the issue of imperialism, and who apparently had said some unkind things about McKinley at the time of the assassination, was excluded from the Republican Senate caucus, but later was given Republican committee assignments. The explanation, which seemed to suggest a kind of associate membership or a probationary status for Senator Wellington, was to this effect: "It does not necessarily follow that Senator Wellington will fully renew his allegiance to the Republican party or participate in the caucuses. It is customary to recognize the request of a senator for committee assignments, the supposition being that he will then act with the party." . . .

The progressive movement, which took on tangible form with the Taft administration, quickly produced cleavages within the Republican party which were manifest on numerous occasions and which frequently raised questions of party loyalty and allegiance. In connection with the Pinchot-Ballinger controversy and the demands in Congress for an investigation, the split between the "regular" and "insurgent" Republicans was such as to require intervention by the President and considerable negotiation to maintain even formal unity in the House party organization, and brought forth, on January 14, 1910, the following White House statement: "It has been agreed between the regular Republicans and the so-called insurgents, represented by Mr. Dwight [of New York, the Republican whip] on the one hand and Mr. Hayes [of California] on the other, after conferences with the President, that a caucus should be held to pass upon the question of the committee in the Interior Department investigation, with the assurance that the insurgents, if they came into the caucus, would be treated fairly, and that a committee of acknowledged impartiality would be appointed. A further agreement was foreshadowed that caucuses should be held from time to time, to which all elected as Republicans should be invited, to take up the various measures recommended by the Administration as performances of party pledges, the subject of each caucus to be announced in advance." . . .

This factional split within the Republican party and the resulting problems with respect to party loyalty and discipline were still more evident in the Senate. On April 3, 1911, the evening before the Republican Senate caucus was held to organize the 62nd Congress, twelve senators met in secret conference, declared themselves "Progressive Republicans" entitled to separate recognition on the basis of their strength as one-fourth of the Republicans in the Senate, and appointed a committee to present their demands to the regular Republicans. In the caucus on April 4, the regulars yielded to these demands, the progressives being allowed four out of eleven members on the Committee on Committees, and two out of eleven on the Steering Committee, those progressive members in each case being named by the progressives themselves in separate conference.

In the Committee on Committees, having as its function the actual assignments to Senate committees, LaFollette pressed a formal resolution "that the insurgent wing be given one in every four Republican committee assignments, and that the insurgents, acting as a body, be given the right to designate what particular members of their group should be assigned and upon what committee he should be placed." . . . In the end, the progressives, although not given every post asked for, were accorded good committee assignments, though without securing formal recognition as a distinct faction.

For some years following the election of 1912, both Senate and House Republicans had less difficulty with the progressive or insurgent group, probably in part because some of the most insistent progressives had bolted to Theodore Roosevelt's Progressive party and were temporarily not wearing the Republican label, in part because the Republicans were now in the minority and it was not quite so important to hold strategic positions within the party organization. . . .

Ten years later, the progressive movement having again become strong, and having again made important inroads upon the Republican party in particular, Republican party differences once more became acute and led to renewed consideration of the appropriate place of the progressives within the Republican party organization. In the Senate, these differences were noted by Senator Jones (Washington), the Republican whip, who, in November, 1923, shortly before the convening of the 68th Congress, issued a formal statement urging the Republicans to get together, apparently being willing himself to accept any member's designation of himself as a Republican. "What we need," he said, "is conferences, not caucuses, attended by all who claim to be Republican, at which views and opinions will be frankly exchanged and an earnest effort made to find a common basis of agreement. We can learn much from each other, and we can afford to make concessions to each other on details and policies, if not on principles, for the good of the country and the party."

In spite of this advice, half a dozen Republicans, being unable to persuade the regulars to yield to their demand for greater recognition, absented themselves from the Republican caucus held on December 1, 1923, to organize the Senate for the 68th Congress. . . . In making this fight, the progressives first voted for . . . [LaFollette for chairmanship of the Committee on Interstate Commerce], which was in itself a considerable revolt, since Cummins [the regular Republican] was entitled to the chairmanship under the rule of seniority and had been selected by the party Committee on Committees and confirmed by the party caucus; but later these progressives even voted for and secured the election of "Cotton Ed" Smith (South Carolina), who thus became the one Democrat to hold an important committee chairmanship in a Republican Senate.

In the House, the Republican situation at this time was, in anticipation, even more difficult and dramatic. . . . Although badly beaten, the progressives in neither house were at that time punished for their irregularity, nor was their standing in the party questioned.

The progressive movement developed for the campaign of 1924 into LaFollette's Progressive party operating as a third party, with many of the progressive Republicans giving it active support and thereby bolting the Republican nominee, President Coolidge; and immediately following the election, won easily by the Republican party, the Republican leaders began to suggest punishing the bolters by treating them, in respect to committee assignments, as members of a third party and no longer as Republicans, and thus depriving them of their seniority on committees, a privilege which had put many of them in good positions. . . .

[To strong progressive arguments that many Republican idols had once been rebels . . .] Senator Watson, chairman of the Republican Committee on Committees, replied that a political party "in reality is organized for one election. If its policies are continuing, the organization may be continuing; but, after all, it is for one contest, one election, subscribing to one platform, one set of principles, and having one body of candidates to represent the people comprising that party and those principles in the ensuing administration. I am not concerned about what men did in 1912 or in 1916 or in 1920; I am concerned about what they did in 1924; and I know that at that particular time and at that particular election these particular individuals left the Republican party." Although there must have been many regular Republicans who winced at this remarkably loose conception of the Grand Old Party, . . . the committee assignments were made as proposed and the four senators were duly disciplined for their irregularity. LaFollette accepted his ouster without comment; Frazier said he felt much more hurt at being barred from the White House breakfasts; Brookhart good-humoredly insisted, over laughter in the Senate, that he was still a better Republican than Watson; while Ladd made a vigorous protest against this application of what he called "rigid and autocratic discipline," and said: "My duty is first to the people of North Dakota, and I deny that the representatives of New Jersey or Pennsylvania shall dictate the limits of my party loyalty."

As a matter of fact, the discipline imposed on these senators was not long continued. . . . [Most of the progressive leaders disappeared between 1924 and 1928 through death and electoral defeat. And after 1926, Republican control of the Senate was so narrow that every possible vote was needed, and the remaining progressives were restored to good standing with all former privileges.]

In the Republican House caucus, held on February 27, 1925, to organize the new (69th) Congress, a formal resolution to make support of the presidential ticket the test of admission to the caucus, and therefore of good Republicanism, was withdrawn after considerable debate; but . . . the Committee on Committees promptly adopted a resolution "that in the selection of the committees we recognize as Republicans only those who supported the Republican national ticket and platform in the last campaign." However, except for two cases, no disciplinary measures of this sort were applied until the new House met in December, 1925. At that time Mr. Longworth, nominated for speaker, and the other Republican leaders, made it plain that the "acid test" of sound Republicanism, which in February had been support of the presidential and congressional tickets, now would be the vote on the speakership and on restoring the stringent discharge rule which had been modified the previous year. . . .

Following these votes in the House, the threatened discipline was applied to the 13 principal insurgents, including Keller (Minnesota) even though he voted for Longworth for speaker, but not including any other Republicans who merely voted against the revived discharge rule; this discipline consisted not only in debarment from the party caucuses, but in demotion from their more important committee posts and assignment to the lowest places on minor committees. That is, the insurgents were denied recognition as Republicans in good standing, but were treated as though they were new members belonging to a third party. . . .

. . . The overwhelming Hoover victory of 1928 brought the regular Republicans into such control of the House that they could ignore these dissident voices out of Wisconsin; and the even more overwhelming Roosevelt victories that followed tended to disrupt still further the insurgent ranks within the Republican party by displacing some of them with Democrats, by presenting a legislative program pleasing to many of those who remained, and also by inducing, for those who still wore the Republican label, a greater regularity in view of their new status as members of a minority party.

There continued to be occasional individuals who broke party discipline and whose party standing was therefore subject to question. . . . William Lemke, of North Dakota, although sitting in the House with the Republican label, ran for president on the Union party ticket in 1936, and was subsequently demoted to lowest place on minor committees. . . .

It is difficult, out of all this, to find any consistent criterion of Republicanism, even for the House alone, and it seems to come out as something to be determined by the circumstances of the moment. In connection with vigorous Republican criticism of President Roosevelt for his failure to include representatives of the minority party in the delegation to the Inter-American Conference in Buenos Aires in 1936, Congressman Hamilton Fish (New York) was asked whom he had in mind for that delegation, to which he replied: "I had not anyone in mind except that he should be a bona-fide Republican, and, that is, not a Republican who has deserted the Party to support the candidate of another party." Upon being pressed further "to start back about 1910 and come down to date, and tell us what a bona-fide Republican is," Mr. Fish replied: "The gentleman is just as good a politician as I am. He knows exactly what I am speaking about. It is one who supports his party's candidate for the presidency." Perhaps that criterion fits the realities as closely as any, so far as the Republican party in the House is concerned.

In the Senate, however, even that simple criterion would not hold. In the 1928 presidential campaign, three Republican senators (Norris of Nebraska, Blaine and LaFollette of Wisconsin) openly bolted Herbert Hoover and took the stump for Al Smith; although they and their several radical colleagues, who also opposed President Hoover's legislative program, were later referred to by Senator Fess, the Republican whip, as "pseudo-Republicans," by Senator Moses, president *pro tem.* of the Senate, as "sons of the wild jackass," and by Secretary of the Navy Adams as "perhaps 12 men in the Senate called Republicans who owe allegiance to no party," they were not formerly disciplined and their excellent committee assignments were continued. Their power on the committees was, however, somewhat diminished by the simple device of increasing the size of the committees, and thus "containing" these radicals within more conservative colleagues. In 1932, four Republican senators (Norris, LaFollette, Hiram Johnson, and Bronson Cutting) again bolted Herbert Hoover and campaigned for Franklin D. Roosevelt; and although Senator Reed of Pennsylvania and other Eastern conservatives desired to read these men out of the party, they were not in the end disciplined in any way, but were left on their committees, invited to party conferences, and treated as Republicans in the best of standing. In 1936, two of these (Norris and LaFollette, the latter now turned Progressive by label as well as by conviction) again supported Roosevelt, but with no resulting punishment; in 1940 Norris (now an Independent by label), and in 1944 Ball of Minnesota, also supported Roosevelt with the same tolerance from their Republican colleagues in the Senate.

In fact, even the conservative Republicans in the Senate seemed to agree, before the party caucus was held in December, 1936, that although "the generally accepted definition of what makes a party man is that he shall have supported the Presidential candidate of the party in which he claims membership," such a test could not well be applied at that time, or there would not have been enough Republicans to serve the party on Senate committees. It was therefore proposed by four of these conservatives, and agreed to by the caucus, that there should "be no rigid test of a Senator's Republicanism, and all those whose political origin was Republican would be invited to attend the minority conference and be considered as aligned with the minority group in the make-up of committees." Under this extremely loose test of "political origin," not only Norris and La Follette, but even the two Farmer-Labor senators from Minnesota (Shipstead and Lundeen) were invited to the Republican caucus and were, for all practical purposes, considered as Republicans. It is not surprising that this action should bring the tart comment that "Republican bewilderment could hardly be expressed more comically," nor that the Grand Old Party should be referred to as a "queer menagerie." Indeed, the trend away from the old test of party membership, support of the party's presidential ticket, went so far that after 1940 repudiation rather than support of Mr. Willkie seemed to become the test of sound Republicanism and, to a lesser extent but nevertheless evident particularly among party leaders in Congress, was a similar test in relation to Mr. Dewey.

Many situations arose out of this loose party system that were irritating to regulars. . . .

The result was to increase the confusion and discord among the Republicans in both houses, especially in the Senate. One writer referred to the independent or liberal-progressive group of Republican senators in the 80th Congress (particularly Morse, Langer, Aiken of Vermont, and Tobey of New Hampshire) as the "New Sons of the Wild Jackass"; a leading Republican newspaper commented that "the so-called Republican majority in the Senate isn't a majority, because it comprises half a dozen different brands of self-styled Republicans"; . . .

II. DEMOCRATIC PARTY

By contrast with the numerous membership problems confronting the Republican party in Congress, the Democrats have had relatively little difficulty, whether because of a more harmonious party, a higher sense of party loyalty, a stricter party discipline, a more tolerant attitude toward party rebels, or for whatever reason. The first case on record involved David Davis, that sturdy independent from Illinois, who was probably a member at one time or another of every political party that operated during his lifetime. After his election to the Senate in 1877, he was pointed out as the only Senator who did not attend either party caucus, and it was said that he "passed a rather lonesome hour on the floor of the Senate, in company with the door-keepers and pages, while the other Senators were talking politics to each other in well-guarded rooms." The Democrats nevertheless considered Davis as one of their own number, or at any rate as one worth cultivating; . . .

Ten years later, the Senate Democrats had to consider what to do about the two Populist Senators, Peffer of Kansas and Kyle of South Dakota. Apparently an understanding had been reached by Democratic and Republican party leaders on a policy of containment with respect to these two Senators, the Republicans to take over Peffer and the Democrats Kyle, and thus reduce their potentiality as independent party men. This division seemed also to be in general accord with the preferences of the two Senators, at least so far as seating arrangements were concerned . . . , but two years later (1893) both were given committee chairmanships as Democrats and generally affiliated with the Democrats on matters of both organization and policy. In fact, the Senate Democrats seemed, on the whole, more tolerant of and more acceptable to the independents than did the Republicans.

During this same Populist period, the status of at least three members of the House (Bell and Pence of Colorado, and Harris of Kansas), elected as both Democrats and Populist, was considered a problem for the Democrats until all three settled the matter by declining to enter the Democratic caucus. . . .

In February, 1906, Senator Patterson (Colorado) supported the Dominican policy of President Theodore Roosevelt on the floor of the Senate, in opposition to the position of his Democratic colleagues, whereupon a Democratic caucus was called and adopted a formal resolution against the Dominican treaty and further "That if two-thirds of this caucus shall vote in favor of the foregoing resolution, it shall be the duty of every Democratic Senator to vote against the ratification of said treaty." Patterson defended his views before the caucus, but was curtly told by Senator Bailey (Texas), the Democratic leader, that he would challenge the right of any Senator to enter the caucus who did not abide by the caucus resolution. Patterson nevertheless persisted, and introduced a resolution in the Senate declaring that such attempt by a caucus to impose party discipline "is in plain violation of the spirit and intent of the constitution of the United States." . . .

. . . To which Senator Bailey retorted: "As I view it, the unity of a party is incomparably more important than the personal fortunes of any Senator. . . . This is merely a rule defining a Senator's duty as a Democrat. The Senator is at perfect liberty, whenever the importance of the question or the force of his convictions, or both, shall render it impossible to obey the caucus, to defy it, and to vote precisely as he would had no caucus action been taken. If he does defy it, he then settles with the Democratic people of his own State. If they agree with him, they return him; if they disagree with him, they may or may not defeat him. Thus the only effect of a caucus action is that it involves the personal fortunes of a Senator. My own opinion is that it is taking an unfair advantage of the Democratic party to call upon its members in the various States to choose members of the legislature, who, in their turn, and under the operation of a caucus rule, choose a Senator, thus giving him the benefit of the party organization, the fruit of the party victory, and then, when elected to the highest legislative assembly in the world, for him to despise the rule that brought him to this exalted station and proclaim his independence of the party." What happened later is not recorded, but Patterson became thenceforth essentially a party outlaw, and this may well have been the most important factor in his failure to be re-elected.

Three years later (1909), in the 61st Congress, the House Democrats agreed in caucus to support the Republican insurgents in their drive to reform the House rules, but Congressmen John J. Fitzgerald and Francis Burton Harrison, of New York, and about twenty other Democrats dissented with respect to certain features, including the proposal for a "committee of 15" (9 Republicans, of whom 4 were to be of the insurgent group, and 6 Democrats) to constitute the Committee on Rules and to propose a revision of the rules; these Democrats voted with the regular Republicans on the floor of the House, and helped save the day, in part, for the conservative group. At the same time, Speaker Cannon named some of these bolting Democrats to important House committees . . . , without consulting Champ Clark, the new minority leader in the House.[1] In at least two of these cases (Fitzgerald and Broussard), it was quite certain that Clark would not have

[1] Clark himself was appointed to both the Ways and Means and Rules Committees. Although the Speaker at that time had full authority to make all committee assignments, the practice had already developed under Speakers Reed and Henderson of consulting the Minority Leader about the minority assignments, and Cannon himself had even allowed the previous Minority Leader (John Sharp Williams) to make these appointments with only a few exceptions.

recommended the appointments that were made by the Speaker, since those men differed radically from the Democratic party position on the rules and the tariff, respectively.

Since this situation involved both a breach of party discipline and suspicion of trading with the enemy, the House Democratic caucus, which had already adopted a resolution "that no Democrat should accept a committee assignment unless it had the approval of the Minority Leader," reconvened promptly to deal with the problem. . . .

. . . The caucus, which lasted several hours, first adopted a set of caucus rules or scheme of government for the Democratic party in the House,[2] intended to define more clearly the rights and obligations of Democratic party membership, prevent such breaches of discipline as had just occurred, and thus promote unified and harmonious party action. The caucus then administered a thorough spanking to those Democrats who had in this instance departed from the party line, by adopting the following resolution:

First—We deplore the action of those Democrats who supported the Fitzgerald plan of saving Cannonism. This action was in conflict with the caucus action of their party, in violation of its platform pledge, and, we believe, of overwhelming Democratic sentiment. The Democratic party in the House disavows their action, and disclaims all responsibility therefor.

Second—Under the guise of giving the Democracy of the House representation on the rules committee and on the ways and means committee, Speaker Cannon appointed on the rules committee, as a Democratic member, the proponent of the Fitzgerald resolution, who is opposed to the Democracy of the House in its fight to reform the rules, and is in accord with the Speaker; he appointed on the ways and means committee, as a Democratic member, a gentleman known to be wholly opposed to any change in the Cannon rule.

We condemn the false pretense of the Speaker, that in these appointments he has granted to the Democracy representation on the said committees and we hereby declare that in neither of these appointments is the Democracy of the House represented, and we decline to recognize such appointees as representatives of our party on said committees. This arbitrary and unjust conduct of the Speaker demonstrates anew the urgent need for a thorough and real revision of the rules, and a better spirit in their application, so as to curb the Speaker, protect the members, and free legislation and legislative procedure from bossism. The issue is too great to be confined within party lines. Of

[2] This was the beginning of the more formal party organization in Congress. [See Berdahl's introductory remarks.—Ed.]

nation-wide importance, it challenges the consideration of every American voter whose neck is free from the collar of a boss, and whose back knows not the machine driver's lash.

Apparently all of the bolters were nevertheless allowed to keep the committee posts to which they had been appointed; and two years later, when the Democrats were in the majority in the House, Fitzgerald again sought in caucus to persuade the Democrats to continue the Speaker in control of committee appointments. This time, however, he accepted his defeat without carrying the fight further, loyally supported the Democratic organization, and, although removed from the Committee on Rules, became chairman of the Committee on Appropriations and one of the wheel-horses of the party in the House. . . .

Almost twenty years later (1928), when Southern Democrats in considerable number bolted the Presidential nominee of their party (Governor Smith), that bolt was led by two Southern Senators, Simmons of North Carolina and Heflin of Alabama. Efforts were made in the different states to punish these Hoovercrats, as the bolters were called, and some were read out of the party, or denied the right to be Democratic party candidates for office, or defeated for office by the rank and file of Democrats. In Congress, however, the Democratic organization did not in any way discipline the two senatorial ring-leaders, possibly because the minority status of the party made such discipline less important; both were, however, shortly punished by their constituents by defeat at the polls.

Senator Rush D. Holt, of West Virginia, who was elected to the Senate in 1934, before he was old enough to take his seat, immediately became a problem child for his fellow-Democrats in the Senate, annoying them continuously by his youthful brashness and disregard for Senate and party traditions. In the campaign of 1936, he apparently had conferences with Governor Landon, the Republican Presidential nominee, and openly fought the re-election of his Democratic colleague from West Virginia, Senator Neely, operating through the new Union party of Father Coughlin, Dr. Townsend, and William Lemke. This was considered a form of party treason, and shortly before the opening of the 75th Congress, Holt was formally notified by Senator Hayden (Arizona), the chairman of the Democratic Patronage Committee, that he might expect to be punished by being deprived of his Senate patronage (which was reported to consist of two policemen and one elevator operator). "It has become my duty to advise you," wrote Senator Hayden, "that when Congress convenes in January, you will in all probability be deprived of the patronage positions now assigned to you. From expressions made to me by Democratic senators, this action will be taken as a result of two facts: First, because you gave aid and comfort to those who were seeking to defeat the Democratic national ticket, and also opposed the election of a Democrat to the United States Senate. Second, because there are newly elected senators who wholeheartedly supported the Democratic party at the last election and who, therefore, have a sound claim to patronage positions among the attaches of the Senate. I am sending you this letter in order that your appointees may not be surprised when they are removed from the places they now occupy. I hope in the meantime they will be able to find other suitable positions." . . . The Democratic caucus . . . sustained its Patronage Committee.

This understandably harsh attitude of the Senate Democrats toward their obstreperous party colleague became in the same 75th Congress one of sympathetic tolerance toward the party independents. Thus, Senator Lundeen (Minnesota), elected as a Farmer-Laborite, requested and was granted classification as a Democrat for the purpose of committee assignments, and in return Lundeen supported the Democrats on matters of Senate organization. . . .

In the 1942 elections, Congressman Vito Marcantonio, that stormy petrel of the House from New York City, secured an easy re-election through having won the nomination, not only of his own American Labor party, but also of both the Democratic and Republican parties as well. In view of the fact that support by the American Labor party had saved several New York congressional seats for the Democrats, the Democratic House leaders felt that some special recognition was due that party, and the Democratic Committee on Committees, by a vote of 9-6, recommended the assignment of Marcantonio to the important Judiciary Committee. This action caused a revolt in the caucus among the Democratic rank and file, particularly the Southern Democrats, who argued that Marcantonio was disqualified for preferred treatment by his record as an isolationist until the invasion of Russia, as a belligerent fighter for anti-lynching and anti-poll tax legislation, and as one disposed to obstructionist tactics in respect to any matter he opposed. It was pointed out also that "Mr. Marcantonio himself owes his election more to the Republicans than he does to the Democrats. . . . When the returns were in, he had more Republican votes to his credit than either of the two parties;" it was therefore felt that he did not deserve any special Democratic recognition.

The Democratic House caucus, after a heated session on January 19, 1943, rejected the Marcantonio assignment, and ordered his name sent back to the Committee on Committees (the Democratic members of the Committee on Ways and Means) for another assignment, which Marcantonio promptly announced he would not accept and which the Committee on Committees therefore did not make. Marcantonio continued as the one Congressman without a committee throughout the 78th Congress; but in the next (79th) Congress he was again recognized by the Democrats and assigned without protest to their last place on the Committee on Interstate and Foreign Commerce, this possibly because in the elections of 1944 the American Labor party carried New York for Roosevelt and Marcantonio himself now became statistically more of a Democrat than a Republican,[3] or because of the tradition that third-party members should be assigned out of the majority quota. In the 80th Congress, the Republicans, now in the majority, argued that Marcantonio should still be assigned as a Democrat, since in 1946 he had been elected with a Democratic label in addition to his regular American Labor party label, but this time without the Republican label at all. However, the Democrats held out against any such Democratic assignment on the ground that Marcantonio was not a Democrat but a third party man; and this the Republicans finally accepted in 1948, giving Marcantonio, after another fifteen months without a committee, the last majority (Republican) place on the Committee on House Administration.[4] . . .

[3] The vote for Marcantonio in 1942 was: ALP-3,501; Dem.-7,553, Rep.-7,890; in 1944; ALP-13,543, Rep.-31,731, Dem.-37,042.

[4] Leo Isacson, elected as the Wallace candidate in a special election on Feb. 17, 1948, was also assigned to a committee (the Committee on Expenditures in the Executive Departments) out of the Republican quota, and without any quibbling, since he was elected only on the American Labor party ticket and was clearly a third party man. "The precedents are clear," said Speaker Martin. "We'll have to make a spot for him. The majority party must take care of the minority [third] party members."

In the 76th Congress, a more serious split developed among Democrats in the House over the Administration policy of continued New Deal legislation, and the party leaders found it increasingly difficult to keep their members on the floor and in line, while the Republicans showed exceptional unity in respect to program and strategy. The result was that a coalition of the Republicans and dissident Democrats was effectively impeding and sabotaging the legislation favored by the large majority of Democrats, and a caucus was called to deal with the matter. At this meeting, held on February 14, 1939, the Democratic leaders, Speaker Bankhead, Floor Leader Rayburn, Mr. McCormack (Massachusetts), chairman of the caucus, and Mr. Drewry (Virginia), chairman of the Congressional Committee, treated the problem as one of absenteeism rather than as a split in the party, pleaded with the members to coöperate with the Administration, and threatened, if necessary, "to crack the whip to compel Democratic members to attend the sessions." A group of the more ardent Administration Democrats also met separately on the same day to press for vigorous action with respect to New Deal legislation, and decided "first, to see that more Democrats attended sessions of the House, and second, to keep them from 'going down the aisle behind the Republican leaders.' "

These efforts to win over the anti-Administration Democrats by persuasion failed, however, and the coalition continued throughout the session. Finally, more than fifty loyal New Deal Democrats, led by Congressman McKeough of Illinois, petitioned for another caucus to deal with the problem. "It is the sense of the members signing the call for the caucus," said Mr. McKeough, "that no adjournment take place until this necessary legislation has been passed, or the responsibility for the failure so to pass is properly placed upon the reactionary coalition consisting of a small bloc of Democrats and practically the entire Republican membership of the House." The purpose clearly was to force through a binding resolution on the anti-Administration Democrats, something which the party leaders very much feared would produce "a party-splitting row." However, at the caucus, held on July 28, 1939, a resolution was adopted "almost unanimously," which strongly, although indirectly, censured the Democrats who had joined the Republicans in opposing New Deal legislation, and formerly pledged the party in the House to continued support of the Roosevelt program. The seriousness of the revolt within the Democratic party during that session of Congress is further indicated by the statement of Congressman Patrick J. Boland (Pennsylvania), the Democratic House Whip, that he was contemplating the dismissal of seven of his sixteen Assistant Whips "because of their disloyalty to President Roosevelt, as evidenced by their opposition to the President's legislative program."

During the war, the Democratic majority was able to maintain a fairly solid and united front in both houses, but with the end of the conflict and renewed emphasis on domestic policy, the coalition was restored on numerous important measures, particularly in the House, Republicans as well as Democrats bolting their regular party line. This revealed the rather meaningless pattern of our so-called two-party system, especially as it operates in Congress, and the situation attracted considerable comment. . . .

This extraordinary looseness in party performance and at the same time the passionate attachment to party labels was also clearly revealed during the presidential campaign of 1948, when Governor Dewey, as the Republican Presidential candidate, felt obliged to urge strongly the election of Republican candidates for the Senate and House, even though those men were opposed to the Dewey policies and would presumably so vote in Congress. Walter Lippmann took notice of this situation, and pointed out that "the concrete issue remaining [in October, 1948] between Mr. Truman and Mr. Dewey is whether the Democrats or the Republicans are to 'organize' the Senate," and that in order to secure a "Republican" Senate Dewey was obliged to campaign for men who were actually his political opponents. "As a matter of fact," wrote Lippmann, "in most if not all of these uncertain States [Illinois, Iowa, Minnesota, New Mexico, Oklahoma, Tennessee, West Virginia, Wyoming] the Democratic candidates [for the Senate] are not only more attractive to independent and progressive voters but are, on the great issues, much closer to Governor Dewey, and more likely to support him. . . . The odd and disconcerting fact about the situation is that in order to keep Senator Vandenberg as chairman of the Foreign Relations Committee, it is necessary for Governor Dewey, and indeed for independent voters, to work for the election of Republican Senators who have always opposed the measures which Vandenberg stands for. Is this not a foolish predicament?"

Mr. Lippmann's solution for this predicament was that Democrats should agree beforehand to allow the Republicans to organize the Senate in case of a Dewey victory, and thus save Vandenberg's chairmanship (and all the other chairmanships as well) and give full responsibility for national policy to the Republican party. Even though this were practically possible (and Lippmann clearly did not expect it to happen), there may well be some doubt as to the usefulness, to either the country or the party, of nominal Republican control unless that control is also Republican in fact, and this again raises the question of what is meant by a Republican or Democrat or whatnot. A better solution of the predicament would therefore seem to be the development of a more genuine and meaningful party system, with fairly precise criteria of party membership, with more closely knit party organizations in Congress, with the House and Senate parties more closely tied together and both closely related to the respective national party organizations, with a keener sense of responsibility as a party, and with a better system of party discipline to keep members mindful of the party position on legislative problems and of their obligations as members of a responsible party group. In some such way only can the two-party system be restored to something like the meaningful system it is presumed to be, and become an effective instrument to reflect the will of the people, who presumably choose Republicans or Democrats to Congress, not solely to "organize" the respective houses, but primarily to enact Republican or Democratic policy.

WE NEED REFORM

Blueprint for a Responsible Party System

AMERICAN POLITICAL SCIENCE ASSOCIATION

II. TIGHTENING UP THE CONGRESSIONAL PARTY ORGANIZATION

Party organization is complex. It also varies from house to house and from party to party. For the sake of simplicity, however, it is here discussed in terms of the party leaders, the party leadership committees, and the party caucuses or conferences.

From "Toward a More Responsible Two-Party System," *The American Political Science Review* (1950 Supplement, Vol. XLIV, No. 3, Part 2, pp. 57-65), American Political Science Association, Washington.

1. *The Leaders.* For more than ten years now the press has carried news about regular meetings between the President and the Big Four of Congress—the Speaker of the House, the Majority Leader of the House, the Vice President and the Majority Leader of the Senate, when the four are of the President's party. Despite their informal character—or possibly because of it—these Big Four meetings have provided an essential tie between Congress and the executive branch. They have given the four congressional leaders an insight into the President's plans and a form of prestige that could not have otherwise been acquired. They have also given the President a valued link with Congress and an important source of guidance and counsel.

In view of the development of this tradition, *it would be an error to attempt to supplant the relationship between the Big Four and the President by some new body* to carry on the same function. An executive-legislative cabinet to provide another bridge between the Chief Executive and Congress would cut down the leadership position of the Big Four.

Whenever it becomes necessary for the President to meet with the leaders of both parties in Congress, it is a simple matter for the Big Four to be expanded into six or eight. This, in fact, has occasionally been done in recent years. On bipartisan issues it should probably be done more frequently. The objective of developing a mechanism for consultation among the party leadership as a whole can best be met by the Party Council discussed in a previous section.

The selection of the Big Four is something that has implications for the entire party. In the case of the Vice President, there is broad party participation through the nominating convention and the election. A somewhat different form of participation is called for in the selection of the remaining three. Neither the Speaker of the House nor the two majority leaders can be regarded merely as representing the party members in the particular house. The same applies to the minority leaders in each house.

In the public eye a party leader like these is a spokesman for his party as a whole. It is necessary, therefore, *that there be broad consultation throughout the national leadership of a party before a party leader is elected in either house.* In particular, this consultative process should include the party organization in both houses and the President.

2. *The Leadership Committees.* The basic trouble at present is not that there are no party leadership committees but that there are too many committees exercising various leadership functions.

Some of these committees are called policy committees, some steering committees, some committees-on-committees. In fact, the Democratic members of a major legislative committee in the House, the Committee on Ways and Means, serve as their party's committee-on-committees—an arrangement that invites some doubt about its effectiveness in either direction. The Republican Committee-on-Committees is made up of one member elected by each state delegation who votes in accordance with that delegation's strength. In the House, also, the Rules Committee carries on certain legislative traffic functions that in the Senate are handled by the policy or steering committees of the parties. There is further the recently created Joint Committee on the Economic Report, which was set up under the Employment Act of 1946. This committee is supposed to bring forth on March 1 of each year a report as a means of coordinating the various legislative committees on matters relating to the economc health and growth of the nation.

The proliferation of leadership committees means that in neither house of Congress is there a body of party leaders who have the power of managing party affairs in Congress and who therefore can be held accountable for it. The result is that many things are left undone or—what is just as bad—are done in a dictatorial manner by individual party leaders. Also, too great a burden is thrown on the overworked Big Four and the Senate and House minority leaders.

To offer a ready-made blueprint to the members of Congress would seem pretentious. However, *we* do *submit these proposals:*

(a) *In both the Senate and House, the various* separate *leadership groups should be consolidated into one truly effective and responsible leadership committee for each party.*

(b) *Each of these four committees should be responsible not only for submitting policy proposals to the party membership, but also for discharging certain functions with respect to the committee structure and the legislative schedule.*

Each of the four committees should be selected or come up for a vote of confidence no less often than every two years, with opportunity for earlier challenge by a sufficiently large body of party members in the house if the committee fails to reflect the party program.

Occasion must be found reasonably often for the leadership committees of each party in the two houses to meet together. This is the only way to discuss common problems of legislative policy. *Furthermore, the rival leadership committees in each house should meet together on a more regular basis.* This is the best way to discuss the legislative schedule. It is not suggested, of course, that the majority party take less seriously the responsibility inherent in its prerogative to schedule legislative business. What we suggest, rather, is that interparty contact in this matter may make responsible scheduling easier.

A case can also be made for the four leadership groups to meet on specific occasions. This would provide an orderly approach to the broadening of areas of agreement between the two parties and to the identification both of party issues and of issues on which no congressional party policy is needed. An obvious occasion for such joint meetings is the transmission of the President's principal annual messages to Congress—the State of the Union message, the economic report and the budget message.

Something of this sort is already presaged in the work of the Joint Committee on the Economic Report. It is no longer a question whether the President's proposals be the starting point of the legislative schedule. They already are. The problem is how to get these proposals responsibily handled. At present they are not.

One of the reasons is that the Joint Committee on the Economic Report is composed of members of Congress who, for the most part, have no formal responsibility for party leadership. No committee of Congress other than one comprising the official party leadership—including the chairmen of the key committees—can serve to coordinate the main policy decisions that arise in the diversified activities distributed over the committee system. This logic points to the need for having the membership of the Joint Committee on the Economic Report include the responsible leaders of both parties—a need recognized early by such leaders as Senator Murry and Senator Flanders.

Another way to approach the same end would be to have the four party leadership committees meet jointly at the beginning of every session as a Joint Committee on the President's Program. Such a committee could consider the entire program embodied in the President's three principal annual messages and furnish guidance to the general line of action on the part of the various legislative committees.

3. *Caucuses or Conferences.* Whether they be called caucuses or conferences, *more frequent meetings of the party membership in each house should be held.* Otherwise there can be no real discussion of party positions and no real participation in or check upon the decisions of the party leadership. Without such discussion and participation, efforts to make party operations more responsible will be futile.

There is no formula to tell how often a caucus or conference should be convened merely to discuss matters and how often it should be held for the purpose of voting upon a position binding on the members. Nor is it possible to prescribe in other than general terms either the conditions under which a party member may be released from abiding by a caucus decision or the consequences to be invoked upon those who disregard the decision without release.[1] Three points, however, are rather clear.

The first is that *a binding caucus decision on legislative policy should be used primarily to carry out the party's principles and program.* Such a decision should not be used merely to support the views of the President or of congressional party leaders when their views do not rest on stated party policy, except in exigencies affecting the public record of the party.

The second is that members who generally stand behind the party program should have reason to know that their service is appreciated by the party leadership. Rewarding party loyalty is a proper way of fostering party unity. On the other hand, *when members of Congress disregard a caucus decision taken in furtherance of national party policy, they should expect disapproval.* They should not expect to receive the same consideration in the assignment of committee posts or in the apportionment of patronage as those who have been loyal to party principles. Their conduct should be brought before the eyes of the public. Their voters are entitled to know about it.

The third is that the party leadership committees should be

[1] The Democratic House Caucus Rules provide that members may be released when they have grounds to consider the decision unconstitutional or when the decision collides with a member's previous campaign commitments or with instructions from his constituency.

responsible for calling more frequent caucuses or conferences and developing the agenda of points for discussion.

III. PARTY RESPONSIBILITY FOR COMMITTEE STRUCTURE

Congressional committees have aptly been called "little legislatures." The bulk of congressional work is done in committee. It is in the committees, therefore, that the parties are put to their highest test.

1. *Selection of Committee Chairmen.* One often hears the lament that the seniority system is bad for the country but that there is just no other way of selecting committee chairmen. But this puts the problem in the wrong way.

The problem is not one of abolishing seniority and then finding an alternative. It is one of mobilizing the power through which the party leadership can successfully use the seniority principle rather than have the seniority principle dominate Congress. Under conditions of party responsibility, with greater clarity of the party's position and broader acceptance of it, deliberate use of the seniority principle for purposes of party unity would be the opposite to personal power exercised by a particular individual or a small clique.

Advancement within a committee on the basis of seniority makes sense, other things being equal. But *it is not playing the game fairly for party members who oppose the commitments in their party's platform to rely on seniority to carry them into committee chairmanships. Party leaders have compelling reason to prevent such a member from becoming chairman—and they are entirely free so to exert their influence.* A chairmanship, after all, is like the position of a quarterback on a football team. It should not be given to someone who refuses to be a part of the team or who might even carry the ball across the wrong goal line. Nor is it satisfactory for either party to find itself saddled with a large number of chairmen representative in their thinking of only one element in the party.

An all-out use of this approach, however, would run up against certain present-day realities. As long as party dissidents succeed in getting elected to Congress, they may hold a balance-of-power position between the two parties. If attempts were made to dislodge them from positions of power they might have gained in their party, they would be able to throw the control of either house into the hands of the opposing party. *The task of party leaders, when confronted with revolt on the part of committee chairmen, is* hence *not easy*. Obviously *problems of this sort must be handled in the electoral process itself as well as in the congressional arena.* Yet these practical limitations are far from insuperable, especially by consistent effort and crystallization of party doctrine. Similar limitations impede action everywhere. If they were regarded as excuses for inaction, progress at any point would be impossible.

To make the obvious explicit, we are not arguing here or elsewhere for parties made up of yes-men. Dissent is not undesirable in itself. It can be wholesome and constructive when it operates on a common basis. We are arguing the need for that common basis. Defiance of that common basis destroys the opportunity for party responsibility.

2. *Assignment of Members to Committees.* The distribution of committee positions among new members is one of the most important functions of party leadership. *The slates of committee assignments should be drawn up by the party leadership committees and presented to the appropriate party caucuses for approval or modification.* This applies to special and joint committees as well as to legislative committees. Where the Vice President and the Speaker of the House are given statutory power to appoint committee members, they should accept the slates offered by each of the parties on such a basis.

The principle of having both parties represented on every legislative committee is a sound one. However, *there is nothing sound in having the party ratio on the committees always correspond closely to the party ratio in the house itself,* which may often mean almost as many committee positions for the minority as for the majority—such as six to seven. This gives individual members of the majority party the balance of power and invites chaos. The results undermine party responsibility.

Regardless of the general proportion of party membership in each house, the majority party in the house should have a comfortable margin of control within each committee. The same applies, for the same reasons, to subcommittees. Of course, in thus taking more direct committee responsibility the majority party will hardly close its eyes to the attitudes in the electorate. Always the majority party will have to think of the next election.

Although much is to be gained in the committee by continuity and experience, there is also an advantage in having a regular review of the committee structure. *Committee assignments* should not be regarded as permanent prerogative. Personal competence and party loyalty should be valued more highly than seniority in assigning members to such major committees as those dealing with fiscal policy and foreign affairs. Previous decisions with respect to committee assignments *should be subjected to regular reexamination by the party caucus or conference with reasonable frequency,* at least every two years.

Adjustments of this kind would make it much easier for either party to come forth with a consistent legislative record. They would reduce greatly the present differences in point of view among different committees, thus giving Congress itself a large measure of unity. They would cause committees to stand less on their vested jurisdictional rights. They would finally cut down the waste of effort that results from the inclination of individual committees to act as small legislatures apart from Congress at large—as when a committee reopens an issue settled by Congress in the course of implementing the prior decision of Congress.

3. *Committee Staff. Staff assistance should be available to minority as well as majority members of a committee whenever they want it.* It should not be within the power of the majority, as it is now, to deny this assistance. The excellent work of the Legislative Reference Service of the Library of Congress should not be expected to take the place of the more intensive type of analysis best done by committee staffs.

Committee staff for members of both parties is essential to provide a basis for sound party operations. It also contributes to the needed minimum of occupational security for professional staff members. *Where all committees staff is controlled by the majority, a change in power threatens continuity of service.* Top quality staff would generally not be available under such conditions.

IV. PARTY RESPONSIBILITY FOR THE LEGISLATIVE SCHEDULE

There is always more work before Congress than can be handled. Not all of the bills reported upon by committees can be taken up on the floor. Only a portion of the bills introduced can be examined at public hearings. One of the greatest defects in present congressional committees is the absence of a truly responsible approach toward the scheduling of what is to be handled and when. Here lies one of the greatest opportunities for party leadership.

1. *The Need for Scheduling.* Scheduling should include not only what measures are to be taken from the calendar for floor action but also the general scheduling of major hearings. *Schedules should be openly explained on the floor in advance.* They should apply to all issues, not just party issues.

No one but party leaders can do this job properly. Policy and steering functions are inseparable. *No committee should be in charge of legislative scheduling except the party leadership committee.*

2. *House Guidance of Legislative Traffic.* For some time up to quite recently, the Rules Committee has held decisive control over the legislative calendar in the House, without attempting to act as a program expediter of the dominant party. At the beginning of the 81st Congress, the rules of the House were changed by allowing committee chairmen to bypass the Rules Committee under certain circumstances. This was a step in the right direction in so far as it partially removed a roadblock in the path of more responsible party control of legislative traffic.

It was far from a wholly satisfactory solution, however. The power taken away from an irresponsible group that did not represent the leadership of the two parties was distributed among the committee chairmen. These, today, do not yet act as a group of responsible party leaders. To safeguard his party the Speaker of the House has been forced on many occasions to deny recognition to individual committee chairmen.

A more *democratic approach would be to substitute open party control for control by the Rules Committee or individual chairmen.* There are many ways to do this. An extreme measure would be to abolish the Rules Committee altogether and have its functions taken over by the leadership committees of the two parties. A more feasible solution would probably be to shift the steering function from the Rules Committee to the leadership committee of the majority party. It might also be feasible to give the Speaker and the Majority Leader jointly the power to bypass the Rules Committee after a given period of time has elapsed, and upon a sufficient showing of support from the membership of the majority party.

3. *The Right to Vote in the Senate.* The present cloture rule goes so far in giving individual Senators the right to speak that it interferes with the right of the majority to vote. It is a serious obstacle to responsible lawmaking.

The present cloture rule should be amended. The best rule is one that provides for majority cloture on all matters before the Senate. This need not interfere with the right of Senators to speak for a reasonable length of time. There is no lack of proposals submitted in the Senate which would hold off the cloture vote for a given number of days or until each Senator has had an opportunity to speak for a reasonable time.

WE DO NOT NEED REFORM

A Dissent from the Floor

JULIUS TURNER

The report of the Committee on Political Parties of the American Political Science Association presents the case for the development of disciplined and responsible parties in a document more complete and more dramatic than any previous summarization of the case. . . .

But the report can be no more than a starting point, for its value is limited by errors in two broad aspects, as follows:

I. The Committee has underestimated present party responsibility.

II. Some reforms which the Committee proposes will accentuate present defects in our party system.

For these reasons, the report should be given the widest possible circulation among students of political science, but its conclusions should be treated with caution.

I. THE COMMITTEE HAS UNDERESTIMATED PRESENT PARTY RESPONSIBILITY

. . . *Do the parties present clear alternatives to the voters?* The Committee believes that the answer is "no." In discussing platforms, the report maintains that "alternatives between the parties

From Julius Turner, *The American Political Science Review* (March 1951, Vol. XLV, pp. 143-152), The American Political Science Association, Washington.

are defined so badly that it is often difficult to determine what the election has decided even in broadest terms." In what appears to be a comment on Congress, the report states that "the sort of opposition presented by a coalition that cuts across party lines, *as a regular thing,* tends to deprive the public of a meaningful alternative. . . . Moreover, on that basis it is next to impossible to hold either party responsible for its political record."

Contrary to the Committee's conclusions, platforms do reveal party differences on national issues affecting many groups. Analysis of the platforms of 1948, for example, reveals collisions in ideology and differences in emphasis which could hardly escape a serious reader. Democrats advocated repeal of the Taft-Hartley act; Republicans commended themselves for having passed it. Republicans advocated "prudent conservation of resources" in foreign aid programs; Democrats boasted that "generous sums have been provided." Republicans promised another reduction in taxes, especially to provide an incentive to new industry; Democrats advocated a reduction, when possible, for low-income groups only. Republicans advocated either voluntary cooperation, or state and local control of public policies; Democrats pointed to a long list of federal legislation enacted by their party.

On many other points, to be sure, the promises, claims, or criticisms of one party were not met squarely by the other. For example, Democratic criticism of tariff, immigration, anti-inflation, housing and "thought control" legislative action in the Republican 80th Congress was met by Republican emphasis on the more popular aspects of the same legislation. Republican criticism of "the tragic lack of foresight and general inadequacy of the Executive" was countered by specific Democratic reference to acts and recommendations of the President deemed valuable in the campaign, such as the Truman doctrine, the recognition of Israel, and the President's civil rights program.

Greater differences in party platforms than those mentioned above would impose a burden which politicians in a republican system could not be expected to bear. If the platforms were to point out clearly all differences between parties, then each party would be forced to reveal not only its assets but also its liabilities. In such a utopian situation, Democrats might be expected to admit that expanded welfare programs require increased taxation or debt, and Republicans would frankly state that an increase in the proportion of Protestant immigrants to the United States necessarily cuts down the proportion of Catholics and Jews admitted. Such political naïveté is not characteristic even in countries with highly disciplined parties, and would not be countenanced by American politicians, however reformed.

The shortcomings of present platforms lie, in other words, not in their failure to present reasonable alternatives, but in a popular belief that platforms have little meaning for the voter. Public belief that platforms rarely reveal party differences probably springs from public ignorance of each platform's contents. Responsibility for this ignorance perhaps may be laid at the feet of uninspired journalists who fail to reduce platform verbiage to terms which readers can understand. Political science, however, can make up in part for the deficiencies of journalists. If the Committee on Parties had included among the scientific studies on which its report is based a point-by-point comparison of the platforms, it might have reversed its conclusions and added to public understanding of party differences.

The Committee has erred to a greater extent in its discussion of Congress than in its analysis of platforms. Contrary to popular impression, the parties usually maintain their ranks on congressional votes, including those of headline significance, with sufficient solidarity so that voters may distinguish between two points of view. In eight modern sessions, for example, party behavior could be scientifically distinguished on 407 of the 455 roll calls recorded in the House of Representatives.[1] Nor were the roll calls on which the parties disagreed confined to issues of minor importance. The accompanying table lists some of the issues on which the parties differed. The list is by no means complete, for it has been culled to avoid repetition or lengthy explanation (for example, votes on public power have separated the parties in almost all sessions examined, but only two such votes are included in the table). This abbreviated list of party issues covers a wide variety of subjects, including the tariff, monopoly, control of business, foreign relations, taxes of several kinds, civil rights, national defense, farm policy, relief, housing administrative reorganization,

[1] The sessions, with percentages of roll calls on which the parties differed significantly, are as follows: 1921, 85.7; 1928, 88.1; 1930-1, 82.8; 1933, 90.0; 1937, 87.1;1944, 85.7; 1945, 95.0; 1948, 95.5. Average for all roll calls, 89.5. Roll call behavior was measured by the chi-square test, with 1/100 as the level of significance.

the size and power of the executive branch and state's rights.

It may be argued that, while the parties differ on some important issues, the compelling issues of the year do not separate the parties for the convenience of the voter. Such a condition may have existed in 1928 when, on three roll calls on the McNary-Haugen Bill, the parties' proportions of "yea" votes were almost identical, and perhaps in 1944, when Lend-Lease failed to arouse partisanship. In all other sessions studied, however, the issues on which the parties failed to differ were matters of routine.

On a national scale, there is little reason for the voter to be unable to distinguish between the parties in Congress. In states and congressional districts, however, the voter may have more difficulty. The national parties as a whole show significant lines of disagreement, but some individual congressmen confuse the voters by support for the policies of the other party. The problem, however, does not affect many districts. Of 4,658 members of the House in eleven selected modern sessions, only 181, or less than four per cent (about sixteen congressmen each year), voted with the opposing party more often than with their own. The proportion was slightly higher in the Senate, where smaller numbers promote independence. Of the 847 Senators in nine sessions, 63, or 7.4 per cent (seven Senators a year), bolted their parties on a majority of the votes.

Voters in some specific districts, such as those of Representative Javits in New York and Senator McCarran in Nevada, may be confused by the incumbent's behavior. In most northern states, however, the insurgent has been forced into that position by the views of his constituents, and faces in the election an opponent who is even more critical of the bolter's party than the bolter himself. Republican liberals such as Javits or Tobey must oppose Fair Deal Democrats; conservative Democrats such as Gillette and McCarran must face even more conservative Republicans. With only occasional exceptions, northern voters have a clear choice, not only between national parties as a whole, but also between individual local candidates in states and congressional districts.

In the South, where most modern insurgency occurs, the problem of voting alternatives is another matter. In most southern districts the parties never present a practical alternative in the general election, since Republican candidates have no chance of election. While the behavior of Southerners rarely corrupts Democratic discipline to the extent that the national parties cannot be distinguished, there is an obvious need for party reform in the South and in all one-party areas. . . .

*Selected Examples of Roll Calls on Which Parties Differed Significantly, Eight Modern Sessions, House**

Page Number in *Congressional Record*	Description of Issue	Roll Call Vote *Democrat* Yea	*Democrat* Nay	*Republican* Yea	*Republican* Nay
	1928				
714	Revenue, amendment, graduated corporation tax	193	1	31	192
2339	Legalize interlocking bank directorates, recommit	123	32	17	160
2851	Army approp., amend to forbid foreign war	113	45	13	188
5604	Howard U. (Negro) approp. authorization, final	60	110	175	0
	1937				
1064	Reciprocal trade extension, final	284	11	3	86
8875	Administrative reorganization, final	262	29	19	52
5232	Relief approp., rec., transfer to state admin.	8	288	82	6
3352	Natl. Housing Act, rec., forbid rates over 7%	34	221	67	5
9662	Deficiencies, conf., amend, add cotton subsidy	217	58	3	80
	1948				
2981	Rent control, amend, local board control	39	123	189	30
925	Revenue, rec., increase personal exemption	158	22	0	236
8473	Fed. Sec. Admin. approp., veto (separate agency)	59	111	229	1
8186	Agr. approp., amend, cut soil conservation	2	155	189	23
8473	Deficiencies, rec., raise rural electrification	169	3	28	201

* Only three selected sessions are included here.—Ed.

II. THE REFORMS WHICH THE COMMITTEE SEEKS WILL ACCENTUATE PRESENT DEFECTS IN THE PARTY SYSTEM

. . . Undesirable results would follow from the implementation of the report of the Committee on Political Parties, for the Committee would give weapons to the dominant groups in each party by means of which 1) the number of one-party areas in the United States would be increased, and 2) the self-destructive tendencies of the minority party would be accentuated.

What are the weapons which the Committee would give to the dominant groups in each party? The report properly stresses democratic, voluntary and cooperative methods for attaining intraparty agreement. But, in addition, the Committee supports (usually as a last resort) techniques which would allow dominant groups to make over each party in their own image. Among other recommendations the Committee proposes that the parties be permitted to define their membership (p. 21)*; that the parties deal with rebellious state delegations by excluding them from National Conventions (pp. 23 and 48) and from National Committee posts (pp. 23, 39, and 48), by using national party funds to defeat local officers (p. 48), and by appointment of temporary state officers (p. 48); that the parties deal with insurgent Congressmen by withholding committee assignments (p. 23), committee chairmanships (p. 62) and federal patronage (p. 61); that a Party Council be given authority to recommend congressional candidates, screen presidential candidates, and interpret the platform (p. 43); and that the platform, when interpreted, be binding on all candidates, including state and local ones (pp. 53 and 56).

The first important effect of the use of these weapons by party leaders would be the spread of one-party monopoly in the United States. Statesmen and political scientists are accustomed to praise the two-party system, on the assumption that competiton between two established groups, each with a reasonable chance of gaining office, increases governmental responsibility to the governed. However, such close competition between established groups exists in the United States only at the national level, where the parties are balanced fairly equally for the election of the President, and in a minority of the constituencies which select the lesser officers of federal, state and local governments. Thus of 435 congressmen in the 81st Congress more than one-third sat secure in the knowledge that only an unprecedented political upheaval would remove them from office, and less than half of this number could expect defeat even if reaction against their party should provoke a landslide comparable to that of 1936. The problem is

* Page numbers in parenthesis refer to passages in the original Report.—Ed.

not confined to the South. In the 81st Congress 141 northern congressmen had received more than 60 per cent of the vote in the preceding election, and stood no reasonable chance of defeat. . . .

A major reason for one-party monopoly in many areas of the United States is the tendency toward sectional polarization on the part of economic, racial, religious and nationality groups. The various groups which make up the American population are not scattered in similar proportions in each constituency. The proportion of Catholics varies widely from Massachusetts to Iowa, and from Railroad Avenue to Hillcrest Drive. The same kind of variation occurs in the distribution of most groups significant in American politics.

To the extent that segments of the population can identify their political desires with the program of one party or the other, competition at the polls will be reduced in the United States, except in those fortunate constituencies where opposed groups are equally balanced. Such identification has already taken place in many districts, so that northern politics tends toward polarization between rural, Protestant, native districts, where Democrats cannot win, and metropolitan, immigrant, industrial districts, where they cannot lose.

The reforms which the Committee proposes would increase the tendency toward one-party districts. If local parties and candidates cannot be insurgent, if they cannot express the basic desires of their constituencies, then those local parties can have no hope of success. Regardless of the organization provided, you cannot give Hubert Humphrey a banjo and expect him to carry Kansas. Only a Democrat who rejects at least a part of the Fair Deal can carry Kansas, and only a Republican who moderates the Republican platform can carry Massachusetts. . . .

Another unfortunate by-product of the Committee's proposals would affect the present opposition party, the Republicans. There is a tendency for party leaders to "put principle above politics" and to insist upon their own economic or social dogmas regardless of the popularity of such dogmas with the electorate. This tendency increases as the party's popularity decreases, because a decline in the party's membership reflects the withdrawal of dissident leaders who had previously moderated the policies formed by the ruling group. This trend, unless interrupted, would lead to the suicide of the minority party.

The self-destructive tendencies of previous opposition parties have been offset, however, by changes in issues and by fortuitous political and economic developments which have thrust the minority into power. With such sharp increases in power as the Democrats received in 1932 come fresh adherents to the party, who bring new and insurgent ideas to modify the party's previously unpalatable program. . . .

Chapter Five

CONSTITUENCY IN CONGRESS: Patterns of Commitment

A PROPER IDEAL?

Speech to the Electors of Bristol

EDMUND BURKE

I am sorry I cannot conclude without saying a word on a topic touched upon by my worthy colleague. I wish that topic had been passed by at a time when I have so little leisure to discuss it. But since he has thought proper to throw it out, I owe you a clear explanation of my poor sentiments on that subject.

He tells you that 'the topic of instructions has occasioned much altercation and uneasiness in this city'; and he expresses himself (if I understand him rightly) in favour of the coercive authority of such instructions.

Certainly, Gentlemen, it ought to be the happiness and glory of a representative to live in the strictest union, the closest correspondence, and the most unreserved communication with his constituents. Their wishes ought to have great weight with him; their opinions high respect; their business unremitted attention. It is

From *Selected Prose of Edmund Burke,* Sir Philip Magnus, ed., pp. 39-41.

his duty to sacrifice his repose, his pleasure, his satisfactions, to theirs—and above all, ever, and in all cases, to prefer their interest to his own.

But his unbiased opinion, his mature judgment, his enlightened conscience, he ought not to sacrifice to you, to any man, or to any set of men living. These he does not derive from your pleasure—no, nor from the law and the Constitution. They are a trust from Providence, for the abuse of which he is deeply answerable. Your representative owes you, not his industry only, but his judgment; and he betrays, instead of serving you, if he sacrifices it to your opinion.

My worthy colleague says, his will ought to be subservient to yours. If that be all, the thing is innocent. If government were a matter of will upon any side, yours, without question, ought to be superior. But government and legislation are matters of reason and judgment, and not of inclination; and what sort of reason is that in which the determination precedes the discussion, in which one set of men deliberate and another decide, and where those who form the conclusion are perhaps three hundred miles distant from those who hear the arguments?

To deliver an opinion is the right of all men; that of constituents is a weighty and respectable opinion, which a representative ought always to rejoice to consider. But *authoritative* instructions, *mandates* issued, which the member is bound blindly and implicitly to obey, to vote, and to argue for, though contrary to the clearest convictions of his judgment and conscience—these are things utterly unknown to the laws of this land, and which arise from a fundamental mistake of the whole order and tenor of our Constitution.

Parliament is not a *congress* of ambassadors from different and hostile interests, which interests each must maintain, as an agent and advocate, against other agents and advocates; Parliament is a *deliberative* assembly of *one* nation, with *one* interest—that of the whole—where not local purposes, not local prejudices, ought to guide, but the general good, resulting from the general reason of the whole. You choose a member, indeed; but when you have chosen him, he is not member of Bristol, but he is a member of Parliament. If the local constituent should have an interest, or should form an hasty opinion evidently opposite to the real good of the rest of the community, the member for that place ought to be as far as any other from any endeavour to give it effect, I beg pardon for saying so much on this subject; I have been unwillingly drawn into it; but I shall ever use a respectable frankness of communication with you. Your faithful friend, your devoted servant, I shall be to the end of my life: a flatterer you do not wish for. On this point of instructions, however, I think it scarcely possible we ever can have any sort of difference. Perhaps I may give you too much, rather than too little trouble.

THE MAKING OF A CONGRESSMAN

The First Richard Nixon

EARL MAZO

Nixon registered as a voter in 1938. He was twenty-five and had missed four voting years. But his job as assistant city attorney of Whittier was a political plum, so to speak, and therefore he had become, in effect, a politician. But it was the late fall of 1945 before he went into politics in earnest.

Whittier and its environs, then the 12th Congressional District of California, was stanch Republican territory. Yet in 1936 it elected a Democrat for Congress, and kept re-electing him. Jerry Voorhis, the Congressman, was mild mannered, conscientious, likeable and extremely popular. He was respected by fellow Congressmen and the press corps in Washington. He worked hard at his job, answered his mail promptly, dealt with personal problems of his constituents on an eagerly nonpartisan basis, and when Congress was not in session he seldom passed by opportunities to be guest teacher of Sunday-school classes or to address church and civic groups. Furthermore, the Congressman faithfully remembered births, anniversaries, and other happy occasions in his district. And, of course, that kept his name in the minds of many voters. In short, Jerry Voorhis was a smart politician.

As was customary for candidates in the crazy quilt of California politics, Voorhis always sought both the Democratic and the Republican nomination. He never ran as an out-and-out, partisan Democrat. In fact, the word "Democrat" rarely appeared in his advertisements and other paraphernalia (just as the word "Republican" almost never showed up on the material of his opponents). Several Republican organization leaders were among Congressman Voorhis' loyal supporters. This galled other rock-ribbed Republicans because, well known to the party faithful, Voorhis was no ordinary Democrat. He was raised in well-to-do circumstances, and that made him all the more sensitive to the woes of the poor. After graduating Phi Beta Kappa from Yale, he took a factory job at 39 cents an hour, worked as a freight handler in a railroad yard, where he saw two fellow workers killed for lack of adequate safety equipment, toured Europe, where he witnessed hunger everywhere, and then, after failing to get a job in a southern textile mill, and working awhile on a Ford assembly line, he married and with financial help from his father, opened a school and home for orphaned boys. In the mid-twenties Voorhis was a LaFollette Progressive. Then he became an active Socialist. And in the early depression years he embraced the "End Poverty in California" program of Upton Sinclair and ran for assemblyman on the ticket which Sinclair headed for governor. By 1936 Voorhis had become a bona fine Democrat and ran for Congress as a follower of Franklin D. Roosevelt. Although he grew increasingly conservative in Congress and became an energetic foe of Communism, his record as a whole was bitter medicine for most stalwart Republicans. Worst of all to them was his espousal of co-operatives and a Voorhis plan for altering the monetary system. They called the latter a "funny-money scheme."

When all else failed, the Republican hierarchy in California turned to the 1940 census for salvation. Since the legislature was Republican, the plan was to gerrymander Voorhis and several other Democratic congressmen out of office simply by redefining their districts. Two communities which Voorhis normally carried by a ratio of 5-1 were sliced from his district. Even so, Voorhis was re-elected in 1942 by a 13,000 vote majority and again in 1944, for a fifth term, by the same impressive margin. Other Democrats also survived the gerrymander. Therefore, in 1945, Republican professionals agreed to let complaining amateurs try their hand. These, most of them successful business, industrial and professional figures, traced the trouble to low-grade candidates, known in the trade as "turkeys." It was decided to form a

Fact-Finding Committee of leading citizens in each troublesome district. This committee would interview potential candidates, weed out the perennials and the misfits, and support with all available resources "sound-thinking, articulate, and respected" individuals, preferably newcomers. Murray M. Chotiner, a resourceful Beverly Hills lawyer-politician whose enterprises included a public relations firm, was designated by the party organization to help the amateurs. Chotiner had masterminded several exceptionally successful campaigns for Republicans, including Governor Earl Warren, and later was to become Richard Nixon's political manager.

Meanwhile the citizen fact-finders in the 12th District bestirred themselves well ahead of schedule. In the late spring of 1945—a full year and a half before the target election—a group met in Arcadia. Stanley Barnes, an attorney who has since been appointed to the United States Circuit Court of Appeals, as chairman and Frank E. Jorgensen, a vice-president of the Metropolitan Life Insurance Company, were the spark plugs. Later, to assure unity, leaders of various regular Republican party organizations were added to the committee in time to hear the first aspirants for nomination. As might be expected, none of the eight applicants were satisfactory. In fact, Jorgensen and his group already knew the man they wanted. He was Walter Dexter, a former president of Whittier College who had become California's superintendent of education. To run for Congress Dexter would have had to resign his state position and, as Jorgensen recalls, "he couldn't afford to risk the financial loss that would result if he was not elected." Dexter therefore suggested one of his former students, Richard M. Nixon, whom he described as one of the most promising young men he had ever known. Jorgensen and two associates, Boyd Gibbons and Rockwood Nelson, drove over to the Nixon grocery store to make inquiries. Frank and Hannah Nixon were more than willing to talk about their oldest living son. They noted that a good friend in town Herman L. Perry, manager of the local Bank of America branch, also had mentioned that their son would be an ideal candidate.

Perry telephoned Nixon in Baltimore, where he was renegotiating Navy contracts while awaiting release from the service. Nixon flew to California, and on December 4, 1945, he formally accepted the fact-finding committee's endorsement in a letter to Roy O.

Day, district Republican chairman. It was evident from his letter that the 32-year old Nixon was eager to be out of uniform and running for office. "I am going to see Joe Martin and John Phillips and try to get what dope I can on Mr. Voorhis' record," he wrote, in part. "His 'conservative' reputation must be blasted. But my main efforts are being directed toward building up a positive, progressive group of speeches which tell what *we* want to do, not what the Democrats have failed to do." The neophyte politician advised Day to "bring in the liberal fringe Republicans. We need *every* Republican and a few Democrats to win. I'm really hopped up over this deal, and I believe we can win."

In January Nixon was released from active duty, and he came west with a satchelful of ideas and a set of electioneering pictures from which he learned a fundamental political truth. It was that the great majority of veterans had been enlisted men for whom a politician campaigning in the uniform of an officer held little attraction. The photographs were thrown out, and the simple words "Dick Nixon" or just "Nixon" replaced "Lieutenant Commander Richard M. Nixon" on proposed literature. Nixon began his active campaign immediately. Shortly thereafter the Nixons' first daughter, Patricia, was born, and within three weeks Mrs. Nixon left the child with her mother-in-law and joined her husband.

Murray Chotiner was the principal professional member of Nixon's campaign organization. Chotiner was Senator Knowland's southern California campaign manager, in itself a full-time job. Roy Day retained him as publicity director for Nixon, on the side, at a fee of $500.

Voorhis and Nixon took advantage of California's peculiar crossfiling system to become candidates for the nominations of both parties. But, while Nixon worked at it energetically, Voorhis sent word that he was very busy looking after the people's welfare in Washington and therefore could not spare the time to campaign in the spring primaries. As usual, that was fine strategy. Voorhis won the Democratic nomination, got a substantial vote in the Republican primary, and gained the psychological advantage of beating Nixon by 7,000 votes in the over-all count. Normally this would have meant sure victory in the November general election. But Nixon's morale went up when a Los Angeles political reporter pointed out that Voorhis' vote, 53.5 per cent of the total, was quite a drop from 1944, when he polled 60 per cent.

"Keen political observers . . . thought we ran a darn fine race, and this was the best Republican primary showing in years," Nixon wrote Chairman Day. "Frankly, Roy, I really believe that's true, and it is time some of the rest of the people began to realize it. All we need is a win complex and we'll take him in November."

The general election campaign flared up early in September, much like many others being fought throughout the country that year of meat and housing shortages, labor unrest and general postwar disenchantment. The Republicans were the "outs," and their battlecry was "Had enough?" The theme of the 12th District campaign followed the national pattern in most respects—that is, the incumbent Democrat was branded as a tool of Sidney Hillman's CIO-Political Action Committee, a promoter of controls, and an enemy of free enterprise who would socialize America.

But the Voorhis-Nixon battle developed distinctive nuances of bitterness. The veteran Congressman had never before been confronted by a buzz-saw opponent, and the tenderfoot candidate had never before debated so totally for keeps. Both candidates electioneered on three fronts. Most exciting to them and the voters were five debates. Meanest of the three fronts was a battle of newspaper advertisements and statements. Most strenuous for the candidates were handshaking and coffee-hour tours.

While Voorhis believes, in retrospect, that he would have lost anyway, Nixon believes the turning point for him, as the underdog, was the first debate. "It was tough," Nixon says. "I was the challenger, and he was the experienced incumbent. Once that debate was over, I was on my way to eventual victory." Nixon went into the debates against the wishes of all his advisers except Chotiner. The others feared Voorhis was too experienced and Nixon too green. Chotiner insisted the gamble had to be taken because, at worst, Nixon would lose and, at best, he might strike the spark his campaign needed so badly.

The first debate did just that—thanks to a Political Action Committee endorsement of Voorhis which is still the subject of controversy. There had been a small Nixon advertisement which declared, in part, "A vote for Nixon is a vote against the Communist-dominated PAC with its gigantic slush fund." Voorhis vigorously insisted he had not sought and didn't have the endorsement of the regional Political Action Committee of the CIO. At this Nixon leaped to his feet, drew a paper from his pocket, and read a report in which the Los Angeles chapter of the *national* Political Action Committee recommended that the national group endorse Voorhis. Nixon also read off the names of officers of the national organization's chapter who were also officers of the regional group. Then, dramatically, he thrust the paper at Voorhis.

Shortly afterwards Voorhis issued a long, poignant statement declaring that, while he cherished the support of labor, he didn't have and didn't want the backing of the California CIO because "under present top leadership of the CIO in California, there is at least grave question whether the Communist Party does not exercise inordinate if not decisive influence over state and county organizations."

A few days later he telegraphed the national Political Action Committee demanding that it withdraw its "qualified endorsement" of him.

For the remainder of the campaign Voorhis expended much of his time and energy denying that he was the CIO's errand boy, while Nixon jabbed or punched, as the occasion demanded, with observations about "lip-service Americans" and high officials "who front for un-American elements, wittingly or otherwise, by advocating increasing federal controls over the lives of the people." In mid-October Nixon warned voters against being "fooled" by the "very conservative" tone Voorhis was adopting. "In the last four years, out of forty-six measures sponsored by the CIO and the PAC, my opponent has voted against the CIO and PAC only three times," declared Nixon. "Whether he wants it now or not, my opponent has the PAC endorsement and he has certainly earned it. It's not how a man talks, but how he votes that counts."

The PAC controversy reached its shrill peak three days before the election, when Republican campaign headquarters issued a statement in behalf of a former lieutenant governor accusing Voorhis of "consistently voting the Moscow-PAC-Henry Wallace line in Congress." The statement also mentioned "the insolence of Moscow in telling the American voter to elect PAC candidates, such as Mr. Voorhis," and it pronounced Candidate Nixon to be "a man who will talk American and at the same time vote American in Congress . . . and fight in and out of Congress to perpetuate American ideals and American freedom."

There were, of course, other issues in the campaign, and in the context of those times it is not unlikely that some were more decisive with voters than exchanges about the PAC. There was, for example, the veteran issue. Nixon pointed to his own wartime service (and indirectly to Voorhis' civilian status) in an often-repeated promise "to preserve our sacred heritage, in the name of my buddies and your loved ones, who died that these might endure." For his part, Voorhis referred to his opponent at times as "the Lieutenant Commander" and the "subtlety" escaped no one.

As an "in," Voorhis was compelled to harp on only one positive theme. It was that he had achieved seniority and experience and to turn him out for a newcomer "wouldn't be good sense and would be damaging to popular government in these critical days."

On the other hand, as an "out," with no record to defend, Nixon was free to attack and promise at the same time. Thus he became "thoroughly committed to a program of federal tax reduction" and promised that a Republican Congress would solve the meat, housing and controls problem.

(It was during this first campaign that Nixon developed the knack of repeating verbatim questions asked of him from the floor. It requires the vocal apparatus to operate on one track while the thinking apparatus operates on another. Nixon does it to give himself time to think of the answer.)

Voorhis had 296 inches of campaign advertising and Nixon 162 inches, in the *Post-Advocate,* the daily newspaper of Alhambra, largest city in the district. It is noteworthy that not one line in a Nixon manifest mentioned the fact that he was a Republican, and none of Voorhis' alluded to his membership in the Democratic party.

Nixon won by a vote of 65,586 to 49,994, and was one of seven Republicans to unseat incumbent Democrats in California. All told, the Republicans picked up fifty-five House seats and won control of the Eightieth Congress. In reflecting on the campaign twelve years later Nixon said the race was, in effect, a contest between a well-known New Dealer and a conservative Republican. "Voorhis lost because that district was not a New Deal district," he said. "Our campaign was a very honest debate on the issues." . . .

At the outset Nixon's favorite work was as a member of a small subcommittee that drafted the Taft-Hartley Labor Law. That was where he became quite friendly with a freshman Democrat from Massachusetts named John F. Kennedy. Nixon and Kennedy were on opposite sides of the Taft-Hartley question, and in the spring of 1947 they went to McKeesport, Pennsylvania, to debate the issue. (Nixon still considers Kennedy "a good personal friend" and says, "I have a very high regard for him as an able senator and campaigner; he's very attractive and formidable." Kennedy does not now reciprocate those feelings. In fact, his attitude toward Nixon is that he would like very much to run against him for president.)

Meanwhile Nixon's interest in the Un-American Activities Committee was not very great. But it warmed up on August 3, 1948, when Whittaker Chambers, a former Communist, listed among his one-time fellow conspirators a man named Alger Hiss.

THE SEARCH FOR MANDATES

The Representative and His District

LEWIS A. DEXTER

We talk frequently of a Representative or Senator "representing" or "failing to represent" his constituents. This is shorthand. The fact is the congressman represents his image of the district or of his constituents (or fails to represent his, or our, image of them). How does he get this image? Where does it come from?

On numerous important policy matters, he hears nothing from his constituency. But whether he hears anything on an issue, what he hears, whom he hears from, or how he interprets what he hears all vary depending upon the kind of person he is, the kind of associations he has had and has in the constituency and in Washington, the public image of his interests and concerns, and the background information or misinformation which he possesses. . . .

A good many congressmen believe that their districts feel very strongly on this, or the other issue, and that they are constrained therefore to vote a certain way. The more sophisticated realize, of course, that legislative procedures and processes are so complex that it is more often than not possible to go through the motions of conforming to such views without helping to enact

From Lewis Anthony Dexter, *Human Organization* (Vol. 16, No. 1). Reprinted by permission of Lewis A. Dexter.

them, when they believe the public preference to be wrong. On most issues, out of a desire to serve the district or from indifference, many congressmen do go along with any view which they believe "the district" holds strongly. When the chips are down, and they have to declare themselves, some will vote against their convictions and for their constituents' (presumed) preferences.

This situation has led to a series of classical utterances on the moral problem of the representative: *Should he sacrifice his judgment to his constituents' inclinations as he conceives them or not?* It would be more accurate to emphasize the ways in which representatives' beliefs about constituent preference are functions of the channels of communication and the special processes of transaction between constituents and representatives rather than of anything else.

If this is in fact so, more students of representation and representatives would concur with Congressman Veteran's interpretation of the representative-constituent picture. The latter has for years been at the center of the legislative issues which provoke the most comment by critics of "pressure," and he told me early in my study of reciprocal trade:

> You know I am sure you will find out a congressman can do pretty much what he decides to do and he doesn't have to bother too much about criticism. I've seen plenty of cases since I've been up here where a guy will hold one economic or political position and get along all right; and then he'll die or resign and a guy comes in who holds quite a different economic or political position and he gets along all right too. That's the fact of the matter.

The first difference between some congressmen and others is how (consciously or unconsciously) they define their responsibilities.

Many of the congressmen interviewed about both tariff and defense matters referred to a personal conception of what they owe their job, of what in some circles would be called "professional obligation." A few made explicit and many apparently hold implicit theories of representation. These theories of representation were not, except for a few instances, so far as I could tell, directly derived from philosophical or academic sources. They resulted from the experiences of men facing the actual moral complexities of a job.

Some members expressed themselves in terms of their obligation to select the right course, regardless of the views of their constituents. For instance, Congressman Stubborn has for a good many years represented a district which (according to interviews with business interests in the district and from an economic analysis of its industrial situation) is inclined to favor the reciprocal trade program. Nevertheless he says:

Oh, knowing my stubborn characteristics, no one ever thinks he can change me, you know . . . some of my people say, "You may not agree with this man, 'Stubborn,' but you know where he stands."

Mr. Stubborn agreed that if fate were to select as his successor a Clarence Randall type "free trader," such a man would be able to vote for a reciprocal trade program without much difficulty, but Stubborn interrupted an effort to probe this point further by declaring:

That's because they (my constituents) do not really understand the matter. During the twenty-one years reciprocal trade has been in effect, it has had . . . [and he named various alleged or actual consequences which he regards as evil]. . . . There isn't any use trying to change me!

Congressman Emphatic on the other hand voted the same way as Mr. Stubborn on the Reciprocal Trade Extension Act of 1955 because of a quite different definition of his responsibility. He said:

My first duty is to get reelected. I'm here to represent my district. . . . This is part of my actual belief as to the function of a congressman. . . . What is good for the majority of districts is good for the country. What snarls up the system is these so-called statesmen—congressmen who vote for what they think is the country's interest . . . let the Senators do that. . . . They're paid to be statesmen; we [members of the House] aren't. (This was said sarcastically, but without humorous intent.)

Mr. Leader, as strong a supporter of reciprocal trade as Mr. Stubborn is an opponent of it, comes fairly close to Mr. Stubborn in his attitude towards constituent opinion. Said Leader:

You're not identifying me on this, of course? It's strictly confidential? Always bear in mind there are those in Congress who lead their districts and those who are led by them. . . . It makes a lot of difference. . . . The "ruanga" growers of my district never opposed me on reciprocal trade. . . . The answer is government stockpiling for them. . . . I think I have convinced these men that a program of high tariffs would not assist them and I think my viewpoint has gained general acceptance from them.

Several times he spoke of himself as having "straightened out" people who had seen the matter "wrongly." . . .

Mr. Fourth represents a district in which there is vociferous anti-reciprocal trade sentiment. This district also has strong economic reasons for supporting reciprocal trade and a particularly influential number of intellectuals predisposed toward reciprocal trade. Mr. Fourth showed how a portion of the district can influence a man when he said:

My impulses when I came down here were in favor of trade not aid, until I started to hear all sorts of things from my district. . . . So, actually, when you stack all these things together, well you're in favor of trade not aid, but, goodness, there comes a time . . . if trade means wholesale layoffs in your district. . . . I've got any number of letters against it . . . carpets, imported rugs . . . there've been around 300 layoffs in a local bicycle plant . . . textiles . . . chemicals . . . electrical equipment . . . glass salesmen. It's difficult to get figures. I assume the Randall Commission report has them. . . . I haven't had time to read it. I don't know. . . . I assume that the people I hear from exaggerate the seriousness of the situation but still that it is serious.

Mr. Fourth ultimately voted against reciprocal trade on the key votes; the decisive factor appears to have been his unwillingness to separate himself from several members from his state, also of junior status, who were definite in their opposition to reciprocal trade. Mr. Fourth, according to his colleagues was wavering as late as two hours before the vote. Had the Chairman of his state delegation (who strongly supported reciprocal trade) personally requested his support, he might well have voted the other way. But he was obviously uncertain, *on the reciprocal trade issue,* whether to adopt the role of servant of his district (as he conceived its desires) or to think in terms of the ideology, implied by the phrase "trade not aid." How he would vote was therefore completely unpredictable. Had he stumbled into any one of three congressmen with strong pro-reciprocal trade views in the lobby or the corridors just before the vote, he might have voted the other way.

Congressman Fourth's vote was unpredictable because on this particular issue he does not have a clear conception of what his obligations are. On some issues—flood control or taxes affecting the major agricultural product of the district—one can predict that he would see his responsibility as being almost exclusively to the district. On others—particularly those under consideration by the very important subcommittee of which he is a member—he would be strongly inclined to emphasize national interest in some form as against district concern.

Congressmen tend to see their obligations as being either to the nation or to their constituency—other equally possible obligations are seemingly not considered.

Obligation seemed to be conceived as national interest versus district interest (district interest was often, as in the case of Mr. Emphatic, related to re-election and therefore to self-interest). No congressman interviewed indicated any feeling of moral obligation to our allies or to any other country, although our allies are regarded instrumentally as means. This is contrary to a theory sometimes expressed that Americans tend to adopt some favorite foreign country as "theirs." Also, reference to representing a region (the South, the West, New England) was very slight. . . .

A congressman's conception of his district confirms itself, to a considerable extent, and may constitute a sort of self-fulfilling prophecy.

Early in my study of reciprocal trade, Congressman Veteran told me:

> You know I am sure you will find out a congressman can do pretty much what he decides to do and he doesn't have to bother much about criticism.

Within the limits of the morally and sociologically conceivable (no congressman from Alabama in 1942 could have advocated integration for instance!), a congressman has a very wide range of choices on any given issue, *so far as his constituency is concerned!* His relationships in the House or Senate and with party leadership, of course, limit these choices severely. It is a fact, however, that there is no district viewpoint as such to be represented on the overwhelming majority of issues. A few will care one way and a few the other, but the issue will be insignificant or unknown to the great majority. Indeed, in many districts, only a fraction of the voters know the name of their congressman, let alone how he voted on a particular issue.

A congressman of my acquaintance took about 100 letters which he received on a particular issue and checked the registration of the writers. He found that almost three-quarters of them were not registered in his district. What difference then would their views make with respect to his prospects for reelection? Mr. Emphatic who insisted that he was representing his district's desires, was led nevertheless, by my questions, to admit that more than likely none of the workers presumably represented by him actually knew how he had voted. . . .

Actually, most of the letters Mr. Emphatic received and most of the comments he heard originated in three large plants in the district and they represented less than 7% of the voters of the district. These plants are organized by national unions which, ironically enough, in chalking up Mr. Emphatic's score in 1956, were inclined to regard his vote against reciprocal trade as an anti-labor vote. Fortunately for him, his stand on other matters and his personal contacts offset this factor. Of the groups in the district, only members of the League of Women Voters wrote to him in favor of reciprocal trade. "They aren't," he averred, "God knows, a potent political force; and all their letters are damn stilted, right out of the same handbook." Actually, however, it was likely that the League members would remember in 1956, and perhaps again in 1958, how he voted. And, because of the "racial" and academic composition of the district, League members may have some influence outside their own membership. It would have been perfectly possible for Mr. Emphatic to take the reverse position favoring reciprocal trade and still to regard himself as representing his district—particularly since the area also has a strong port interest. . . .

A congressman has great difficulty in deciding what the viewpoint of the district is even on such an issue as reciprocal trade. Most persons with an interest or belief in the tariff will have interest or beliefs in other issues as well. Thus, the most effective representation of their overall interests may necessitate concessions on some matters, in order to get along with party leadership, colleagues, or prominent committee members in Congress. "Joe Martin and Charlie Halleck in their heart of hearts," said a prominent Republican, "certainly go along with us, not with the White House on this; and they can swing twenty-five votes, at least, anytime they want; we lost by less than twenty-five votes, so they beat us." Martin is the Republican leader; Halleck is his likely successor as Republican leader or Speaker when he steps down. Is a congressman doing a better job of representing his district when he keeps in the good graces of such powerful men (and thereby helps to get a bridge or a new post office or a dam for his district) or when he opposes them on an issue, the details of which no one will remember six months later? The Republican who told me this is one of the most persistent enemies of reciprocal trade in the party and he is probably the most effective in a quiet way. He is opposed to reciprocal trade in part because of its "harmful" effect on his district. However, he cheerfully admitted, "It wouldn't make any difference what my congressman does on this matter," insofar as his re-election is concerned. Afterwards he qualified this by saying that perhaps the incumbent ought not stick his neck out strongly *for* reciprocal trade, but there is no call for activity of any kind.

A congressman hears most often from those who agree with him.

A congressman's relationships with his district tend to be maintained through a small group whom he knew before he was elected or through a group who have since then worked closely with him. Generally speaking, the views of those whom he knew prior to his election tend to be more like his than do the views of the "average" voter. It is a well-known fact that we tend to be like the people with whom we associate and vice versa. Also, most of the people who have worked closely with the congressman since his election—because he is a congressman—have a particular axe to grind. They will naturally tend therefore to stress agreement with him on issues about which they are not concerned—just as salesmen typically do not disagree with their customers on politics. For several years, I wondered about the unfavorable references congressmen frequently made to the League of Women Voters and several times to delegations from labor unions. Ultimately, it occurred to me that these two groups are probably the only ones which seriously, on a face-to-face basis, year after year, go over with a congressman the issues on which they disagree with him. Because their efforts cannot be entirely discounted as "politics," they make congressmen uncomfortable. . . .

Some men automatically interpret what they hear to support their own viewpoints.

Mr. First of New Hungary does not think he hears much about foreign imports. Mr. Second, coming from the same sort of district in the same city, says:

It's either the first or second most important issue with me. Unemployment is the other. And, of course, they're really the same thing.

The last sentence is the clue to why Mr. Second hears so much more than Mr. First about foreign imports. When Mr. First hears about unemployment, he hears just about the invidious differential effect which accelerated amortization and certain other tax provisions have had on industry in the area. In fact, when I talked to him about the tariff, he advised me that I really ought to study accelerated amortization. Mr. Second, however, interprets almost any statement about unemployment as a plea for relief from foreign imports. Sometimes it is, but sometimes it isn't. So, seeing the same men and hearing the same things said, Mr. Second will "hear" about tariff matters, Mr. First will not. (Mr. Third, their colleague from an adjoining district, is vitally interested in wilderness preservation, hunting, and fishing. He sees many of the same men, but they are likely to talk to him about his interests, and if they do talk to him about unemployment, he is less likely to draw any special conclusions from the talk.) . . .

In more general terms, what congressmen hear and how they interpret what they hear depends on who they are.

Conventional discussion of the relationship between congressmen and constituents assumes that the kind of man the congressman is does not influence what he hears from the district and that the question is whether he follows or contravenes district sentiment. The notion of the congressman representing "the" district at least needs restatement *in terms of a particular congressman* who represents what he hears from the district as he interprets it. And his interpretation results from his being the particular kind of person he is and is reputed to be. . . .

Pressure is how you see it.

"Pressure" and "pressure politics" are regarded by most "sophisticated" people today as "explaining" a great deal that happens. But it was frequently impossible to find any admission of or apparently any awareness of "pressures." That was not because shrewd and worldly politicians were concealing what really goes on from this naive and innocent interviewer and his naive and innocent colleagues.

The reason is explained by Senator Service's assistant:

There are very few people actually pressuring us, even if you count all we hear about all issues. Seriously, the sense of being pressured is a matter of reaction. Other people who get no more mail than we do in this office would say, "See how much pressure is on me." We don't feel it. . . . Sure, you get mail. It's just that so-and-so makes more 'phone calls than somebody else. The result is purely physical. It isn't a representation of what or how or when people are going to vote in elections. My personal opinion is that members of most organizations make up their minds on what they read in the papers without reference to organizations.

With this theory of voting behavior, Senator Service's assistant naturally will not be too much worried by a good deal of effort to get him or his boss to change policies—he simply will not regard it as pressure.

Congressman Widesight amusingly illustrated the point made by Service's assistant. Mr. Widesight has moods when he reaches way out into left field looking for things to worry about, things which might possibly defeat him. One day, discussing reciprocal trade, he said that things were very bad indeed. His reason was that he was getting "so much" mail against it. "I, whom they never used to bother at all." When I checked with his secretary later, I found he couldn't possibly have received more than 50 letters (representing glass, electrical equipment, and 2 or 3 bicycle interests) opposing reciprocal trade. This was only a fraction of the mail Senator Service receives on the same matter. It was also a fraction of what Congressman Widesight himself has several times heard on other matters such as postal pay increases. However, Widesight is accustomed to communications on that issue and he wasn't accustomed to them on the reciprocal trade issue. . . .

Even where there is a considerable amount of what the outsider would consider pressure, the point made by Senator Service's assistant is entirely valid. What you call pressure . . . or what you feel to be pressure . . . depends on how thick your skin is. Mr. Second, for instance, told me that he had been subject to no "pressures—that is, no threats." To many men in politics threats alone represent the only real pressure because they know very well that few votes are actually lost on any one given issue such as reciprocal trade. But, of course, what is a threat to one man is not a threat to another. (For comparison, we should have studied some explosive issues like "McCarthyism" or *humane slaughtering* or perhaps some issues in which the profit-and-loss relationship is clearer like the question of pay increases for postal employees.)

The most strongly felt kind of pressure on the reciprocal trade issue came, apparently, from Speaker Rayburn and the Democratic leadership against the potentially recalcitrant Democrats. Speaker Rayburn attended a breakfast for freshmen congressmen shortly before the vote and said, in effect, that he'd discovered that those who go along, get along. One new member regarded this as pressure—a threat. Another new member (actually probably more vulnerable in terms of his factional position and his position within the delegation) did not. Both of them failed to "go along." Aside from this speech, most of the "pressure" on the doubtful members seems to have come through the grapevine or from their own apprehensions as to what might happen if they bolted the party leadership.

One reason why fairly few members seem to have felt pressure on this matter is to be explained in terms of their background and associations in local politics. In many states, "pressure" on matters like highway contracts or patronage or even for or against gubernatorial programs, must be relatively heavy—that is, threats are far more common at the state level than they are in Washington. Many congressmen come from such a background and a good many are still involved in local conflicts about patronage, contracts, etc. As a result, Washington to them seems very mild.

Nagging may also be called pressure, whether done by mail or in person. When a congressman has definitely announced his stand and does not intend to switch it, he resents being bothered by avoidable pleas (pressures) to change. The resentment point, obviously, is highly individual so one man's pressure is another man's routine. . . .

PRESSURE GROUPS AND THE ENGINEERING OF OPINION

Group Interest versus Public Interest

HOUSE SELECT COMMITTEE
ON LOBBYING ACTIVITIES

(a) *On defining lobbying.*—The term "lobbying" has been in common usage for approximately 100 years, and has been given

From *General Interim Report of the House Select Committee on Lobbying Activities,* House of Representatives, Eighty-First Congress, Second Session, 1950, pp. 1-50.

many definitions. In the 1870's and 1880's, "lobbying" means direct, individual solicitation of legislators, with a strong presumption of corruption attached. The lobbying of the 1880's demanded this kind of definition; the lobbying of today demands something quite different. Unfortunately, most present-day definitions are both inaccurate and unrealistic; they generally fail to recognize that modern pressure on legislative bodies is rarely corrupt, that it is increasingly indirect, and largely the product of group rather than individual effort. With these limitations, the ordinary definition of lobbying provides an unsatisfactory basis for either congressional inquiry or statutory regulation. . . .

. . . Webster's New International tells us that lobbying is "to address or solicit members of a legislative body in the lobby or elsewhere, as before a committee, with intent to influence legislation." With the passage of the Regulation of Lobbying Act in 1946, numerous groups and persons claimed this kind of definition as their own in an effort to escape full disclosure under the act. The National Association of Manufacturers typically maintained that in passing the act Congress had only intended to reach and include:

> . . . activities which seek more directly and specifically to secure the support or opposition of individual Members of Congress toward legislation actually pending in either House. Such an interpretation, in addition to avoiding constitutional questions, is more nearly in accord with the general concept of "lobbying."

The NAM followed this "general concept of lobbying" to its logical conclusion by reporting on only the 1.97 percent of its 4.3 million dollar budget which the association conceded should be charged to "legislative activities." The association's $2,000,000 public relations program was claimed to be totally unrelated to legislation, and no part of it was reported under the Lobbying Act. Yet this is the same NAM whose president told a Senate committee in 1946 that his organization had spent $395,850, "largely on advertising," in its campaign to abolish OPA.

And so goes the refrain from group after group after group: "Millions for 'education' or 'public enlightenment,' but not 1 cent for lobbying—as we define it." If this committee had followed the lobbyists' definitions of lobbying, we would have had relatively little to investigate.

. . . our investigation started with an existing lobbying law on the books. The framers of that statute, The Federal Regulation of Lobbying Act did not use the word "lobbying" anywhere in the act except the title. Instead, they referred to attempts to influence the passage or defeat of legislation for pay or any consideration. Our Committee regards all such attempts as "lobbying" and has generally so used that word during our investigation.

(b) *The extent of lobbying activity.*—Whether defined narrowly or broadly, lobbying is extremely difficult to measure objectively. The members of this committee knew, as all Members of Congress cannot help but know, that lobbying in the past few years has become more widespread and intensified than at any other time in our history. We recall the Taft-Hartley issue, OPA, rent control, public housing, and a whole host of other recent issues which have been the subjects of terrific pressure campaigns. We knew then as we know now that intense efforts and many millions of dollars were expended in connection with these measures; but these are things which cannot be computed with mathematical precision.

A few useful gages of the extent and cost of lobbying are available, however. Primary among these are the sums reported and registrations made under the Federal Lobbying Act since 1946. The following analysis summarizes the quarterly reports of lobbying contributions and expenditures filed by organizations and groups pursuant to section 305 of the act.

From: Analysis of Reports Filed under Sec. 305 of the Federal Regulation Lobbying Act

Year	Number filed	Contributions	Expenditures
1946*	138	$ 1,612,735.62	$ 2,297,281.21
1947	642	14,825,440.26	6,969,897.08
1948	971	18,387,869.02	7,844,668.86
1949	1,127	20,369,504.07	10,319,670.65
Grand Total	2,878	$55,195,548.97	$27,431,517.80

* Third and Fourth Quarters only.

More than $20,000,000 has been reported under another section of the Lobbying Act (sec. 308) for the same period. Most of this amount is not included in the figures in the table above.

Seventy-five million dollars for 3½ years of lobbying is a large and impressive sum but it does not begin to reflect all that is actually collected and spent in efforts to influence legislation. Many groups submit only fragmentary reports in which they omit the costs of publications, public relations, and advertising directly related to public issues. The National Association of Home Builders, for example, has not reported the cost of its public relations program which it estimates has aggregated $250,000 in the past few years. Many more groups do not report at all, taking the position that they are exempted by the "principal purpose" clause of the Lobbying Act, or that their agent's registration relieves them of the responsibility of reporting. Witness the fact that the 2,878 quarterly reports were submitted by only 495 groups, a fractional proportion of the permanent national organizations which are vitally interested and continuously active in seeking to shape public policy.[1] In still other cases, a national organization, such as the National Association of Real Estate Boards, or Americans for Democratic Action, will file reports while the State and local adjuncts will not, this despite the fact that legislative operations on the several levels are inseparably meshed. Many other types of nonreporting and partial reporting under the Lobbying Act could be added.

In sum, these reported figures give us a very incomplete picture of the realities of lobbying. To accept this picture as complete would be equivalent to saying that no money is gambled on horse races other than that paid through the pari-mutuel windows in the 27 States which have legalized such gambling. If the full truth were ever known, this committee has little doubt that lobbying, in all its ramifications, will prove to be a billion-dollar industry. This figure is not offered in an effort to shock the complacent but as a sober estimate. Consider the costs of letter and telegram campaigns; the thousands of pages of institutional advertising; the purchase and distribution of millions of highly charged books and pamphlets on public issues; the salaries of executives, lawyers, and publicists; the operating budgets of all the thousands of organizations throughout the Nation whose central purpose is to influence what Government does—all of those costs

[1] W. B. Graves lists 1,800 permanent national organizations. See W. B. Graves, *Administration of the Lobby Registration Provisions of the Legislative Reorganization Act of 1946* (Washington, Government Printing Office, 1950). The new Department of Commerce list includes 4,000 organizations. Jay Judkins, *National Associations of the United States* (Washington, Government Printing Office, 1950), p. 634.

and many more are chargeable to lobbying, whether we like the word or not.

So far as reported expenditures for lobbying are concerned, organized business far outspends other interests. This fact, however understandable, points to a situation which tends to undermine the props on which American thinking about lobbying has traditionally rested. We believe lobbying to be every man's right. But some men are more able to make their rights meaningful than others. In practical terms, this has meant that those interests with the most to spend for protection have proclaimed "lobbying for all men" as an almost sacred article of faith. It is not unlike the elephant shouting "Everybody for himself," as he stomps up and down among the chickens.

. . . The pressure groups continue to receive large contributions, but increasingly the great corporations are mounting their own major lobbying efforts.

(c) *Money for lobbying.*—. . . The means by which groups raise funds for lobbying are infinitely varied but there are two general patterns which cover the fund-raising activities of most lobbying organizations. The first might be called "orthodox" solicitation, largely because it conforms to standard practice among the well-established, membership groups. Labor unions, trade or business associations, farm groups, veterans' groups, and professional societies are typical membership groups, that is, groups where membership rests on the basis of occupation, profession, service, or trade. Fund-raising by these organizations is usually simple and straightforward. . . .

Frequently, particular legislation demands intensified group effort, and inevitably, more money to sustain it. This is a time for special levies for what the press has called war chests. Thus in 1949, the American Medical Association waged a heavy and generally successful campaign to obtain $25, sometimes not without elements of coercion, from each of its 140,000 members in order to support the all-out drive against national health insurance. This kind of tactic is unusual; most groups approach their members without threats. The National Association of Real Estate Boards, for example, uses its local organizations as collection agencies for its special assessments. In a letter dated December 17, 1948, the association's president-elect wrote to presidents of member boards:

We need to know now if your board will support the Realtors' Washington Committee by sending money or by sending in its pledge immediately in an amount equal to $5 per active member. *How your board raises this money is its own affair.* [Emphasis supplied.] . . .

Another technique . . . is to solicit money through influential persons. A letter from Merwin K. Hart, president of the National Economic Council, to Lammot du Pont, dated February 17, 1949, outlines this method of operations:

It has occurred to me to wonder if you would consider addressing a letter to perhaps 100 or 200 carefully selected corporations, mentioning our work and stating that one moderate-size corporation has subscribed in that manner (1 cent for each share stock); and asking them to consider making a subscription on the same basis. If we got only a few subscriptions out of such a letter, it would be well worth while. . . .

Although foundations and committees seldom solicit funds for specific purposes, the appeal for money is usually geared specifically to the interests of prospective contributors. Distinctly different appeals are aimed at distinctly different groups. The Committee for Constitutional Government, for example, uses a wide variety of mailing lists for specific fund-raising campaigns. At various times this group has sought funds from and sent materials to lists of—

1. 200,000 corporation presidents.
2. 8,000 persons worth between $500,000 and $1,000,000.
3. 10,000 millionaires. (Mr. Rumely maintained that this was his "least productive" list, "because nobody is more shy—the only thing more shy than a millionaire is a man with two million.")
4. Farm leaders. (Mr. Rumely said: "We spent about $15,000 compiling a list of about 40,000 farm leaders. That list is productive. We get action on it.")
5. Labor leaders.
6. Press, radio, and other publications.
7. Industrial groups.
8. Other organizations.
9. Catholic and Protestant Clergymen ("That list is so good . . . We get back a little of our cost by renting the list out.").
10. Members of Congress, State legislators, and jurists.

In fact, the CCG's typewritten list of lists is 12 pages long. . . .

Techniques of Lobbying

. . . The National Association of Real Estate Boards . . . has systematized all means of direct contact between its members and legislators more completely than any other group appearing before this committee. This group conducts letter and telegram campaigns. It also prepares, sometimes on request, specific letters which local members transmit to their Senators and Representatives. The association has developed through its local member boards remarkably extensive lists of congressional "contacts," persons who are expected to wield particular influence with the Representative or Senator from the district or State concerned. . . . The expectation is, of course, that the "contact's" political, business, or personal acquaintance with the Member of Congress —and it is on this basis that he is selected as contact—will enable him to make a decisive impression on the Member's thinking. Six to seven hundred of these contacts make up the membership of what the National Association of Real Estate Boards calls the enlarged committee of the Realtors' Washington Committee, which handles and directs much of the lobbying for the association. . . .

In the days when lobbying meant little more than unabashed bribery, committees of Congress were the favorite focus of the old lobby barons. Then as now, crucial decisions were made in committee, and men having entree to them could quietly make the necessary arrangements. The committees are even more important in the modern legislative process, but with the institution in 1911 of open hearings on all major legislation the possibilities of easy influence diminished. The lobbyist who appears formally before committees today is generally obliged to argue on the merits. Despite public scrutiny and the watchfulness of competitors, however, some misrepresentation is still possible. In a letter dated January 17, 1949, to Herbert U. Nelson, of the National Association of Real Estate Boards, Art Barrett of Detroit had an interesting suggestion along these lines:

"My thinking is simply this: I believe our case opposing the extension of rent control would be helped tremendously if we could parade in a few small property owners from around the country, a little bedraggled and run-down-at-the-heels-looking, who could get their story over to Congress that the small man who owns a little property is taking one hell of a beating." This sort of stagecraft fully developed could turn the congressional process into a masquerade ball. . . .

The service function in lobbying takes many different forms. When representatives of organized groups appear before committees of Congress, for example, they are not only presenting their own case but they are also providing Members of Congress with one of the essential raw materials of legislative action. By the same token, the drafting of bills and amendments to bills, the preparation of speeches and other materials for Members, the submission to Members of detailed memoranda on bill-handling tactics—all of these are means by which lobby groups service the legislative process and at the same time further their own ends.

In addition to these services rendered to Members of Congress in their official capacities, lobbying organizations often perform favors of a more personal sort. Three generations ago, when standards of congressional morality were less exacting than they are today, the lobbyist could favor the Member in ways which strike the modern mind as crude. The lobbyist of the 1880's was a bountiful host, a social guide, a financial confidant, and a free-handed companion at the gaming table. But times change, and, while the theme of personal attentiveness still runs through modern pressure tactics, the forms which it takes have changed. Formal dinners for Members of Congress and, in addition to these, more casual and intimate gatherings, remain part of the lobby group's stock in trade. But apart from these vestiges of the old "social lobby," the personal service aspects of lobbying have been considerably revamped. Today, the resourceful pressure groups may seek to serve themselves as well as Members of Congress by arranging remunerative speaking or writing engagements for them, or by such friendly acts as helping the new Member to secure housing in Washington.

The relationships between Members of Congress and groups interested in legislation are infinitely varied. Many Members have spoken before such groups, frequently for no remuneration whatsoever. In other cases, Members have arranged for groups to reproduce their writings on public issues. One Member, for example, has regularly written a weekly Washington column which has been distributed by a group filing reports under the Lobbying Act. He has received no pay for this writing, but he has received "research expenses" which have ranged from $250 to $500 per month. Obviously, those groups which cannot work on equally close terms with Members are left at a considerable disadvantage.

There is a final long-standing lobbying technique which, without any modernization at all, has become increasingly prevalent during the past 40 years. We refer to the use of the franking privilege for mass mailings of printed matter.

It is unlawful for Congressmen or Government officials to lend the frank or "permit its use by any committee, organization, or association. . . ." Yet the Committee for Constitutional Government obtains mass distribution of various materials through the use of congressional franks in the following manner. A Member inserts in the Congressional Record an article or speech that may or may not have been furnished him by the committee. It is reproduced by the Government Printing Office much less expensively than at commercial rates. The printing is paid for by the Member, who in turn is reimbursed by E. A. Rumely's group. The matter is mailed in bulk, sometimes already stuffed and sealed in franked envelopes, to the Committee for Constitutional Government in New York, where it is stored. At the moment deemed most timely and convenient for the committee, the individual envelopes are addressed and mailed postage-free under the congressional frank. . . . Close to 2½ million pieces of franked material of one Member of Congress were obtained by this one organization in a single year for distribution postage-free at the taxpayers' expense. This same organization publicly advocates Government economy. . . .

Mass distribution of books and pamphlets is only one of the means by which the pressure groups have sought to influence legislation through the creation and exploitation of a charged public opinion. Wherever public opinion is made, the pressure group is likely to be found. . . .

. . . The National Association of Real Estate Boards, for example, has induced colleges and universities to set up special courses in which its general point of view was taught. It has also stimulated the writing of textbooks on real estate, home building and management, and real estate economics, which it estimates are currently used by 127 colleges and universities. . . .

The pressure groups have long been aware of the power of the press and have sought to harness this power for their ends. One of the prime conditions of successful public relations is anonymity of the source; thus it is not surprising that the effort to use the Nation's newspapers and periodicals as instruments of pressure politics has been concentrated on gaining access to editorial and news columns. One way in which this can be done is discussed in the following exchange between Representative Doyle and Mr. Rumely:

Mr. Doyle: One other question: I noticed, in many California papers, what I would call standard editorials, of exactly the same text. In your processes, do you send out stereotyped editorials?
Mr. Rumely: No; we do not send out canned editorials. We send out informative information which we hope the papers will print. In a fight like this one, we picked out about 20 editorials that told our side, and sent them to all newspapers in the United States."

Labelling this process is less important than ascertaining its results. In this case, Mr. Rumely's material apparently proved attractive to the several dozen editors, in California and elsewhere, who printed it verbatim. . . .

No discussion of the use of the press to influence public opinion on legislative issues would be complete without reference to the meteoric growth of institutional or editorial advertising, that is, paid advertisements for ideas rather than for products, and particularly for ideas which relate directly or inferentially to public issues. This practice developed phenomenally during World War II when the tax structure made it prudent to keep operating costs high and profits down. It developed, in fact, to such an extent that the format of the American newspaper and magazine has been quietly revolutionized. It is no longer any novelty to see full-page advertisements in which the Association of American Railroads reminds us that the truckers should pay more for their use of the highways; or in which local affiliates of the National Association of Home Builders warn that public housing is pure socialism. But editorial advertising of this kind is not limited to lobbying organizations. It is, rather, increasingly the province of separate business concerns, labor unions, and other such organizations not established primarily for the purpose of influencing legislation.

Two different problems arise in connection with these efforts to affect public thinking. The considerations involved in public issues are not always reducible to one-page summaries; overstatement and oversimplification are apt to create a condition in which reasoned public thinking and calm legislative judgment become increasingly difficult.

The second problem relates one again to full disclosure under the Lobbying Act. Few corporations have reported under the act, and those few generally neglect to state their institutional advertising expenses. Lobbying organizations which report have shown similar reluctance to disclose their expenses in this area. The relevancy of most of this advertising to public issues is quite clear and, consequently, its cost should properly be made a matter of public record. . . .

Chapter Six
EXECUTIVE AND CONGRESS: A Reversal of Roles

INSTITUTIONALIZING PRESIDENTIAL INITIATIVE

Planning the President's Program

RICHARD E. NEUSTADT

Early in 1954, President Dwight D. Eisenhower presented to the Congress—and the country and his party—some 65 proposals for new legislation, over and above appropriations. This presentation was a massive affair. First came six weeks of well-publicized preliminaries: cabinet deliberations, congressional briefings, press conferences, and a fireside chat. Then, in three annual messages to Congress—a State of the Union Address, a Budget Message, and an Economic Report—the President set forth his bundle of proposals, elaborating certain aspects, outlining the rest. Along with these came seven supplementing special messages, each filling in details on some particular: Taft-Hartley, farm price supports, social security, health, housing, atomic energy, foreign aid, and trade. And following the messages Administration-approved

From Richard E. Neustadt, *The American Political Science Review* (1955, Vol. XLIX, No. 4), American Political Science Association, Washington.

bills, conveyors of the ultimate details, were introduced in Congress.

Throughout, one theme was emphasized: here was a comprehensive and coordinated inventory of the nation's current legislative needs, reflecting the President's own judgments, choices, and priorities in every major area of Federal action; in short, his "legislative program," an entity distinctive and defined, its coverage and its omissions, both, delimiting his stand across the board. And—quite explicitly—this stand was being taken, this program volunteered, in order to give Congress an agenda, Republicans a platform, and voters a yardstick for 1954.

Thus, one year after his inaugural, Eisenhower espoused a sweeping concept of the President's initiative in legislation and an elaborate mechanism for its public expression; developments which no one seemed to take amiss. Both in governmental circles and in the press, the whole performance was regarded almost as a matter of course, a normal White House response to the opening of Congress. The pattern, after all, was quite familiar; the comprehensive program expressed in ordered sequence, with some sort of publicized preliminaries and detailed follow-up, had been an annual enterprise in Truman's time. Indeed, while Eisenhower had undoubtedly improved upon the earlier mechanics, his 1954 procedure seemed expressive less of innovation than of reversion to accustomed practice. In 1953, he had been criticized in many quarters for failing to produce a defined program of this kind; now that "failure" was made good, a general expectation satisfied in the "customary" way.

Customary, perhaps; yet as recently as 1946 an informed observer had remarked, accurately enough, on the "absence of cohesion in the legislative program of the chief executive—absence, in fact, of a program clearly designated as such." Presidential reports and recommendations to Congress were as old as the Constitution; presidential sponsorship of specific measures, high-lighted in special messages and spelled out in Administration bills, had been a commonplace in Franklin Roosevelt's time and by no means unknown much earlier. But the elaborate paraphernalia of a comprehensive and specific inventory, contents settled and defined as regards substance no less than finance, *presented in detailed fashion and packaged form at the opening of each session of Congress*—this was a "custom" scarcely nine years old, a postwar phenomenon evolving under Truman and now carried forward under Eisenhower.

Here is an institutional development of no mean proportions, with a great preparatory effort obviously involved in advance of every session. Three questions are suggested: First, currently, what are the mechanics of this program preparation; how is the job done and by whom? Second, historically, what gave rise to such institutionalization in the postwar decade; how did it evolve and how did it survive the change of Administration? Third, prospectively—and speculatively—what may the whole development imply regarding powers, opportunities, of President and presidency in the legislative process? This paper attempts answers to these questions; its starting point is the making of the Eisenhower program of 1954.

I. PREPARING THE EISENHOWER PROGRAM OF 1954

"The presentation of a legislative program," wrote Truman in his farewell message to the Congress, "falls properly to my successor, not to me . . . and I would not infringe upon his responsibility to chart the forward course." This was easier said by the outgoing President than done by the incoming, with his first Congress already in session (courtesy the Twentieth Amendment). In 1953, for the first time in years, there was no "legislative program," no charting of the course in the specific sense conveyed by Truman's words and prior practice.

At the outset, Eisenhower did present to Congress his own report on the State of the Union, but he chose throughout that address to keep most of his legislative references general to the point of homily. The new regime, while reducing appropriations requests—as in the case of the Air Force—forebore to present a complete new budget document and message; while revising some economic policies—as in the case of credit and controls—it attempted no new Economic Report. During the spring of 1953, a number of Administration stands on legislation were developed and expressed, piecemeal, in special messages or bills, or both. But for the most part these encompassed only inescapable necessities—like foreign aid, taxation, reciprocal trade—where scheduled expirations of authority forced the presidential hand. More characteristic were the surveys, investigations, and study groups brought forward by the President or his subordinates in lieu of action recommendations on numbers of great issues, foreign and domestic.

What accounts for this lack of firm programming in the congressional session of 1953? . . .

. . . [W]hatever Eisenhower's personal position, there seems no doubt that certain members of his entourage were then distinctly predisposed against a comprehensive program presentation along anything like Truman's lines. "We always meant to have a program," appears a considerable overstatement, at least if "we" refers to the whole White House entourage in 1953. Conciliating Congress was the order of the day; by some, apparently, this was interpreted as *not* doing whatever Truman might have done. Moreover, some of the new White House aides appear to have been seriously concerned about the constitutional proprieties; others disturbed about the range of Democratic intervention in domestic spheres; still others doubtful of the need for further emphasis on lawmaking, *per se*. Such attitudes as these add up to general bearishness toward widespread volunteering of firm presidential stands on current or prospective legislation—especially when controversial. "Let Congress struggle with it; keep us out." Here was, reportedly, an often-sounded White House theme through most of the first session of the 83rd Congress.

Yet scarcely five months after that session's close, there came the Eisenhower legislative program of 1954. Whether as an outcome of deliberate plans, or of changed attitudes, or both, this represents a distinct alteration in approach from one session of Congress to the next. How did it come to pass? How was the newness tempered, the bearishness reduced, the program put together?

In May, 1953, the Bureau of the Budget sent to the multilith machines—in preparation for June 30 distribution—its annual call for estimates from Federal agencies, in this case for fiscal 1955. Included in that document as an instruction to each agency was Section 86, entitled "Legislative Program":

> A statement will be submitted [September 15] describing the preliminary legislative program of the agency for the forthcoming session of Congress. This statement should include *all* items of legislation [other than appropriations] which the agency contemplates proposing during the ensuing twelve months. . . .
>
> The statement should be in three parts:

1. Those items in the President's legislative program which have not yet been enacted . . . limited to proposals . . . specifically identified by the President as part of his program, or specifically held [by Budget through central clearance] to be "in accord with the program of the President."
2. Legislative proposals not included in part 1 . . . which would cause no increase in budgeting requirements.
3. Legislative proposals not included in part 1 . . . which would cause an increase in budgeting requirements . . . arranged to reflect relative priority among items on the list and also . . . with respect to other portions of the budget. . . .

With respect to each item of proposed legislation, this statement should set forth (1) the subject matter . . . together with a summary statement of the objectives . . . and the need . . . (2) the state of readiness of legislative drafts and other supporting material; (3) a reference to the numbers of pertinent bills and . . . reports [in recent sessions] . . . together with a brief appraisal . . . (4) a forecast of both the appropriations and the expenditures required . . . and (5) the names of other [interested] departments and agencies. . . .

This language was identical with that included in the 1952 call for estimates issued a year earlier before the close of Truman's term. Indeed, section 86 and its requirements had been a feature of each Budget call since 1949. Their renewal in 1953 marks not an Eisenhower innovation but a bureaucratic continuum, an attempted restoration of routines, an action taken on the Budget's own initiative without advance assurance as to either agency response or ultimate White House reaction.

This was a venture with no guarantees attached; it was, however, something more than a leap in the dark. The Budget Bureau's renewal of section 86 was powerfully reinforced by two other acts of initiative, one preceding, one following preparation of the new call for estimates.

The first of these involved the agencies. As early as January, 1953, the new Budget Director, Joseph M. Dodge, had corralled cabinet colleagues, one by one, for orientation briefings by his career aides. In a number of cases these sessions were held even before Inauguration Day, providing several cabinet members-designate their first glimpse from inside into the complexities of their new assignments. And at each briefing Budget staffers took occasion, with Dodge's assent, to inform the department head about "his" legislative program (compiled the preceding fall), its existence in form and fact, its usefulness for orientation, its potential for planning and control, its liability to renewal on Budget's call.

Thereby, a piece of left-over machinery idling in the departmental depths was impressed on the consciousness of new department heads at a uniquely favorable moment. This had its due effect; by late summer 1953, when lower-level bureaucrats began preparing agency responses to Budget's new call, their top superiors, in almost every case, were reasonably well acquainted with the departmental "program," quite acclimated to its presence as a fact of departmental life, and quite prepared to oversee its renovation and renewal in advance of 1954.

Meanwhile the Budget had taken a further act of initiative, this time involving the White House. Early in July, 1953 President Eisenhower had voiced some concern about means to bring together, well in advance, data and suggestions for his January, 1954 State of the Union message. Budget aids were asked to brief him on his predecessor's practice; they took the opportunity to urge some White House recognition for the programming requirement in Section 86 of the new call for estimates. In Truman's time it had been customary for the President to write each agency in early autumn, requesting message data and, at the same time, reiterating over his own signature the main terms of section 86. Message and program requests had long been joined; that was made clear to the new President.

The result was an identical letter to each cabinet officer over Eisenhower's signature and bearing signs of his own dictation. Dated July 30, 1953—a month after formal issuance of Budget's call—the letters asked for substantive ideas appropriate to the State of the Union Message, these ideas to be based on a "thorough rethinking of the mission of your department and the . . . means to achieve it." And, quite explicitly, that review was to "complement attention you are giving the 1955 budget and the formulation of a carefully planned, specific legislative program."

If there were any doubts remaining at top departmental levels about the propriety—and the priority—of Budget's legislative call, this missive from the President appears to have resolved them. By mid-September, 1953, agency legislative programs were flowing to the Budget. By early October, departmental message memoranda were en route to the White House, many of them referencing or appending these programs to concretize suggested points of emphasis. The President had called for a "thorough rethinking." Here, in this double-barrelled presentation, was the visible response.

Cumulatively, it was an astonishing response, at least to those White House staffers disinclined toward executive initiatives in legislation. For here were departmental declarations of intent to sponsor literally hundreds of measures great and small, *most of which the President was being asked to make his own by personal endorsement in a message.* And among these were dozens of proposals, espoused now by one or another of Eisenhower's own department heads, closely resembling—in general purpose, if not always precise form—predecessor measures urged in Truman's time and bearing then a Fair Deal label: an expansion of social security, an increased minimum wage, a revision of immigration laws, a broadening of unemployment compensation, and many more. Mostly these represented improvements in going programs long advocated by career administrators (and their clientele) to modernize or clarify the application of public policies in their charge. Agency legislative programs in 1953 were not sheer replicas of those in 1952 and earlier—some items were stricken, others added, still other revised—but their content makes plain that mixed with the rethinking from on high was a good deal of educating from below.

For eight years past—save only 1953—there had been a presidential charting of the course in Truman's terms: an executive inventory of specifics (agenda and yardstick both) for action by the Congress. Now, in October, 1953, these agency submissions forecast that some such executive charting would be done in 1954—if not by Eisenhower comprehensively, then by his cabinet members piecemeal; if not in his name, then in theirs. At his own invitation they had defined their ambitions, drawn their plans, and these now turned out to encompass controversial innovations of national concern, inextricably involving the President's position and prestige. Were he therefore to influence scope, scale, priorities, and presentation, he needs must act upon their requests for endorsement, thereby asserting his own rule in program-making, *his* plans, *his* charting of the course as against theirs.

The implications were not lost for long upon the presidential staff. . . .

Within the White House . . . there was no escaping action

upon agency submissions. By mid-October it was generally conceded that whatever major issues they might raise would have to be acknowledged in some form or fashion—negatively, at the very least—by or before Eisenhower's annual messages. This necessitated first of all a close look at the contents of the pile well in advance of message preparation. And by early November, such examination was preoccupying half the members of the White House entourage.

Their initial "look-see" became a rather elaborate affair. Under the aegis of the Assistant to the President, Sherman Adams, with his deputy, Wilfred E. Persons, and the then Special Counsel, Bernard M. Shanley, actively in charge, anywhere from six to ten members of the entourage—depending on subject-matter—joined in an item-by-item review around the conference table; over a two-week period this involved some 12 meetings of two to three hours apiece. . . .

[From mid-October through December of 1953, program making went through various stages, briefly summarized here. With the help of Roger Jones, career chief of the Budget Bureau's Office of Legislative Reference, the staff sorted through some 33 "major" proposals, pros and cons of each were sought from congressional and "outside" sources and priorities among the proposals were established. From late November through mid-December several cabinet presentations were made, consensus was sought, with Eisenhower actively participating. This served educative and co-ordinative purposes and also as a dress rehearsal for what was to be many cabinet members' first full-scale approach to a legislative committee.—Ed.]

In the course of these various proceedings late in 1953—staff reviews, presidential briefings, cabinet presentations, and attendant negotiations—the White House grew increasingly committed to an Eisenhower legislative program, the more so as its practicable scope and character came clear. By the end of November there was no longer any question that a program would ensue, or that it should appear in annual messages, or that it should be at once comprehensive and concrete. Amidst the concentration on specifics, these things came to be taken for granted. In part, this is attributable to the sheer momentum of those staff and agency proceedings once started on their way. In part, it seems related to the intra-party power struggle in which Senator McCarthy had engaged with increasing directness since the death of Senator Taft the preceding summer. On December 2 and on December 16 the President at press conference took pains to assert that his own forthcoming program, *not* McCarthy's chosen issue, would measure Republican performance in the election year of 1954; this hard upon the Senator's press statements to the contrary. The presidential program, once, perhaps, a questionable undertaking or a necessary chore, was now become a prime political imperative, its relative readiness a godsend, one expects, to the regime. . . .

On December 17, 18, and 19, 1953, Eisenhower formally unveiled his program to the Republican congressional leadership, in an unprecedented series of carefully staged briefings at the White House. With the President presiding, these ran a full eight hours daily, covering a subject-matter agenda fixed in advance and rigidly enforced from the chair. The Vice-President, the Speaker, the Majority Leaders, and the Whips were in attendance at all times, as were most members of the cabinet and the White House entourage. Committee chairmen and their ranking (Republican) associates participated when their subjects were discussed, arriving and departing on a pre-determined schedule; so did a number of executive officials below cabinet rank. In deference to Eisenhower's own communiques, issued each afternoon, and honoring his personal request, those moving in and out avoided detailed comment to the press; thereby, the White House got ideal publicity in presidential terms—headlines about Eisenhower and his program but no scoops on particulars. . . .

Less than three weeks intervened between these leaders' meetings in December, 1953 and the President's State of the Union Address to Congress; it was a busy season for the message drafters. In policy terms there was by this time little left to be decided, but the contents of the several messages remained to be coordinated, their relative scope and coverage fully defined, specific drafts agreed upon—or, indeed, written—and final language snarls worked out. In carrying these matters forward, actual drafting of the Budget Message was left largely to the Budget Bureau, the White House checking mainly general tone and precise wording of concrete proposals. Similarly, drafting of the Economic Report remained largely in the hands of the Economic Council chairman, himself a prime participant in earlier staff consultations. But for the psychologically most important annual message, the President's personally delivered State of the Union address, the drafting was from first to last a White House undertaking. . . . the first consolidated State of the Union draft was so crowded with specifics that it would have taken some three hours to deliver. In consequence, large portions were pulled out to form the first five of Eisenhower's 1954 special messages, his personal address becoming in the end a sort of preparatory note and table of contents for the supplementing documents to follow.

Meanwhile, the departments concentrated on bill drafting in order that each definite proposal conveyed by these messages might be backed promptly by a detailed draft of legislation bearing an Administration label and ready for transmission (formally or not) to Congress. . . .

Neither by content nor tone were documents like these well suited to the task of dramatizing for the country and his party the President's own personality and purposes. Yet if there was but little drama in the messages themselves, there was, perhaps, much to be gained by focussing attention on their presentation as a collectivity, seeking dramatic impact in the sheer fact of "program," aside from the nature or the statement of its parts. To this the White House—President and staff together, it appears—devoted a great deal of thought and care during December, 1953.

In the five weeks before the State of the Union address, there emanated from the White House a steady stream of press communiques and dope stories concerning the program's preparation. Specific plans were guarded rather carefully—the aim, no doubt, to generate suspense—but generalized official comments on the special cabinet sessions, and in particular the legislative leaders' meetings, were arranged and facilitated by the White House press office with all the fanfare usually reserved for first-rank international conferences. After the conclusion of those meetings, December 19, the President removed to Georgia over Christmas, whence came almost daily stories of last-minute conferences on the impending messages with officials flown down from Washington. On January 4, 1954, all this was capped by a radio and television address to the nation, in which Eisenhower plugged his program and urged everyone's attention to its imminent unveiling. In dramatic appeal this discourse was scarcely an unqualified success; trying to reach the country in the evening hours without depriving Congress of its first crack at details, he avoided scooping his congressional address at the expense of over-generalizing. Nevertheless, the notion that something portentous impended, Eisenhower's own, received top billing once again in newscasts and the press.

On January 5, the President met minority legislative leaders at the White House for a courtesy preview of his recommendations; thereby the press got one last "program" story before the opening of Congress. Then on Thursday, January 7, came the President's State of the Union Address to the Congress, another radio and television presentation, if at noon. There followed on three successive Mondays and Thursdays no less than seven of his supplementing messages, spaced for optimum press play and in a sequence obviously intended to strengthen the impression of a vast executive creation, highlight its most generally appealing features, blur the rest: Taft-Hartley and farm messages sent up at the same time on the same day (with a Korean defense treaty sent the Senate simultaneously); social security, health, and housing messages each featured in a separate package on a separate day; housekeeping and limited-interest requests buried by the dozen in the Budget Message; tax reduction dominant in the Economic Report. . . .

IV. LEGISLATIVE PROGRAMS AND PRESIDENTIAL LEADERSHIP

Survival is the acid test of institutional development within the White House orbit. At this writing, in 1955, the Budget's call for estimates for fiscal 1957 has just gone to the agencies, a Section 86 included as before. The President may now abandon letters of request for message data—in 1954, a reminder at cabinet table served instead—but there is every expectation in his entourage that 1955's budget and message seasons will proceed along the lines of prior years, with January, 1956's annual messages conveying to the Congress and the country a comprehensive program presentation, Eisenhower's third—thus marking the tenth anniversary of Truman's trial compendium of 1946. . . .

Traditionally, there has been a tendency to distinguish "strong" Presidents from "weak," depending on their exercise of the initiative in legislation. The personal appearances in the hall of the House, the special messages, the drafted bills, the public appeals, so characteristic of contemporary program presentation, have all been represented in the past—no farther back than Franklin Roosevelt's time—as signs of a President's intention or capacity to "dominate" the Congress. If these were once relevant criteria of domination, they are not so today. As things stand now they have become part of the regular routines of office, an accepted elaboration of the constitutional right to recommend; as such, no more indicative of presidential domination than the veto power, say, in Herbert Hoover's time.

Indeed, from the congressional point of view, "service," not domination, is the reality behind these presidential undertakings. In practical effect, they represent a means whereby Congress can gain from the outside what comes hard from within: a handy and official guide to the wants of its biggest customer; an advance formulation of main issues at each session; a work-load ready-to-hand for every legislative committee; an indication, more or less, of what may risk the veto; a borrowing of presidential prestige for most major bills—and thus a boosting of publicity-potentials in both sponsorship and opposition.

That Congress wants these things and finds them useful for its purposes may be judged from the almost total absence nowadays of vocal criticism or surprise at annual presentations of the President's program; an indicator reinforced by irritated comments, privately expressed on both sides of the aisle, when Eisenhower stayed his hand in 1953. Outcries against "dictatorship" and "speeches-from-the-throne" have long been stilled in responsible quarters. In 1947, Senator Taft told a Budget aide that as a matter of orderly procedure Republican committee chairmen *ought* to have the Democratic President's own views across-the-board and in detail, else the committees would lack solid ground from which to gauge the pleadings of departments and their clientele. In 1953, the very senior chairman of a major House committee reportedly admonished an Administration witness, "don't expect us to start from scratch on what you people want. That's not the way we do things here—*you* draft the bills and *we* work them over."

As that remark suggests, the Congress deals not in abstract ideas but in bills. It comes to grips with substance in terms of phraseology. The process cannot start without a draft. And since executive expertise is often indispensable, while executive wishes are data to be weighed—though quite conceivably ignored—a "downtown" draft has tangible advantage as the starting point. But more than drafting service is provided by contemporary presidential programs. Annual programming serves also to identify, to render timely, in effect to choose, most *legislative* issues on which serious attention is to center at a session; the President becomes agenda-setter for the Congress, the chief continuing initiator of subject-matter to reach actionable stages in committee and on the floor, whether or not ultimately passed. Of course, as Lawrence Chamberlain and others have made plain, most major measures are the product of long germination, much cross-fertilizing. Quite so; the service of contemporary Presidents has been less creativity than crystallization; a matter less of seeding new terrain than of tracing new lines in old ground, thereby to mark the field for current cultivation.

In this respect, the presidency is performing for the Congress a task apparently beyond that body's institutional capacity to carry on its own account. When one looks at the legislative record of the last decade, the major controversial measures brought to focus, debate, and near-passage, or enactment on congressional initiative *alone*, are small scatteration relative to those highlighted by—or with assistance from—the President: most prominently, perhaps, the Taft-Hartley Act, the two McCarran Acts, and the perennial Bricker Amendment.[1] Of these, at least Taft-Hartley may be ascribed actually to a reverse sort of presidential initiative —Truman choosing *not* to propose action in an area where momentary public sensitivity was certain to evoke response of some sort from the 80th Congress.* . . . presidential silences no less than statements may serve to delineate the actionable issues.

But note that setting an agenda is not the same thing as enforcing it; selecting issues for consideration is not equivalent to

[1] Other items which reached the point of passage include the tax reduction measures of 1947 and 1948, the first tidelands bill in 1947, and the natural gas and basing point bills of 1949. Of course, there have been infinite numbers of amendments to, adjustments in—and sheer denials of—Administration proposals, over the years, as matters of distinct congressional initiative, oppositional to presidential purposes or claimed intent. But these are in a different category. The fact that Presidents are now so largely raisers of the issues does not signify that they are safe from penalties for having done so; quite the contrary, both in and out of Congress.

* See below, "Policy Formulation in the Executive Branch: The Taft-Hartley Experience."—Ed.

having bills enacted into law. For evidence one has but to review the course of any recent congressional session. As a matter of fact, the most institutionalized aspects of the President's involvement in the legislative process are precisely those least concerned with actual campaigning for his program once presented: legislative programming and legislative clearance, *not* legislative infighting and signal-calling, day-by-day. To be sure, periodic White House meetings with congressional party leaders have become the norm; agendas prepared for the President in Truman's time; minutes kept as well in Eisenhower's. And Eisenhower has established in his entourage an Army-type liaison operation, its several staff aides covering each corner of the Hill on regular patrols. But formal leaders' sessions tend to be ambassadorial encounters; organized liaison tends to create its own chores, if not, indeed, to confuse liaisoners' loyalties. So far as one can judge from the outside, it remains true in Eisenhower's time—as in Truman's and F.D.R.'s before him—that when the chips are down, there is no substituting for the President's own footwork, his personal negotiation, his direct appeal, his voice and no other's on the telephone. Naturally, such methods cannot guarantee success; to overwork them would be self-defeating; to institutionalize them may well be impossible. Yet these, not programming devices, must bear the weight, provide the test, of presidential "domination" over Congress.

Indeed, a presidential purpose to control the congressional *product* may actually be impeded, not advanced, by legislative programming as presently evolved. Those massive, annual presentations have a tendency to blur the public impact of particulars, scatter attention, divert interest—as with Eisenhower's messages of 1954, or Truman's, year by year. Regularized repetition tends to dilute the dramatic, focussing effects of personal appearance and appeal. White House sponsorship spread wide tends to reduce the import of each presidential label. Manifold commitments tend to complicate the task of striking particular bargains. Multi-item programs tend to encourage score-keeping by parties, press, and public, ordinarily with the result of stressing losses over gains on a strict by-the-numbers basis. . . .

But whether or not always advantageous in those terms, the annual presidential inventory and its attendant mechanics have now become so rooted in responsibilities of office, so customary in the view of press and public, so satisfactory to the Congress, so institutionalized in the executive, that major alteration of the present pattern, much less its permanent abandonment, would appear no light matter for a President, nor likely. . . . And these are backed now by accustomed practices each year becoming more entrenched—not only as responses to congressional and public expectations, but as prime means to policy decision and control in the executive. To disavow them now might be to trade more flexibility with Congress for fewer hand holds on departments—this difficulty among others. . . .

THE LIMITS OF PRESIDENTIAL DISCIPLINE

The Purge of 1938

WILLIAM RIKER

As the primary campaign started that year it did not seem to differ significantly from earlier primaries. President Roosevelt did, it is true, try to smooth out intra-party disagreements. For example, he persuaded Representative Disney of Oklahoma not to run in the primary against Senator Thomas. He repeatedly and unsuccessfully urged John L. Lewis and the party regulars in Pennsylvania to support the same candidates in the primary; but he was unable to prevent a vicious, mud-slinging campaign fight between the two factions, a fight disastrous to the Democratic ticket in the fall. He took much trouble to help two Southern New Dealers, Senators Pepper of Florida and Hill of Alabama, in the spring primaries—for Pepper, the President's eldest son formally announced "we are interested" in seeing him return. Early in March, Roosevelt took a part behind the scenes of the Kentucky primary, persuading erstwhile supporters of Governor Chandler, who coveted Senator Barkley's place, to desert Chandler for Barkley. All this activity was quiet maneuvering, however, not extensively reported in the newspapers; all the public statements were made by other people, not directly using the President's name; and his so-called interference was either in support of sitting Senators or in the interest of party harmony. What Roosevelt did, therefore, was no more than what many of his predecessors had done. It would have been very strange indeed had he not helped his loyal floor leader, Barkley; and it would have been stranger still if he had ignored Pepper, who was one of the few Southern Democrats in favor of the very controversial and—in the President's view—extraordinarily important wage and hour bill, and whose renomination would certainly swing some wavering Southerners to its support.

The first intimation that Roosevelt intended a real break with political precedent came during a vacation at Warm Springs, Georgia, at the end of March. Reporters were quick to notice that he praised Governor Rivers and Representative Weichel without mentioning Senator George who was up for renomination. Another hint was dropped a month later when Jim Farley, still then Postmaster-General and Chairman of the Democratic National Committee, was quoted as saying that Maryland Democrats should defeat Senator Tydings in the primary. Several Maryland politicians, eager to be the President's candidate, promptly scurried to the White House to beg for approval. By the end of May the President's new role in the primaries was clear to journalists, if not to the public generally, and the word "purge" had begun to appear in the headlines. When the Governor of Oregon, a very conservative Democrat, implied that the President favored his renomination, Roosevelt's press secretary issued a sharp denial and a few days later Secretary of the Interior Ickes advised Oregon Democrats to vote for the other, more liberal Democrat in the primary. At the same time Governor Johnson of South Carolina, a New Dealer, emerged from an interview with the President to announce that he would try to get the Democratic senatorial nomination over the incredibly reactionary Senator "Cotton Ed" Smith; and Governor Rivers of Georgia, also after seeing the President, intimated to reporters that he had been urged to run in the primary against Senator George. These were clear enough indications that Roosevelt was trying to defeat those Democratic Senators who were lukewarm about the New Deal.

Then came the first clear evidence of a plan to purge. Harry Hopkins, then the Administrator of the WPA, told a reporter that, if he were voting in the Iowa primary, he would support, not Senator Gillette who was seeking renomination, but Representative Otha Wearin who was seeking promotion. Senator Gillette, and other Democratic Senators who fearfully visualized a similar pronouncement about themselves, were outraged and excited by what they thought was a threat to use WPA money against Democrats. They spent the whole day debating it in the Senate. Faithful Administration Senators, like Barkley and Mrs. Caraway, defended Hopkins, saying that he had been badgered by reporters into an indiscretion; even they did not then conceive of arguing that the Administration ought to campaign publicly against sitting Democratic Senators in the Democratic primaries.

After the excitement aroused by Hopkins' remark, Roosevelt evidently wavered. The next day, coming out of a conference with the President, Representative Eicher of Iowa, announced his support of Wearin; but a few days later at a press conference Roosevelt refused to discuss the Iowa primary and said that Hopkins' comment was off-the-record and ought not to have been published. Roosevelt's wavering reflected the division among his official intimates. While Hopkins, Corcoran, and Ickes were evidently urging aggressive action, Jim Farley seemed to support Gillette; and Henry Wallace, the only Iowan high in the Administration, kept discreetly, even noticeably, silent. Roosevelt, uncertain and unwontedly indecisive, did nothing, Gillette won, and a few days later the two sat down to a hatchet-burying luncheon, in shirtsleeves, so reporters said.

If Roosevelt intended to appeal to the people for support, the Iowa primary was an inauspicious start—ill-prepared, ill-timed, ill-managed, and necessitating at the end an embarrassing reconciliation. Perhaps Roosevelt was piqued by the failure; perhaps he had gone too far to stop—he had, for example, already selected Governor Johnson of South Carolina to oppose Senator "Cotton Ed" Smith; he had already given his blessing to one Lawrence Camp in the Georgia primary against Senator George; and Senator Guffey of Pennsylvania—always loyal, but always too blunt—had already been forced off the Democratic Senatorial Campaign Committee for proposing a purge of all those Democratic Senators who had voted against the Court reform bill. In any event, whether piqued by a messy failure or trapped by events which in his hesitancy he allowed to slip from his control, he told the people in a fireside chat that he intended to intervene in Democratic primaries:

> As the head of the Democratic Party . . . charged with the responsibility of carrying out the definitely liberal declaration of principles set

forth in the 1936 Democratic platform, I feel that I have every right to speak in those few instances where there may be a clear issue between candidates for a Democratic nomination involving these principles. . . .

Do not misunderstand me. I certainly would not indicate a preference in a State primary merely because a candidate, otherwise liberal in outlook, had conscientiously differed with me on any single issue . . . [but]. . . . We all know that progress may be blocked by outspoken reactionaries and also by those who say "yes" to a progressive objective, but who always find some reason to oppose any specific proposal to gain that objective. I call that type of candidate a "yes, but" fellow.

Soon thereafter he started out on a trip through the South to California, presumably to campaign in the Democratic primaries for New Dealers and against the " 'yes, but' fellows," the ones who had opposed not only the Court bill, but also the wage and hour bill, the administrative reorganization bill, and the public utility holding company death sentence clause. He made four speeches for Senator Barkley in Kentucky; but after that the "purge" was, as an editor of *Nation* complained, allowed "almost to peter out." Instead of campaigning forthrightly for his supporters, he ceased to mention primaries, substituting:

an elaborate code of graduated approval—with candidates designated as "friend," "old friend," and "dear old friend" according to the degree of White House enthusiasm for their respective nominations.

In Covington, Kentucky, he had asked Democrats to renominate the Senate floor leader because:

We in this country operate principally through what we call the party system. We so operate because we believe that party responsibility eliminates a large part of the confusion which would result from a complete lack of party leadership.

But by the time he spoke for Senator Thomas in Oklahoma, he had cheapened the argument from an appeal for executive democratic government to an appeal to sordid self-interest:

Senator Thomas has been of enormous help to me and to the Administration in keeping me advised as to the needs of your State, and as to how we, in Washington, could help meet them.

In Colorado and Nevada, where Senators Adams and McCarran, two who really qualified for the "yes, but" category, were up for renomination, he ignored their opponents and referred to McCarran as a "friend," albeit the lowest degree of approval.

Back again in the Old South, and encouraged perhaps by the news of Barkley's victory, he was more forthright. At Barnsville, Georgia, he made a full dress speech for Lawrence Camp, the Federal District Attorney whom he had encouraged to run against Senator George. In South Carolina he obliquely supported Governor Johnson who was running against Senator "Cotton Ed" Smith. In Maryland, he made the most powerful and partisan speech of the campaign endorsing Representative Davey Lewis, who was trying to unseat Senator Tydings. Finally in a New York City Congressional district, he strongly supported one James Fay, a deputy collector of internal revenue, against Representative O'Connor, a Tammany Democrat, chairman of the House Rules Committee, and the man who more than anyone else delayed consideration of the wage and hour bill.

And the result of his campaigning? Senator Barkley won in Kentucky, Senator Caraway, whom he had mildly supported, won in Arkansas, Senator Thomas won in Oklahoma. Three victories. But Senator George won in Georgia, Senator Smith won in South Carolina, Senator Tydings won in Maryland. Three defeats. James Fay won in the New York 16th District. A victory. As many journalists and scholars have pointed out, every sitting Congressman, with the exception of O'Connor, won—which suggests that Roosevelt's campaigning had no significant effect, except perhaps in New York City. Of course, 1938 was a bad year for the New Deal in the fall elections and it may be that he did at least save Barkley and Thomas from defeat. Otherwise, however, he did not accomplish very much, certainly not enough to compensate for the bad feeling he engendered among conservative Democrats.

Why the meagre result?

Perhaps in part Roosevelt failed because of simple lack of preparation. While some of his advisors may have conceived the plan in 1937, Roosevelt himself probably did not decide just what to do until late in the campaign year. How else can one explain his wavering over the Iowa primary? How else can one explain the elaborate trip West, starting out just after the promise made in the fireside chat to "indicate preferences," a trip taking him through eleven states during their primary campaigns, and yet a trip on which he indicated a preference plainly in only three states and hinted at a preference in only two more? Reconstructing the events now, it seems likely that, with his advisors divided, he planned at first merely to have certain recognized intimates speak out, as his son James did in Florida, or as Harry Hopkins did in Iowa, but that he changed his mind after the Iowa fiasco. No doubt it is futile now to pry into long-forgotten thoughts, but one fact is certain: He did not select his candidates in Georgia or Maryland until sometime in May, unfortunately after the junior Senator in each state—both good New Dealers—had agreed to campaign for the men he was trying to purge. Yet one rule upon which most experienced politicians would agree is that, in a primary campaign to unseat a fairly popular officeholder, the aspirant ought to work full-time at his campaign for at least six or nine months before the election. By this standard the purge was ill-planned; the hesitancy on his trip West indicates that the affair was ill-managed. In his own campaigns, Roosevelt was extraordinarily astute; but here he blundered.

The blunder is understandable. He was attempting something entirely new in American politics. Furthermore, he was running counter to the tradition of localism and state sovereignty in American politics. So it is not strange that he blundered in an unexplored land. Consider the blank amazement and unbelief displayed by Hiram Johnson when Hopkins' remark about the Iowa primary was reported to the Senate:

Mr. Johnson. . . . I take it Mr. Hopkins is a resident of Iowa.
Mr. Wheeler. I do not know.
Mr. Johnson. He must be, or he would not think of doing such a thing.
Mr. Wheeler. No, he is not, I am told.
Mr. Johnson. The Senator must be in error. Mr. Hopkins must be a resident of Iowa, or he would not think of doing such a thing.
Mr. Wheeler. Mr. Hopkins, I am informed, votes in New York . . . he is being talked of as a candidate for Governor of the State of New York.

And having considered Johnson's incredulity, consider then how difficult to plan and execute was Roosevelt's self-imposed assignment.

It is a superficial explanation, however, to say that the meagre result of Roosevelt's campaign was due only to blundering. Behind the blundering lies the fact of federalism. What this whole episode demonstrates more than anything else is the resistance of local politicians to national leadership. With their own well-oiled local machines, all the sitting Senators won, whether Roosevelt favored or opposed them. The only place where Roosevelt unseated a Congressman was in his own state of New York; and there he was perforce a local politician himself, the leader of a local faction; so his victory must be attributed as much to his residence as to his national leadership.

A CASE OF BUREAUCRATIC LOBBYING

Congress and Water Resources

ARTHUR MAASS

Should Twitch Cove, Maryland, be improved at Federal expense for the protection of the few crabbers who live near this Eastern Shore community? This past May, Congress decided yes; they confirmed a recommendation of the Chief of Engineers, U. S. Army. The United States Engineer Department as the Corps of Engineers is called in the exercise of civil functions, recommended in favor of Twitch Cove after evaluating alternative plans of improvement and selecting that one which appeared to balance best the factors of "economic feasibility"—i.e., the ratio of benefits to costs, "engineering feasibility," and the "desires of local interests."

This last item is of interest for the moment. For any major improvement, even for Twitch Cove, there will be many groups of "local interests," and their "desires" will differ, may even conflict. Thus, the Engineers seek to adjust these interests and to come up with a recommendation that will maximize the total desires of the community.

Congress for a great number of years has followed a procedure of legislative self-restraint with respect to water resources developments. It will not authorize any improvement which has not received a favorable report from the Chief of Engineers. And since the Engineers attempt to maximize local desires, it may be said that Congress has transferred important responsibility for the adjustment of group interests from its own body to the U.S. Engineer Department, as executive agency.

The Engineers have recognized the nature of the responsibility which Congress has delegated to them. They have conducted

From Arthur Maass, *The American Political Science Review* (1950, Vol. XLIX, No. 3), American Political Science Association, Washington.

their organization and operations in a manner designed to allow a rather full articulation of local group interests. The project planning procedure, from the time Congress authorizes the Corps to undertake an examination of a given area, involves twenty distinct stages at which group interests are able to present their views to the Corps. At three of these twenty, public hearings are regularly provided for; at two additional stages, Engineer Department instructions require consultation with local interests; and at the remaining fifteen, the extent of consultation varies with particular circumstances, but the necessity of a constant awareness of the current attitudes of local interests is emphasized in all Engineer Department publications.

Recently, the Chief of Engineers said:

> The authorization of a river and harbor or flood control project follows a definitely prescribed, democratic course of action. It is based upon the activation of the desires of local interests, who are most vitally interested. Local interests, as individuals or groups through the actions of their representatives in Congress, make request for an item to be included in a rivers and harbors or flood control bill (i.e., authorization to conduct an examination). . . . The District Engineer, mindful of the need for developing all public opinion, holds an open public hearing at which not only those interests that are active in obtaining the authorization of the proposed work but also all other views are obtained and encouraged. Having thus developed the desires of the local citizens, the District Engineer makes a study. . . .

I. PRESENT ARRANGEMENTS AND THE LEGISLATIVE PROCESS

Several important consequences for the legislative process flow from this project planning procedure. These include the participation by members of Congress in the "executive" planning process; legislation by committee resolution; service by the Corps of Engineers as consultants to, and contractors for, the Congress, certain congressional committees, and individual members of Congress; by-passing of the President and friction among executive agencies; and the interlocking of pressure groups, the Corps, and members of Congress.

Though Congress as a group has largely disassociated itself from the process of project planning by transferring responsibility for adjustment of group interests to the Engineer Department, individual members of Congress have not been so abstentious. Representatives and Senators, knowing they cannot obtain congressional authorization for the projects they are sponsoring without a favorable report from the Engineers, have attempted to pressure them into approving these projects by appealing to District Engineers and to the Board of Engineers for Rivers and Harbors in Washington in public hearings. . . .

If the Engineers submit an unfavorable or partially favorable report, the proponents of a project seek a re-examination, for the Congress will, as noted, not authorize an improvement without a favorable Corps recommendation. At the same time, the Corps by law may not initiate a survey unless Congress has specifically authorized it, usually in an omnibus rivers and harbors or flood control bill. However, to make it easier for members of Congress to require the Engineers to re-examine unfavorable reports in the hope that "changed conditions" may justify a favorable recommendation, the Congress has devised a truly unique procedure amounting to legislation by committee resolution.

After a report of the Chief of Engineers is one year old, any Representative or Senator may present a resolution to the appropriate congressional committee which, if adopted by the committee, requires the "Board of Engineers for rivers and harbors . . . to review the report with a view to determining whether any modification should be made at this time in the recommendation heretofore made." The committee resolution has the effect of law, and, it should be noted, is not subject to presidential veto.

Review resolutions have been quite common. As the Congressmen proposing the reviews enjoy no opposition to their requests in most cases, and as the Engineer Department has not been called upon often to report on the desirability of conducting reviews, the committees have been disposed to grant the requests, on occasion disregarding even the one-year waiting period. It is physically impossible for any one member of a committee to be informed on the history of all navigation and flood control projects. The Representative from Arkansas, for example, in all probability never heard of Mill Creek, Virginia, to say nothing of having any judgment as to whether or not the Engineers should be asked to review the report on this Creek; he will vote, Yes. Of 83 investigations completed by the Corps in fiscal year 1946, 20 were authorized by regular legislation and 63 were re-examinations submitted in response to committee resolutions. . . .

The Congress, in its long history of legislating internal improvements, has developed close relations with the Corps. (The Corps was the engineering department of the Government which planned and executed the national internal improvement programs of the 1820's.) Congress considers the Corps to be *directly* responsible to it. By resolution Congress directs the Board of Engineers for Rivers and Harbors, an advisory board to the Chief of Engineers, to conduct reviews of surveys. It does not direct the chief executive officer, the President; nor does it even provide the President with an opportunity for veto.

The Corps concurs heartily in this relationship. The Engineers call themselves "the engineer consultants to, and contractors for, the Congress of the United States." The theoretical consequences of such a direct legislative-agency relationship are familiar to students of government and administration; they need not be repeated here.

As might be expected, Congress as a whole is not equipped to exercise direct responsibility over the conduct of Engineer Corps civil functions. It is rather certain congressional committees—those with competence over navigation and flood control matters—that attempt to hold the Corps accountable. It is to them that the Engineers are directly responsible. Witness the review resolution procedure in which Congress in effect allows a committee to legislate for it.

Traditionally members of Congress from the Mississippi delta area, where flood protection, drainage, and river navigation problems assume great importance, seek positions on the committees which handle Corps legislation. Through regular re-election they attain positions of seniority. . . .

Direct relations between Congress and the Corps mean, of course, that the Engineers by-pass the President. This is obviously bad, for the only place where related executive functions can be coordinated effectively is in the President's office. Prior to the 1930's there was no major problem as most river improvements were for single purposes and did not impinge directly on the activities of other agencies. In the early '30's, however, the Corps began planning multiple purpose projects throughout the country involving flood control, power, irrigation, drainage, and other uses, and coordination in order to produce the best multiple purpose plan for the development of major drainage basins seemed essential. The history of resources legislation and of the development of planning procedures between 1934 and this date constitutes very largely the history of efforts by Presidents Roosevelt and Truman to break down direct agency responsibility to the Congress and to substitute for it a pattern of responsibility to the Chief Executive. Only in these terms can recent developments in the resources field be interpreted.

The agency with which the Corps has had greatest friction due to lack of coordination is the Bureau of Reclamation in the Department of the Interior. In this inter-agency feud, which has been really intense since 1939, the Corps . . . has enjoyed the strong support of the Congress. The Secretary of the Interior and the Bureau of Reclamation, on the other hand, have received less consistent congressional support and have sought to balance the advantage of the Corps of Engineers in this respect by obtaining the support of the President and his Executive Office. The general pattern may be expressed as follows: Corps of Engineers + Congress v. Secretary of the Interior + Executive Office of the President.

The fact that Congress as a body has transferred to the Engineers responsibility for adjusting group interests in proposing water developments, but that individual members of Congress continue to take an active part in the planning and adjusting process is revealed in an interesting manner by the national water pressure groups—particularly the National Rivers and Harbors Congress. This comprehensive lobby counts in its membership the "local interests" (state and local officials, local industrial and trade organizations, contractors), the U.S. Congress (Representatives and Senators are honorary members), and the Corps of Engineers (officers of the Corps engaged in rivers and harbors work are all ex-officio members). The members of Congress, though they are in a real sense the lobbied, take a very active part in the Rivers Congress. Today, for example, the President is Senator John McClellan of Arkansas, a member of the Public Works Committee and of the sub-committee of the Committee on Appropriations which handles Engineer Corps funds, and chairman of the Committee on Expenditures in the Executive Departments—to which the Hoover Commission recommendations proposing reorganization of the Corps of Engineers have been referred. McClellan, as a member of the Hoover Commission, dissented from those recommendations which would divest the Army of rivers and harbors functions. The national vice presidents of the pressure group are Senator Wherry of Nebraska, Republican floor leader and a member of the Appropriations sub-committee on Engineer Corps funds; Representative Whittington of Mississippi . . .*; and Representative Case of South Dakota, a member of the Committee on Appropriations and, at the time of his selection as vice president, of the subcommittee which considered appropriations for the Corps.

In the past the ex-officio members, officers of the Corps, also have taken part in the proceedings of the lobby, though today they are somewhat more circumspect. The Rivers Congress remains, however, the most active pressure group in support of the [Corps].

Perhaps the most interesting and important aspect of the Rivers and Harbors Congress is the work of the Projects Committee. When the National Congress was formed in 1901, its slogan was "a policy, not a project." The purpose was not to urge any specific waterway improvements but to interest the public and the Federal Congress in the development of waterways in general. In 1935, however, the Rivers and Harbors Congress reversed its policy, agreed to promote certain waterway improvements actively, and for that purpose organized a Project Committee. The Committee meets once a year for several days preceding the annual convention to act upon all applications for endorsement. It holds hearings on each project, classifies it in one of several orders of priority, and presents its recommendations to the full Rivers and Harbors Congress for adoption.

Senators and Congressmen who are sponsoring waterway improvements in their districts appear before the Committee in order to obtain from that organization of which they are honorary members favorable recommendations for their projects. . . .

II. THE NEGLECT OF WATER RESOURCE PLANNING

. . . Today we have no rational national water policy, even apart from the unrelated consideration of individual projects. President Truman recognized this in January, 1950, when he set up a temporary Water Resources Policy Commission under Morris L.

* In 1950 Chairman of the House Committee on Public Works.

Cooke to develop one. Why is this true? Why are we spending hundreds of millions of dollars each year on water developments without a plan?

That ultimate responsibility rests with Congress, there can be no question. But Congress and congressional committees are not equipped to develop a national water plan out of whole cloth. They are admirably equipped to examine, approve, disapprove, and amend any intelligent programs presented to them which focus on the great issues. It is the Chief Executive who is best able to prepare such broad programs and assume responsibility for placing them before the elective body. For the greatest part of water development, however, the President has been short circuited. The Congress and the Engineers work together, but as related, this combined labor has produced no plan.

The Corps of Engineers in reporting to Congress makes no special effort to point up the broad policy questions or to recommend or encourage the enactment of laws containing a careful definition of national policy in the water field. As the "Engineer consultants to and contractors for the Congress of the United States," they have, they say, no responsibility for initiating policies and broad programs; that is the function of Congress. . . .

President Roosevelt tried hard to fulfill what he considered his duty—to develop a national water policy and to submit this to Congress for action. He created and supported the National Resources Planning Board and its Water Resources Committee. But in this position the President enjoyed the intense opposition of the Congress and of the Corps of Engineers. The Corps failed to give full and genuine cooperation to the Water Resources Committee in its efforts to develop a policy. It dissented from most policy reports of the Committee, most notably from the important 1941 Report on National Water Policy. The Congress was always unsympathetic to the NRPB; refused, despite frequent personal appeals from the President, to give the Board permanent statutory status; and finally abolished it by denying appropriations in 1943. The single most important reason for congressional opposition to the Board was probably resentment on the part of the so-called rivers and harbors block in Congress to any effort by the President to interfere with the direct relations between Congress and the Corps. Furthermore, Congress failed to pay any heed to the policy recommendations of the Water Resources Committee which, though they contained dissents from the Corps, were supported by the President. . . .

III. CONGRESS AND EXECUTIVE BRANCH ORGANIZATION

The fact that organization for water resources development is so inadequate today is in large part a result of the congressional attitudes we have outlined.

Theodore Roosevelt, Herbert Hoover, Franklin Roosevelt—all have tried to bring rationale into administration of water functions. And all have failed, failed because Congress will brook no interference whatsoever in its direct relations with the Corps. As one writer has said, "The civil functions of the Army Corps of Engineers constitute a veritable Rock of Gibraltar against all executive attempts to introduce any organizational integration of flood control and river development with the land use, irrigation, and electric-power activities of other federal agencies."

In recent years the Bureau of the Budget, as a coordinating agency for the President, has tried to break into the direct channel between the Corps and Congress. It has required that survey reports (in the same manner as proposed legislation) be submitted to the Executive Office of the President, prior to submission to Congress, so that the Corps can be informed of the relationship of the reports to the program of the President. But when the Executive Office informs the Corps that a project does not conform with the President's program, the Engineers pay no heed. They recommend to Congress, nonetheless, that the project be adopted. . . .

. . . The same obstacle prevents the President from consolidating important resources functions. Theodore Roosevelt recommended to Congress in 1908 that responsibility for water development be centralized. Congress, expressing full confidence in the Corps of Engineers, failed to implement his recommendation. Herbert Hoover proposed to Congress in 1932 that the civil functions of the Corps of Engineers be transferred to the Department of Interior. His reorganization plan, submitted under the Economy Act of 1932, was roundly defeated in the House. The members of the House Committees on Flood Control and on Rivers and Harbors, Democrats and Republicans alike, opposed the reorganization. Franklin Roosevelt in 1937 proposed that Congress enact legislation permitting him to effect reorganizations within the executive branch. No agencies of Government were to be excluded. When in 1939 Congres finally passed the Reorganization Bill authorizing the President to submit plans to Congress which would become law unless vetoed by both Houses of Congress within 60 days, the Corps of Engineers was one of a very few purely executive agencies placed beyond application of the legislation. Harry Truman in 1945 asked that Congress re-enact reorganization legislation (it had lapsed some years previously) and that no agencies be exempted from its provisions. Congress did exempt some eight agencies, seven of them independent commissions or boards, and the eighth, the Corps of Engineers. . . .

Continued congressional opposition to Valley Authorities has been in part a consequence of the traditional legislative handling of water business. Congressional supporters of the Army Engineers, particularly members of the congressional committees to which the Engineers report, have been among the most violent opponents of Valley Authority legislation. They argue that the Engineers are doing a fine job and should not be displaced by independent corporate organizations.

It will be remembered that in 1937 President Roosevelt sent to Congress his famous message on regional authorities—the "8 little TVA's," as it came to be known. This much misunderstood proposal called for dividing the nation into eight regional areas for the purpose of developing integrated plans for resources development and management. At least in the early years, regional authorities with responsibilities broader than just planning would be set up or continued in only three areas. These were the TVA, the Columbia Valley Authority, and the Mississippi River Commission.

A careful reading of the hearings on this legislation before House and Senate committees reveals that almost all opponents of the bill, no matter whether their hostility to the legislation was inspired principally by opposition to hydroelectric power, by fear that the favored position of navigation interests in river development might be adversely affected, or by other causes, expressed complete confidence in the Engineer Department and an unwillingness to see any tampering with its duties in regard to rivers and harbors and flood control.

Significantly, the only Valley Authority legislation which has passed the Congress, that creating the TVA, was not handled by the committees which write navigation and flood control legislation, but rather in the Senate, by the Committee on Agriculture and Forestry, and in the House, by the Military Affairs Committee. These committees, particularly the Senate Committee on Agriculture, have been infinitely more sympathetic to Valley Authorities than the committees with which the Engineer Department has cooperated. Thus the fate of Valley Authority legislation, at least in so far as getting a sympathetic committee hearing is concerned, has depended in large part on the committee of reference.

The classic example is the legislation proposed by the President, and introduced by Senator Murray, to create a Missouri Valley Authority (S. 555, 79th Cong., 1st Sess. [1945]). Senator Murray wished this bill referred to the Committee on Agriculture which had handled TVA legislation. The opponents of an MVA wished it referred to the Committee on Commerce, which then handled navigation and flood control. The Committee on Irrigation and Reclamation was also interested. Senator Murray lost, and this meant sudden death for the MVA. In an almost unprecedented action, the Senate adopted a resolution (Sen. Res. 97, 79th Cong. 1st Sess. [1945]) referring the bill to all three committees—*first,* for a period of 60 days to the Committee on Commerce with respect to navigation and flood control; *second,* for an equal period, to the Committee on Irrigation and Reclamation with respect to their competence; *last,* to the Committee on Agriculture. Within 60 days the Commerce Committee had reported back unfavorably; some five months later the Committee on Irrigation reported unfavorably. There was no necessity for the Agriculture Committee either to hold hearings or to make a report—the bill was dead. . . .

THE CONDITIONS OF EXECUTIVE POWER

Policy-Making in the Executive Branch: The Taft-Hartley Experience

SEYMOUR Z. MANN

Almost all the line departments and a number of the independent commissions and agencies participated in the legislative history

From Seymour Z. Mann, *The Western Political Quarterly* (1960, Vol. XIII, No. 3, pp. 597-608), Salt Lake City.

of the Taft-Hartley Act. The principal participants were the National Labor Relations Board, the Department of Labor, the Bureau of the Budget, and individuals in the Executive Office of the President. Proposals were offered, rejected, or modified. Important in determining official policy, at both the executive and the congressional levels, were the activities of individuals who occupied influential positions in the network of communications. A case analysis of the complex interplay involved in formulating the executive policy on the Taft-Hartley Act seems to show that the decision-making process, while shaped in its general contours by the major institutions of government, takes on special characteristics peculiar to the particular policy problem, the individuals involved, and the consequent communications process that develops. Certainly one does not perceive centralized deliberative activity.

The National Labor Relations Board

More than any other single agency the National Labor Relations Board had reason to anticipate—and fear—legislative developments in the Eightieth Congress. The labor policy expressed in the Wagner Act had been its most intimate concern and responsibility for twelve years. The Board had been the subject of bitter attack from many sides throughout these years. A portion of the divided labor movement had stood strongly against it for at least the first five years of its life. In 1946 and the early weeks of 1947 the Board was aware of the difficult defensive position it was in.

The members of the Board were faced with several related problems. First, what position were they going to take on revision of the Wagner Act? Were they to announce publicly for change? If so, for how much revision? Secondly, what kind of case were they going to make against the decade-old and now renewed charges against them of bias and maladministration? Thirdly, in view of their position as an independent agency, how vigorous a stand could they take and how active and open a relationship could they establish with the Democratic administration and the Democratic minority in Congress? Fourthly, they were faced with the problem of orienting one completely new member of the Board at this critical time.

Immediately after the 1946 election Chairman Herzog wrote the President a rather long letter advocating the adoption of a bipartisan technique for working out a long-run labor policy. He adverted to the President's success in establishing a bipartisan foreign policy and the receptivity of Republican Senator-elect Ives to bipartisanship on labor questions. Chairman Herzog won the informal support of Secretary of Labor Schwellenbach, and actively advised the President for a time; but the bipartisan approach never materialized. After his first weeks in the Senate Ives gave no support to such a program. It was clear that the Republican majority would not accept it, and Herzog and Ives were forced to follow different courses. Although they remained friends, they battled each other on the "hill."

John M. Houston was the second member of the Board. James Reynolds replaced Gerard D. Reilly as third member late in 1946. Reilly had come increasingly to disagree with the majority of the Board during the latter part of his term, and there was doubt as to the point of view Mr. Reynolds might adopt. General Counsel Van Arkel felt that with Mr. Herzog relatively new and Mr. Reynolds brand-new it was essential for the Board to examine its record for consistencies and inconsistencies, and to agree on a position. He was anxious to confront Congress with a unanimous Board. With the failure of the bipartisan approach, Chairman Herzog gave his approval to the "self-study" proposal. . . .

The areas studied were those in which the Board had been most frequently criticized and amendments most often proposed. The inquiry was directed at the trend of Board decisions, to determine whether a consistent and orderly policy could be discerned. The results of the studies were organized in a series of twenty memoranda which were presented to the Board, where they became a basis for discussion. Each memorandum covered: (1) an examination of previously proposed legislation on the topic; (2) previous reports and statements made on behalf of the Board; (3) a summary of Board positions on the matter, particularly case decisions when they existed; (4) whatever relevant statistical and economic materials were available.

After a really serious study the Board concluded that its past decisions and actions were coherent and consistent. The members unanimously concluded that the Wagner Act should not be changed; the Board should defend both the Act and its own administration of the Act. This conclusion did not ignore, however, the possibility of improved administrative practices and changing lines of decisions that would ease pressure and remove criticism without impairing the consistency of Board policy. They also considered the tactical desirability of a limited program of amendment. Should the Board agree officially and openly on some course of amendments in the hope of tempering the kind of legislation that might otherwise occur? Or would a yielding on amendments indicate that there was more wrong than the Board itself was conceding? The legislators might use the limited program merely as a starting point rather than a terminal point for legislation.

The Board position was summed up in a memorandum signed by Herzog and sent to the President on December 11, 1946. This memorandum was made available at the same time to the group in the Bureau of the Budget working on the State of the Union message discussed below. The memorandum argued that the public interest required the maintenance of the rights of labor under the Wagner Act. Any other course "is not likely to prevent strikes [but] it may well reinstate old causes of strikes." The Board considered that the public interest would be served by only one amendment, "legislation that would protect both employers and employees from the use of pressure by labor organizations to compel an employer to violate or ignore certification or order of the N.L.R.B."

Nevertheless the Board did not rule out other anticipatory proposals. "But the administration may conclude that for certain reasons of strategy and equity they should move first without waiting for counter proposals. We do not presume to prophesy whether initiating such action might not have the result of encouraging more extreme proposals from some other sources. Some of us think that probable." If the President desired to follow such a course, limited amendment of the Act to allow employer petitions, to remove foremen from the coverage of the Act, to broaden free speech, and to impose upon unions the duty to bargain collectively might be included. The Board did not consider these changes necessary or useful. "We say merely that they would not destroy the fabric of the Act if ultimately enacted in the law. We do not consider it advisable for the President to go into any of the detailed suggestions in his Message on the State of the Union." . . .

Officially, then, the Board was to stand almost completely on the Wagner Act. Unofficially it felt that a program of limited amendment had to be ready to counter the extreme legislation that would inevitably arise in 1947. This latter unofficial program, however, never took firm hold with the administration until quite late; some close to the situation would argue that it was never employed.

It was on the basis of this activity that the statements presented to the labor committees of the two houses were prepared and developed, and to a great extent it was upon these materials and the conclusions reached therefrom that the Murray substitute, which was finally agreed upon by the minority as counterlegislation to the Taft bill in the Senate, was grounded.

It is important to note the manner in which the Board reacted to the situation in late 1946 and their prognostications concerning the Eightieth Congress. The Board undertook an organized approach to the determination of policy. The procedure was in itself important, as were the manifold objectives of their organized efforts. It gave them a sure footing on their own part. Despite conclusions based on the facts of their administrative life, there was a recognition of the practical political situation and eventually a decision as to the course of action it would be necessary to follow. The manner in which they went at their work and the unanimity of policy they achieved paved the way for the active role which the Board, through the Chairman and various Board personnel, was able to play in respect to the development of administration policy throughout the legislative development and the aid they were in a position to render the minority members in the legislative battle. The importance of this and the individuals concerned are discussed further in the final section of this paper.

One other question, one which was never fully answered to the satisfaction of the Board personnel closest to the development of Board policy during this period, was how strongly the Board should act on the policy they had agreed to adopt. Should they act vigorously and with great force in the defense of their past and the Wagner Act itself? Or should they make their case continuously and in all areas in a quiet, courteous, behind-the-scenes manner? Tied to this was the question of how active Board members and Board personnel should be in administration circles and in work with individual legislators. One school, which centered around the Chairman, felt that they had to work quietly and without offense, largely because the status of the Board as an independent agency had to be protected. Others felt that the Board was fighting for its life (a Democratic victory in 1948 was unforeseen) and it had to shout and shout loudly that as an agency it knew more than others about the nature of the Wagner Act and labor relations under it and without it. Actually a middle course was followed. Official contacts with the legislature were made in a fashion to protect the independent, nonpartisan character of the agency. Behind the scenes the Chairman was very active, particularly in administration circles, as the Taft-Hartley Act came closer and closer to passage. But he insisted that this was done only at the request of the President and was therefore not wrong or unusual. Board personnel were very active in working with the official Committee minorities in the Senate and House and were particularly active with individual legislators.

The Department of Labor

As an administrative agency the Department of Labor was not so concerned with the substantive content of the labor legislation to be formulated as was the NLRB. As a clientele agency serving labor, however, it was naturally concerned with the outcome of the Act. It was its function, moreover, to deal at the political level with the labor organizations and interests. The Secretary of the Department was an official member of the President's family. It should be expected, then, that the Department, particularly at the secretarial level, would be involved in the formulation of administration policy. There was some effort in this direction, but for many reasons the Secretary did not play a decisive role in influencing the President's policy until the veto stage in the history of the Act had been reached.

Actually two groups or levels in the Department were involved. The first was at the secretarial level and consisted of Schwellenbach, his special assistant Louis Sherman, Assistant Secretary David Morse, and Millard Cass, Morse's assistant.[1] The other group centered around the Solicitor of the Department; aside from the Solicitor, Mr. Tyson, those most actively concerned were Kenneth Roberts and Kenneth Mikeljohn. This group was

[1] It should be noted that David Morse had been the NLRB General Counsel in 1945-46. It was natural for the Secretary to turn to him on such questions.

most active in working with the NLRB people during the legislative battle itself.

The letter Herzog addressed to the President in early November of 1946 indicates that Schwellenbach agreed with him on the need for a specific legislative program. Given the temper the Republicans were bound to bring to the Congress after the 1946 elections, it was certain that they would insist on the passage of some legislation. An administration that was going to pursue a non-partisan policy on labor problems would have to go along at least part way on the question of amendatory labor legislation. While the Secretary and those about him undoubtedly wished to protect the essentials and the principles of the Wagner Act, Schwellenbach did not then have the strong feeling that he displayed at the time of the veto. His earlier position was probably based solely on an assessment of the political situation. The administration, facing a hostile Congress over which it had lost even nominal control, was in no position to adopt a stand-pat attitude on the matter of revised labor legislation. In fact the Secretary was informally active during the whole period in attempting to bring the unions to the same point of view.

Those working on the problem in the Solicitor's office did not see eye to eye with the group at the secretarial level at any time. The former group, in fact, was strongly opposed to giving in at all on the Wagner act. The Act was still needed. Its principles were still sound; and opening it up at all threatened to bring a flood that would sweep aside more moderate amendments in favor of extreme proposals.

In the Department, as in the Board, a study group was set up in the late months of 1946. David Morse was in charge; he was to examine the stand of the Department and to begin the preparation of the statements which the Secretary would be called upon to give to the congressional committees. This same group prepared tentative drafts of a proposed labor section for the forthcoming State of the Union message. Schwellenbach did not have great influence with some of those close to the President at this early stage, and the Department's suggestions were not so closely heeded as were those of the NLRB in the preparation of the message.

The official stand of the Department came to be resistance to any legislation that would amend the Wagner Act except in rather minor instances. At all times, however, the Secretary tacitly encouraged those around him continually to be thinking and working on the problem of counterlegislation. Officially he supported what came to be accepted as administration policy of no amendment; but informally he began early to sound out former senatorial colleagues on the possibility of support for some kind of administration legislative proposals. Until the Department actually began active participation in what came to be the Murray substitute, the Secretary and the Solicitor were at variance with regard to the desirability of an administration legislative program. It may be because he did not make adequate contact with people in the Department, or it may be from a lack of accessible documentary materials; but this writer came to the opinion that there was never the intensive institutional or collective examination of the issues that occurred in the NLRB. This was, perhaps, partially a result of the conflict just noted, and most certainly it related in some ways to the kind of man the Secretary himself was. While Labor Department people would say otherwise, except at the last stages of the veto period the Department of Labor never commanded the influence in the formulation of administration policy that the NLRB and the Bureau of the Budget personnel discussed below did.

The Bureau of the Budget and the Executive Office of the President

Primarily the consideration here is with the Bureau of the Budget and its activities in the preparation of the 1947 administration policy as embodied in the State of the Union message to the Eightieth Congress. Since the Bureau seldom deals directly with the President on other substantive legislative questions than the budget, the question involves the relation of the Bureau to others in the Executive Office of the President. More narrowly, the participation of the Budget Bureau was almost entirely confined to the G7 (labor estimates) section of the Estimates Division.[2] This group became quite active again at the veto stage and

[2] The persons who did the work in this area in 1945 and 1946 were David Bell, David Stowe, Ross Shearer, and Harold Emerson. For this whole section of the study, the writer is most indebted to Ross Shearer, who gave generously of his time and interceded with Mr. Stowe (later on the White House staff) for access to the latter's files in the White House and consulted Stowe on questions when the writer was unable personally to see him.

was principally responsible for the form and content of the President's Taft-Hartley veto message. It is important to note as well that this was one of the first instances in the administration of President Truman that Bureau people were used as staff aides on substantive legislative questions other than budget matters and routine and advisory functions at the enrolled bill stage. Groups within the Bureau were later used frequently in this capacity by the President.[3]

At this time, the Bureau group worked most closely with Clark Clifford, then Special Counsel to the President, and Charles Murphy, who later succeeded to Clifford's position and at that time acted for the most part as an assistant to Clifford. Clifford actively supervised the work on, and was most responsible for, the labor section of the State of the Union message. It is to be recalled that this time there was a kind of split in the President's immediate family along "conservative-liberal" lines. It was largely a question whether the President was going to follow the advice of Clifford and those around him or the more conservative views of Secretary of the Treasury Snyder and his following. It ought also to be recalled that policy in this controversial area had to be fashioned at a time when the President was at the nadir of his political life prestige-wise. With November 1946 elections Harry S. Truman was already widely described as the "defeated 1948 Presidential candidate."

While the G7 people were essentially technicians, it is obvious that they were aware as early as 1945 that some kind of amendatory labor legislation was inevitable. They were not blind nor could they ignore the activities of the second session of the Seventy-ninth Congress. They were, of course, during this early period most concerned with the settlement of dispute problems. They were preparing official memoranda on the subject; and a number of them were informally at work with some NLRB people in the preparation of legislation on this problem at the request of individual legislators. . . .

But even in this area the proposals of the people in the Bureau would not undermine or substantially change the protection and practice of collective bargaining under the Wagner Act. . . . By

[3] It is interesting to note that Stowe and Bell later went from this group to the President's White House staff. (Bell has since become President Kennedy's Budget Director.—Ed.)

1947 the G7 section position might be summed up as follows: "There were some definite abuses existent insofar as industrial relations and labor union activities were concerned. Limited amounts of legislation might be supported within the limits of the President's broad program or what the President's broad program ought to be."

Accordingly the Bureau people set out to make a thorough assessment of the current situation and to prepare a series of memoranda that would suggest proposed courses of action for the administration. In the early weeks of December these were sent to the Director of the Bureau. The first memorandum reviewed all the proposals and suggestions that were then current. These included a review of scholarly and academic approaches as well as of bills introduced in the national and state legislatures. In another memorandum in early December the G7 group had begun to outline what should be included in legislation that might be proposed by the President. Included would have been a provision to place upon both parties the duty to bargain collectively (embracing a four-point definition of collective bargaining) and a proposal for the redesigning of the federal machinery in the settling of disputes (including status quo provisions, arbitration without compulsion, a Federal Mediation Board within the Labor Department, a Federal Arbitration Commission, and Boards of Inquiry, purely informative, to be appointed by the Secretary of Labor in cases of national significance). The sum total of the suggested legislation had begun to revolve around the four points which were contained in the 1947 presidential message, but the proposals were elaborated in more detail and with more specific suggestions than appeared there.

About December 9, David Bell of G7 had prepared a tentative draft of what could be included on labor in the 1947 message. At this point the Bureau was asking for specific recommendations from NLRB and the Labor Department on the proposed items that most concerned those two agencies. It is not necessary to examine the early drafts in detail, but some of the text of this one draft may profitably be compared to the message finally delivered.

I feel now that we can take another long step forward by expanding the Wagner Act to require unions to bargain, to prohibit unions from certain specific unfair labor practices—such as violence, occupation of private property and interference with free choice of individuals to work or not to work—and to require unions to accept settlement of jurisdictional disputes by impartial government decisions under careful legislative standards. (This to be revised when NLRB recommendations are available.) I recommend that by law there be placed on both parties to collective bargaining the duty to exert every reasonable effort to make and maintain collective agreements.

The message itself, of course, never mentioned the Wagner Act and did not use the phrase unfair labor practices. It proposed specific legislation in regard to union activities for only three matters; jurisdictional strikes; unjustifiable secondary boycotts; and the use of economic force, by either labor or management, to decide issues arising out of the interpretation of existing contracts. Other matters were to wait upon the report of the proposed investigating commission. In many other ways the message finally took on a more general tone than the Bureau drafts.

Sometime shortly after the preparation of this December 9 draft Clifford was informed of the work the G7 group was doing. He then asked for their materials and a conference with Stowe (and possibly others) to review their work and suggestions. Shortly afterward the group was detailed to the White House staff to work with Clifford. Clifford later described his feelings in pretty much the following manner:

I realized in 1947 after the elections that there was a tremendous amount of confusion and a good deal of viciousness in the air concerning labor relations and reconversion problems. I tried to give it an objective, sensible and unemotional consideration. We could see that our problem was to forestall the movement toward an unstable labor law. By that time I had been on the job about a year and the lines were clearly drawn between Clifford and Snyder. Here was an issue on which I was going to win out.

Clifford used the G7 section to make the kind of appraisal of the situation which he thought necessary. On December 24 it submitted an extensive final memorandum to him. This was divided into four parts: first, the problems in terms of sources or causes of unrest; second, the group's reactions to proposed courses of action, including the suggestion that Congress create a Commission to study the problem (the makeup and activities of the Commission were outlined); third, a description of the disputes machinery which would constitute a part of the process; fourth, the identification of certain practices of labor and management which should be ended, along with the proposals for eliminating these abuses. Draft legislation for points three an four was supplied.

In this outline of the December 24 memorandum the labor section of the 1947 State of the Union message is clearly seen. In the days immediately following the message was written, but in considerably more general language than was proposed originally by the G7 group, with no reference to the submission of proposed legislation, and with the question left open as to whether any of the proposed action would actually amend the Wagner Act or not. The Bureau people as technicians felt quite definitely that legislation on these matters should have been submitted. They were not completely aware of—perhaps not greatly concerned over—the political dangers that might be incurred if Congress used a specific bill or bills submitted by the President merely as starting points.

It is not clear why a legislative program was not endorsed. Clifford seemed to indicate that he was in favor of an early administration bill or at least a counterproposal after the majority legislation was ready or close to ready. The President was deferred to here, and while the story does not completely jibe from the legislative side, it seems that the President was following the recommendations of advisors on the "hill" who said the President ought not to take the risk of what the Congress would do to such a bill. It was believed, and Clifford shared this opinion, that no counterlegislative action was possible until the public support of the labor groups could be won. Although this might have been true, minority legislators keenly felt the lact of Presidential leadership during the legislative struggle. The general statements of January did not suffice. Such leadership did come at the veto stage—but then it was too late.

Summary and Implications

Summing up, it is pertinent to point out that this Bureau group, while believing that the Wagner Act could work, felt more disposed on technical and professional grounds that those in the other agencies to suggest the need for amendatory legislation. Even on disputes machinery they were certainly prepared to go further than even the Labor Department. But they were not so aware of the political problems to be faced in the new Congress.

Their education on this matter progressed rapidly under the tutelage of Clifford when close relations were established. Their relationship proved of even greater importance during the veto stage, when Clifford assumed more the upper hand in the President's intimate official family.

We must call attention to the individuals from these agencies who were concerned in the effort. Representatives of the Board and the Solicitor's group in Labor became active in working for the minority, and supplied much of the committees' staff help as the legislative battle proceeded. Van Arket from the NLRB was particularly active—sometimes with and sometimes without the knowledge of the NLRB Chairman. People close to the Secretary of Labor as well as NLRB personnel worked behind the scenes to attempt agreement on an administration counterlegislative program. Clifford later became active here and at one stage tried to get the national party organization to take some action in this direction.

At no stage of the legislative battle, however, was there any kind of effort to co-ordinate and direct the work of these groups and individuals. Congressmen, even those of the President's party close to him, were for the most part unaware of the early administration effort that went into the formulation of the President's policy. Certainly they were totally unaware of the kind of effort made in preparing the labor section of the 1947 State of the Union message. Neither the President nor those around him undertook to communicate this.

At every point these individuals and groups entered into the communicative relationships that were part of the process that led to individual decisions by a number of congressmen. Out of the Eightieth Congress, however, came an act establishing a national labor policy repugnant to the President and to most of the men herein discussed who had striven in some way to influence what the administration's stand on labor policy in 1947 was to be. It is very possible that this might not have been the case had the President, or a clearly designated emissary, earlier supplied a clear and unwavering co-ordinating effort in the consideration of basic policy issues.

Few pieces of legislation either in the ten years before or in the thirteen years since the Taft-Hartley Act have assumed such controversial proportions. It is still in many ways a live issue, and even today persons who played some active role in the legislative struggle preceding its ultimate passage speak or write about the experience with feeling and with vigor. Many of the practices, strategies, and tactics that Truman and many of the executive branch agencies displayed or practiced during this period were new or unusual reactions to the special nature of the policy proposals at hand. Presidential and agency activities during this period, however, fully illustrate the extensive formal and informal network of roles in the executive branch that operate to establish or influence basic public policy decisions.

SECTION IV *Congress as an Instrument of Government*

Chapter Seven

THE FORMULATION OF POLICY: Representation, Result

DOMESTIC POLICY: Government Regulation or Business Self-Regulation?

Legislative History of the Securities Act of 1933

JAMES M. LANDIS

The act naturally had its beginnings in the high financing of the Twenties that was followed by the market crash of 1929. Even before the inauguration of Franklin D. Roosevelt as President of the United States, a spectacularly illuminating investigation of the nature of this financing was being undertaken by the Senate Banking and Currency Committee under the direction of its able counsel, Ferdinand D. Pecora. That Committee spread on the record more than the peccadillos of groups of men involved in the issuance and marketing of securities. It indicted a system as a whole that had failed miserably in imposing those essential fiduciary standards that should govern persons whose function it was to handle other people's money. Investment bankers, brokers and

From James M. Landis, *The George Washington Law Review* (28 Geo. Wash. L. Rev. 1959). Reprinted by permission.

dealers, corporate directors, accountants, all found themselves the object of criticism so severe that the American public lost much of its faith in professions that had theretofore been regarded with a respect that had approached awe. As the criticism mounted, doubts as to the value of the very system of private enterprise was generated, and a wide demand was prevalent for the institution of procedures of governmental control that would in essence have created a capital issues bureaucracy to control not only the manner in which securities could be issued but the very right of any enterprise to tap the capital market.

It is of interest to note that Mr. Roosevelt declined to endorse this demand. His message to the Congress on March 29, 1933, contains these two paragraphs:

> Of course, the Federal Government cannot and should not take any action which might be construed as approving or guaranteeing that newly issued securities are sound in the sense that their value will be maintained or that the properties which they represent will earn profit.
>
> There is, however, an obligation upon us to insist that every issue of new securities to be sold in interstate commerce shall be accompanied by full publicity and information, and that no essentially important element attending the issue shall be concealed from the buying public.

Meanwhile the task of drafting the legislation to carry out this message had been assigned to Houston Thompson, a former member of the Federal Trade Commission, whose draft bill introduced on that very day was totally inconsistent with the President's expressed desires. That bill, which sought to institute a system of registration of securities proposed to be offered, provided "that the Commission [the Federal Trade Commission] may revoke the registration of any security by entering an order to that effect, if upon examination . . . it shall appear . . . (e) that its [sic] or their affairs are in unsound condition or insolvent; or (f) that the enterprise or business of the issuer, or person, or the security is not based upon sound principles, and that the revocation is in the interest of the public welfare."

The Thompson bill introduced by Mr. Rayburn in the House of Representatives and by Senator Robinson (for Senator Ashurst) in the Senate was referred respectively to the House Committee on Interstate and Foreign Commerce and the Senate Committee on Banking and Currency. Mr. Sam Rayburn was Chairman of the former and Senator Duncan U. Fletcher of Florida of the latter. The committees thereupon proceeded to hearings upon the bill.

The hearings before the House committee were brief but sufficient to disclose the unworkability of the Thompson bill. Its draftsmanship was of decidedly inferior quality. It has based itself in large measure on the blue sky* legislation of the states, but went beyond the most severe of these state statutes in lodging extensive powers to control the issuance and sale of securities in the federal government. . . .

The hearings before the House committee on the Thompson bill convinced Mr. Rayburn and his committee that that bill provided no basis for sound federal securities legislation. His deep concern over this matter was communicated to the White House and the White House in turn went to other sources for help.

Professor Felix Frankfurter, now Mr. Justice Frankfurter, had been in close touch with the Roosevelt campaign of 1932. His associations with the President-Elect and particularly the reputed head of his "Brain Trust," Professor Raymond S. Moley, became even more frequent after the election. His wide knowledge of public law, his fertile mind, and his intimacy with the younger generation of lawyers upon whose help he could always count, made him invaluable to the new administration. I happened to have had the good fortune of being closely associated with him both as a student and later as his colleague, having cooperated with him in the production of a book and several articles, none of which, however, dealt with securities legislation. As a recently appointed Professor of Legislation at the Harvard Law School, I had spent considerable of my time and that of my small class in an attempt to explore the nature and variety of the sanctions available to government to bring about conformance with its statutory mandates and in dealing with the nature of standards capable of reasonable enforcement. An understanding of both problems seemed to me essential in order to grasp the elements of

* This name derived from the belief that irresponsible securities dealers would sell shares not only in the Brooklyn Bridge but even the blue sky. Generally state securities laws provided (1) criminal penalties for fraudulent sales and permanent injunctions from future sales in the state; (2) the licensing of sellers of securities subject to revocation, based on the "good repute of the dealer; and (3) the registration of all securities with full information on the company and the security, in most cases requiring state commission approval before a sale could be made. This generally involved the commission in a judgment of the soundness of the security.—Ed.

legislative draftsmanship. A particularly illuminating field, filled with challenge, had been state blue sky legislation. For the last years my seminar, as well as I, had been exploring this field. Little in the way of scholarly research had characterized that field and it had precipitated few judicial decisions of any consequence. Consequently, when in response to Rayburn's concern, Moley turned to Frankfurter for assistance, he, in turn, asked me to assist him. I can recall well the morning of that request. It was a Thursday in early April and my next classes were scheduled for the following Monday. Frankfurter, however, thought that the job could be done over that week-end. We consequently left on the night train for Washington.

The next morning in Washington we met with Benjamin V. Cohen and Thomas G. Corcoran. Cohen had been summoned by Frankfurter from the ranks of active practitioners. I was told he was a most brilliant man, knowledgeable in the field of securities, and that he possessed a gentle personality. My information was correct. Corcoran I had known intimately since law school days. I knew of his experience with the law firm of Cotton & Franklin in New York City and of his work with that firm in the securities field. Considerably disillusioned after 1929, Corcoran had come to Washington abetted by Frankfurter and was then serving as counsel to the Reconstruction Finance Corporation. It was a strange team—Corcoran ebullient, moving easily with the new forces in the administration; Cohen reserved and almost shy; but both brilliant and indefatigable workers.

After a brief session with Frankfurter, where we determined to take as the base of our work the English Companies Act with which Cohen was very familiar, Cohen, Corcoran and I set to work. Frankfurter had other political duties to attend to. By late Saturday night we had a draft of the bill in reasonable shape. We had to work under certain limitations imposed upon us by the fact of the Thompson bill. Tactically it seemed wise to shape our proposals as "perfecting" amendments to that bill, with the result that our original bill embodied a number of proposals contained in the Thompson bill that were subsequently happily discarded. The core of the Securities Act of 1933 is, however, to be found in that hurried draft of ours.

Our draft remained true to the conception voiced by the President in his message of March 29, 1933 to the Congress, namely that its requirements should be limited to full and fair disclosure of the nature of the security being offered and that there should be no authority to pass upon the investment quality of the security. This, of course, is the theory of the English Companies Act, but to the sanctions of that act we added the right of the Commission to suspend the registration of any security if inadequate compliance with the stated requirements for disclosure of misrepresentations of fact were found to exist in its registration statement. . . .

On Sunday, Frankfurter informed us that Rayburn had called a special meeting of his Committee for Monday to consider our draft. I arranged to put off my classes for a day, trusting to be able to take Monday's night train back to Cambridge. . . .

In addition to the members of the House Committee, there were present at this private hearing Frankfurter, Thompson, Cohen, Beaman, Perley and myself. Middleton Beaman had been for many years a chief legislative draftsman for the House of Representatives. Members of both political parties trusted him, and rightly so, for his complete impartiality and his competence. His function, as he always saw it, was to put into effective statutory language the ideas, whatever they might be, of the sponsors of such legislation as might be referred to him. Allan H. Perley, who later succeeded him, was only slightly less able than Beaman.

Frankfurter took the lead in the exposition of our draft. It was a brilliant performance. Questions of detail were referred by him to Cohen and to me, but he handled the main structure of the bill magnificently as well as the relationship of this bill in the nature of a "perfecting" amendment to the Thompson bill. The session, punctuated by questioning from members of the Committee, continued throughout the morning. We adjourned for lunch and resumed in the afternoon. It was difficult for me to assess the effect of our draft upon the Committee, particularly on Rayburn, whom I had never seen before. About five o'clock the meeting ended and the Committee held a brief executive session from which every non-member was excluded except Frankfurter. At its close, Rayburn and Frankfurter came out to talk to Cohen and myself, and Rayburn asked us to continue to work with the Committee and with Beaman's office as consultants to perfect our draft. Upon Frankfurter's assurance that my classes at Cambridge could be covered, I agreed to do so. Cohen also was willing to continue. That night Frankfurter, I believe, left for Cambridge. Cohen and I stayed on, for what I believed would be only another few days. It became almost two months.

Middleton Beaman is a difficult man to describe. I had thought I knew something of legislative draftsmanship until I met him. The next days were spent in continuous conference with him and Perley at his offices deep in the bowels of the old House Office Building. For days Beaman would not allow us to draft a line. He insisted instead on exploring the implications of the bill to find exactly what we had or did not have in mind. He probed always for the extent and nature of these hiatuses that any proposed important legislation necessarily possesses. It was exasperating to both Cohen and myself. We would meet Corcoran in the evenings, inasmuch as his duties prevented him from giving his full time to this project, and give vent to our suspicions that this delay bore symptoms of sinister Wall Street plotting. We were wrong. It was these discussions that first evolved the exact scope that we wanted the Securities Act to cover. . . .

The House committee had created a subcommittee to deal with this legislation, consisting of five members, three of whom were Democrats and two Republicans. Its chairman was Sam Rayburn. It had been agreed between them that no publicity of any nature would be given to our work until a draft satisfactory to the subcommittee was reported out to the full committee. That agreement was faithfully kept until almost the very last, despite the fact that Wall Street was aware that the Thompson bill had been discarded and that we were preparing a new draft. In addition to the new print of our original draft, five successive confidential committee drafts were printed and circulated among the subcommittee members. None of them "leaked," with the exception noted below, although there was considerable speculation and concern about the nature of our work in the *Wall Street Journal* and other financial columns, particularly in the light of the dismay, not to say terror, that the Thompson bill had aroused. It amuses me in retrospect to recall that Cohen and I during those days had a room on the seventh floor of the Carleton Hotel. Just above us was J. P. Morgan, Jr., and his staff, who had been summoned to testify in the Pecora hearings. We frequently met in the elevator in the morning or in the evening. We naturally recognized him, but we passed unnoticed, happy that our burrowing into the structure of that empire had no noticeable reverberations above.

Four revisions of our draft were completed before we were ready to meet with the subcommittee. Members of that subcommittee had, however, dropped in frequently in their individual capacity to make a suggestion or to inquire as to the meaning of a particular section. The number of exempted securities had been expanded. Municipal bonds, which we sought to include in our original draft, were made exempt for obvious political reasons. Securities of building and loan associations, savings and loan associations, and homestead associations were also excluded for similar reasons. Securities of common carriers issued subject to the provisions of section 20a of the Interstate Commerce Act were exempted to the theory that otherwise there would be a dual jurisdiction by the Federal Trade Commission and the Interstate Commerce Commission over these securities. Rayburn insisted on their exclusion despite our contention that the Interstate Commerce Commission exercised no controls over the manner in which railroad securities authorized under section 20a of the Interstate Commerce Act could be sold.

Two sessions of the subcommittee were held and further changes made, but none of major consequence other than the reduction of the statute of limitations from six to two years.

When the bill was ready to be reported to the full committee a somewhat extraordinary circumstance occurred. Wall Street's concern over our work and its inability to see it in its formative stages has already been noted. Some friends of Moley, however, stirred him up to such a degree by misrepresenting to him the character of our work as well as our motives to the point that he insisted with Rayburn that a select group of New York lawyers versed in security matters should be given a copy of the bill and have an opportunity to express their views on it to the subcommittee. Rayburn was loath to agree to this procedure but finally acquiesced in it upon the condition that Cohen and I should be entitled to be present and make such comments as we might choose in defense of our handiwork.

This meeting occurred on a Saturday morning. John Foster Dulles, A. I. Henderson and Arthur H. Dean constituted the group of New York lawyers.[1] Dulles started the attack. His preparation, however, had not been adequate. Allegations he made

[1] They represented the Wall Street law firms of Sullivan & Cromwell; and Cravath, DeGersdorf, Swaine and Wood, firms active in security matters of large moment.

as to the import of the bill were incapable, as we pointed out, of substantiation. Rayburn, who is an expert in judging experts, exhibited considerable annoyance at these accusations, not merely on our account, but at Dulles' allegations that Rayburn was sponsoring legislation that would undermine our financial system. Rayburn insisted that all that was being demanded was that the system should live up to its pretensions.[2] Henderson and Dean were far better acquainted with the details of the bill. Their criticism went primarily to certain technical features and much of it had merit. The subcommittee adjourned shortly after noon with the understanding that Henderson and Dean would meet with Cohen and myself that afternoon and consider their suggestions in detail. Rayburn led us to understand that whatever we accepted need not go back to the committee for formal approval but could be incorporated in the bill as submitted to the full committee. We spent a long, hot afternoon with Henderson and Dean, ending with a number of technical changes particularly in the schedules to the bill that had not had a thorough going over by the subcommittee.

The hearing before the full committee was public. Little basic opposition to the bill developed publicly. The changes made by the full committee were few. Two were, however, important. The first added to the list of exempted securities, which already included those issued by national banks, the securities and state and territorial banks if supervised by their respective governmental banking officials. The second expanded and also contracted the list of exempt transactions by exempting transactions by an issuer with or through an underwriter only so long as they

[2] Similar allegations were not uncommon. A memorandum circulated by the Investment Bankers Association on the bill as passed by the House, dated May 6, 1933, stated that its "practical results . . . will be to suspend the underwriting or distribution of many capital issues by responsible persons. . . . The bill as a whole might be exceptionally deflationary in its effects because it affords unreasonable interference with honest business. . . . The Act goes beyond publicity and, despite its protestations, would encourage the public to believe that the Government had accepted the duty of passing officially upon the safety of investments." Admittedly the Securities Act of 1933 in its original form did hamper the normal flow of capital into enterprise, a check which was not overcome until the 1934 amendments were enacted. That check, however, in my opinion was due less to the provisions of the original act than to their misinterpretation, deliberate to a great degree, by the widely publicized utterances of persons prominent in the financial world together with their lawyers.

did not involve a public offering. Underwriters could consequently participate in private offerings without the need for registration, but issuers could not make a public offering of their securities even though no underwriting might be involved.

The report of the House committee, drafted by us, is an analysis of the bill. . . .

In the House the bill went under a special rule because of its complexities and the danger that an unstudied amendment, apparently fair on its face, might unbalance the careful articulation of its various sections. This rule permitted the consideration of amendments only if they had the approval of the committee chairman. With Cohen at his side, Rayburn had complete control of the situation. The bill passed with scarcely a murmur of dissent.

In the Senate an entirely different story was unfolding. The Senate had nothing but the Thompson bill to work on. Moreover, the Senate Committee on Banking and Currency was busy with its investigation of securities transactions and securities markets. Pecora and his staff were occupied with this investigation and had no time to devote to other matters. Two lawyers formerly active with Thompson were attached to the Senate Committee but they had admittedly neither the time to devote to it nor the experience that would allow them to be regarded as experts. The Senate legislative drafting service operates on different lines than that of the House. No one on its staff had the same authority and prestige as Beaman had on the House side and, furthermore, its services could be availed of by any Senator with the result that it did not have the time to spare for another major job.[3] It became apparent fairly early that on the Senate side the bill would bumble along and that our hope for the side-tracking of that bill would have to rest upon an agreement in conference that the House bill would be the basis for the final draft.

In the Senate, however, one major development had taken place. Senator Hiram Johnson of California had become interested in the debacle of the billions of foreign governmental securities that had been sold to the American public, primarily those issued by Latin American governments. They had been hawked to investors in the Twenties by many of the larger New York investment banking firms. Not only were most of these securities

[3] In the House only chairmen of committees could generally command the services of its legislative drafting staff.

in default but the circumstances attending their issuance and sale reflected seriously upon the integrity of these underwriting houses. Senator Johnson naturally had a sympathy with those provisions of the proposed securities legislation that would subject foreign governmental issues in the future to controls of a type roughly comparable to those dealing with private offerings. But he also wanted to do something for the outstanding bondholders in the hope that their investments might to some degree be recouped. The existing intrusion of various protective committees had developed abuses almost as bad as those that surrounded the original issuance of these securities. With this in mind, he introduced into the Senate a bill to create a Corporation of Foreign Bondholders, whose directors would be appointed by the Federal Trade Commission and whose initial financing would come from the Reconstruction Finance Corporation. The directors would act as representatives of these defaulted bondholders in negotiating with the foreign governments involved and see that the flow of any funds that might be made available, should go to the defaulted bondholders. Admirable as Senator Johnson's motives were, his proposal immediately ran afoul of the State Department. That Department had a natural aversion to the creation of any independent governmental agency empowered to deal directly with foreign governments. Such an agency was only too likely to pursue negotiations and take attitudes with our Latin American friends in direct conflict with those that the State Department was evolving in the development of its new Good Neighbor Policy. The State Department in lieu of the proposed Corporation of Foreign Bondholders, wanted to see the creation of a responsible non-governmental group to handle these problems so that the United States as a government would not have to take inconsistent positions at the same time and to the same nation.

President Roosevelt stood in the midst of this conflict. Both policies were in a sense integral to his program but both could not be satisfied at the same time. Senator Johnson's cause was a popular and worthy one and in line with the general trend of the New Deal. On the other hand, his new Secretary of State, Cordell Hull, was not a person to offend with impunity. To place him and his Department in potential conflict with another agency of the government might in the long run be disastrous. Proponents of both sides of this issue sought the aid and assistance of the President, and both sides were given that aid and assistance but not quite at the same time. On one day the President would be quoted, probably correctly, in favor of Senator Johnson's proposal. On the next, he would be found in the State Department's camp. Senator Johnson, however, somehow succeeded in getting his bill tacked on as an amendment to the Senate's securities bill as a new Title II. He was backed up in all probability by many Senators who were willing to vote for it on the theory that its ultimate fate would be determined by the House and Senate Conference Committee which would have to reconcile the differences between the two bills.

The rules of a Conference Committee are apparently not unlike those rules that govern collective bargaining negotiations. If they exist, and documentary evidence to that effect is to be found in *Hine's Precedents,* they are observed as much in breach as in conformance. In theory the Conference Committee is supposed to reach some sort of a mean between the positions taken by the two Houses and should abjure the introduction of new matter. In fact, new matter, either consisting of new ideas or of extensive emendations to what the two Houses may have passed without too thorough a consideration, again and again finds its way into their reports and is adopted without opposition by both Houses. In theory also, the House and the Senate members of the committee each vote as a unit; in fact, the weakening of any member on either side tends to bring about agreement. The atmosphere of a Conference Committee is tense where the committee is concerned with legislation that is other than routine. Its members are always members of the committees who have most actively sponsored the legislation in their respective chambers and have consequently developed strong predilections for the points of view that their hard won bills represent.

It was in an atmosphere such as this that the Conference Committee met on a Monday morning in May. Senator Fletcher was the chairman of the Senate group and Sam Rayburn headed the House delegation. Cohen and I were present, and Beaman and Perley were still with us. The two Senate advisers also were present at most of the sessions. The Senate, however, was most ably represented by a former student in my seminar in legislation, then attached to the Senate drafting service and later to become a chairman of the Securities and Exchange Commission, namely Ganson Purcell. On the Senate side, there were such distinguished names as Carter Glass of Virginia, James Couzens of Michigan and Hiram Johnson of California.[4] Senator Fletcher of Florida also commanded considerable prestige for his conduct of the Pecora investigations and his unwavering support of his counsel amid a number of trying circumstances. The House, on the other hand, had no such distinguished personalities except for Sam Rayburn, although each of its members was far better acquainted with the subject matter at hand than the representatives of the Senate.

Jockeying occurred at the beginning as to the procedures that should be adopted. In its midst Senator Glass, who had been rapidly scanning the House bill, broke out into a tirade to the effect that he was the proponent of legislation dealing with banks and their relationship to the sale of securities and that he wanted no interference with his handling of these issues.[5] We pointed out to him that the House bill had carefully excluded from its operation all securities issued by banks, whether state or federal, as contrasted with the Senate bill which exempted only the securities issued by national banks, and also that nothing in the House bill in any way conflicted with the proposals contained in his bill to divorce banks from their security affiliates. He growled, thumbed the bill for any further reference to banks, found none, and shortly thereafter left the committee never to reappear.

Senator Fletcher, with the courteousness that always characterized him, suggested to Rayburn that he should accept the chairmanship of the committee at least for the first meeting. Rayburn agreed and shortly thereafter suggested that the first business was to come to a determination of which bill should become the basic working draft for the committee.[6] Rayburn quietly asked Senator Fletcher if he did not desire to make a motion on this matter. The

[4] Senator Robert Wagner of New York was also a member of this Conference Committee. Although he signed its final report I cannot recall his appearance at any of the sessions. He was, of course, busily occupied at the time with other phases of the "Recovery Program."

[5] This bill introduced by Senator Glass became the Banking Act of 1933. . . .

[6] The two persons attached as experts to the Senate Committee had anticipated that this question would arise. Their loyalties being to the Senate, they had prepared and had printed a "Confidential Conference Committee Print" based on the Senate bill and embodying portions of the House bill that they believed might be sufficient to bring about acquiescence on the part of the House representatives. The result was an unbelievable patchwork. Their attempt to get this draft circulated in the Conference Committee was rudely but firmly brushed off by Rayburn. . . .

Senator replied by moving that the Senate bill should be made the working draft. Rayburn took a vote on this motion and, finding that all the Senators voted for the motion and all the members of the House voted against the motion, applied the unit rule and declared that *since the vote was a tie the motion failed of adoption and consequently the House bill would become the basic draft.** That was the last we heard of the unit rule, and the last of Title I of the Senate bill except for an occasional reference to its provisions as a basis for comparison.

Work moved reasonably smoothly thereafter and Title I was completed by Friday. Senator Fletcher never requested to alternate the chairmanship and, absent any request from him, Rayburn continued to guide the proceedings. The committee met daily. Its sessions carried on throughout the mornings, the afternoons being occupied by sessions of the full House and Senate. The representatives of the House were assiduous in their attendance, the Senate members less so. The tenseness of the first day's session became relieved as Rayburn made it plain that any suggestion of any Senator would receive the most careful consideration. A goodly number of suggestions came from Senator Townsend of Delaware, a Republican, who was in close touch with the financial world but who under no circumstances would take their suggestions as commands or as ideas to hold on to in the face of a compelling argument to the contrary. In fact, friendship and mutual respect under Rayburn's guidance developed friendships not only among the members but between the members and the staff.

Cohen, Beaman, Perley and I took the opportunity these days gave us to improve further the House bill. The Investment Bankers Association had suggested a series of amendments to the House bill, all of which had to be scanned carefully and most of which were discarded. The Federal Trade Commission submitted a carefully detailed memorandum, which I later learned was prepared by Baldwin B. Bane, later to become the first chief of its Division of Securities, commending the House bill despite the fact that the Commission's Chief Counsel, Robert E. Healey, later to become one of the original members of the Securities and Exchange Commission, had favored and still favored the Thompson bill. Numerous other memoranda were filed with the com-

* Emphasis added.—Ed.

mittee or with the individual members. Requests were also made through them for consultation with the staff by lawyers and others, to which it was difficult not to accede.

Four drafts of the bill found their way into print before the final draft was accepted. There were numerous changes made, of which the significant ones are noted in the Statement of the House Managers contained in the Conference Report as submitted to the House. . . .

The Conference Report also deliberately contained language commenting upon the meaning of certain of the most contentious provisions of the bill in the hope that that language as an expression of the "intent" of Congress would control the administrative and judicial interpretation of the act. This is particularly true with respect to the nature of the fiduciary obligations assumed by officers and directors of a registrant. It seemed impossible to define in statutory language the extent to which a fiduciary might lawfully delegate his duties to others. In lieu of such an effort, resort was made to general language in the report to indicate that a goodly measure of delegation was justifiable, particularly insofar as corporate directors are concerned.

The bitterest struggle between the House and Senate members of the Conference Committee concerned the civil liability that should be imposed upon the officers and directors of the registrant. The Senate bill imposed a liability akin to that of insurer's liability with respect to the accuracy of the statements made by them in the registration statement. The House bill, on the other hand, held this liability to the standard of due care, recognizing that the due care involved was that of a fiduciary. The victory of the House representatives on this issue was important. A contrary result would obviously have imposed an unjust and insurmountable burden on those who have the responsibility for the conduct of corporate enterprise.

With the conclusion of the conference work on Title I, the committee on Saturday morning turned to the problem of Title II —the Corporation of Foreign Bondholders Act. For some days the question of what to do with Title II had bothered Rayburn. It had also worried Cohen and myself who wished no part of the controversy between Senator Johnson and the State Department but were worried by the fear that that controversy might imperil the Title I legislation. Rayburn, who was quite willing to follow any suggestion that the President might make, had asked Senator Johnson to get a definitive answer one way or the other upon the question. Saturday morning no such answer had yet been received and Rayburn was in a quandary as to what to do. After some discussion Senator Johnson suggested to Rayburn that he should telephone the President directly and see if he could get an answer to the problem. Rayburn requested me to accompany him to an adjoining room presumably on the theory that I might be helpful in answering such technical questions as might arise. I listened in on the conversation. The sum and substance of it was that the President had no idea as to what to do and ended up by telling Rayburn to do whatever he thought best.

This left Rayburn in exactly the same position in which he had been all week. This was when I thought of adding to Title II the provision that that title should take effect only if, and when the President determined that it should do so in the public interest and issued a declaration to the effect. Rayburn recognized that, if Johnson would accept this provision, it would put the problem squarely back in the lap of the President and make possible the immediate passage of both Title I and Title II. I hastily drafted the provision and we returned to the committee room. I explained the provision to Senator Johnson and the committee. Beaman started to question the constitutionality of the provision as being an unconstitutional delegation of legislative power to the President. Although I had my doubts as to its validity and still retain them, I argued in behalf of its constitutionality. Cohen joined me, and Beaman, realizing the quandary in which the President had put Rayburn, ceased to advance any further objections. We turned hopefully to Senator Johnson to get his agreement. To our amazement he accepted it without further argument. The Conference Committee's labors thus came to an end. There remained only the passage of the bill.

. . . All of the Republican representatives of the House had signed the Conference Report. None of the Republican Senators had done so, although they voiced no disagreement to the report. It passed both Houses with no substantial opposition and on May 27, 1933, became a law. . . .

FOREIGN AND MILITARY POLICY: Some Conditions of Congressional Entrée

The Day We Didn't Go to War

CHALMERS M. ROBERTS

Saturday, April 3, 1954, was a raw, windy day in Washington, but the weather didn't prevent a hundred Americans from milling around the Jefferson Memorial to see the cherry blossoms—twenty thousand of them from watching the crowning of the 1954 Cherry Blossom Queen.

President Eisenhower drove off to his Maryland mountain retreat called Camp David. There he worked on his coming Monday speech, designed, so the White House said, to quiet America's fears of Russia, the H-bomb, domestic Communists, a depression. But that Saturday morning eight members of Congress, five Senators and three Representatives, got the scare of their lives. They had been called to a secret conference with John Foster Dulles. They entered one of the State Department's fifth-floor conference rooms to find not only Dulles but Admiral Arthur W. Radford, chairman of the Joint Chiefs of Staff, Under Secretary of Defense Roger Kyes, Navy Secretary Robert B. Anderson, and Thruston B. Morton, Dulles's assistant for Congressional Relations. A large map of the world hung behind Dulles's seat, and Radford stood by with several others. "The President has asked me to call this meeting," Dulles began.

Urgency and a Plan

The atmosphere became serious at once. What was wanted, Dulles said, was a joint resolution by Congress to permit the President to use air and naval power in Indo-China. Dulles hinted that perhaps the mere passage of such a resolution would in itself make its use unnecessary. But the President had asked for its consideration, and, Dulles added, Mr. Eisenhower felt that it was indispensable at this juncture that the leaders of Congress feel as the Administration did on the Indo-China crisis.

Then Radford took over. He said the Administration was deeply concerned over the rapidly deteriorating situation. He

From Chalmers M. Roberts, *The Reporter* (September 14, 1954, pp. 31-35).

used a map of the Pacific to point out the importance of Indo-China. He spoke about the French Union forces then already under siege for three weeks in the fortress of Dienbienphu.

The admiral explained the urgency of American action by declaring that he was not even sure, because of poor communications, whether, in fact, Dienbienphu was still holding out. (The fortress held out for five weeks more.)

Dulles backed up Radford. If Indo-China fell and if its fall led to the loss of all of Southeast Asia, he declared, then the United States might eventually be forced back to Hawaii, as it was before the Second World War. And Dulles was not complimentary about the French. He said he feared they might use some disguised means of getting out of Indo-China if they did not receive help soon.

The eight legislators were silent: Senator Majority Leader Knowland and his G.O.P. colleague Eugene Millikin, Senator Minority Leader Lyndon B. Johnson and his Democratic colleagues Richard B. Russell and Earle C. Clements, House G.O.P. Speaker Joseph Martin and two Democratic House leaders, John W. McCormack and J. Percy Priest.

What to do? Radford offered the plan he had in mind once Congress passed the joint resolution.

Some two hundred planes from the thirty-one-thousand-ton U.S. Navy carriers *Essex* and *Boxer*, then in the South China Sea ostensibly for "training," plus land-based U.S. Air Force planes from bases a thousand miles away in the Philippines, would be used for a single strike to save Dienbienphu.

The legislators stirred, and the questions began.

Radford was asked whether such action would be war. He replied that we would be in the war.

If the strike did not succeed in relieving the fortress, would we follow up? "Yes," said the chairman of the Joint Chiefs of Staff.

Would land forces then also have to be used? Radford did not give a definite answer.

In the early part of the questioning, Knowland showed enthusiasm for the venture, consistent with his public statements that something must be done or Southeast Asia would be lost.

But as the questions kept flowing, largely from Democrats, Knowland lapsed into silence.

Clements asked Radford the first of the two key questions:

"Does this plan have the approval of the other members of the Joint Chiefs of Staff?"

"No," replied Radford.

"How many of the three agree with you?"

"None."

"How do you account for that?"

"I have spent more time in the Far East than any of them and I understand the situation better."

Lyndon Johnson put the other key question in the form of a little speech. He said that Knowland had been saying publicly that in Korea up to ninety per cent of the men and the money came from the United States. The United States had become sold on the idea that that was bad. Hence in any operation in Indo-China we ought to know first who would put up the men. And so he asked Dulles whether he had consulted nations who might be our allies in intervention.

Dulles said he had not.

The Secretary was asked why he didn't go to the United Nations as in the Korean case. He replied that it would take too long, that this was an immediate problem.

There were other questions. Would Red China and the Soviet Union come into the war if the United States took military action? The China question appears to have been sidestepped, though Dulles said he felt the Soviets could handle the Chinese and the United States did not think that Moscow wanted a general war now. Further, he added, if the Communists feel that we mean business, they won't go "any further down there," pointing to the map of Southeast Asia.

John W. McCormack, the House Minority Leader, couldn't resist temptation. He was surprised, he said, that Dulles would look to the "party of treason," as the Democrats had been called by Joe McCarthy in his Lincoln's Birthday speech under G.O.P. auspices, to take the lead in a situation that might end up in a general shooting war. Dulles did not reply.

In the end, all eight members of Congress, Republicans and Democrats alike, were agreed that Dulles had better first go shopping for allies. Some people who should know say that Dulles was carrying, but did not produce, a draft of the joint resolution the President wanted Congress to consider.

The whole meeting had lasted two hours and ten minutes. As

they left, the Hill delegation told waiting reporters they had been briefed on Indo-China. Nothing more.

This approach to Congress by Dulles and Radford on behalf of the President was the beginning of three weeks of intensive effort by the Administration to head off disaster in Indo-China. Some of those at the meeting came away with the feeling that if they had agreed that Saturday to the resolution, planes would have been winging toward Dienbienphu without waiting for a vote of Congress—or without a word in advance to the American people.

For some months now, I have tried to put together the bits and pieces of the American part in the Indo-China debacle. But before relating the sequel, it is necessary here to go back to two events that underlay the meeting just described—though neither of them was mentioned at that meeting.

On March 20, just two weeks earlier, General Paul Ely, then French Chief of Staff and later commander in Indo-China, had arrived in Washington from the Far East to tell the President, Dulles, Radford, and others that unless the United States intervened, Indo-China would be lost. This was a shock of earthquake proportions to leaders who had been taken in by their own talk of the Navarre Plan to win the war.

In his meetings at the Pentagon, Ely was flabbergasted to find that Radford proposed American intervention without being asked. Ely said he would have to consult his government. He carried back to Paris the word that when France gave the signal, the United States would respond.

The second event of importance is the most difficult to determine accurately. But it is clear that Ely's remarks started a mighty struggle within the National Security Council, that inner core of government where our most vital decisions are worked out for the President's final O.K. The argument advanced by Radford and supported by Vice-President Nixon and by Dulles was that Indochina must not be allowed to fall into Communist hands lest such a fate set in motion a falling row of dominoes.

Eisenhower himself used the "row-of-dominoes" phrase at a press conference on April 7. On April 15, Radford said in a speech that Indo-China's loss "would be the prelude to the loss of all Southeast Asia and a threat to a far wider area." On April 16 Nixon, in his well-publicized "off-the-record" talk to the newspaper editors' convention, said that if the United States could not otherwise prevent the loss of Indo-China, then the Administration must face the situation and dispatch troops. And the President in his press conference of March 24 had declared that Southeast Asia was of the "most transcendent importance." All these remarks reflected a basic policy decision.

It is my understanding, although I cannot produce the top secret NSC [National Security Council] paper to prove it, that some time between Ely's arrival on March 20 and the Dulles-Radford approach to the Congressional leaders on April 3, the NSC had taken a firm position that the United States could not afford the loss of Indo-China to the Communists, and that if it were necessary to prevent that loss, the United States would intervene in the war—*provided* the intervention was an allied venture and *provided* the French would give Indo-China a real grant of independence so as to eliminate the colonialism issue. The decision may have been taken at the March 25 meeting. It is also my understanding that this NSC paper has on it the approving initials "D.D.E."

On March 29, Dulles, in a New York speech, had called for "united action" even though it might involve "serious risks," and declared that Red China was backing aggression in Indo-China with the goal of controlling all of Southeast Asia. He had added that the United States felt that "that possibility should not be passively accepted but should be met by united action."

The newspapers were still full of reactions to this speech when the Congressional leaders, at the April 3 secret meeting with Dulles and Radford, insisted that Dulles should line up allies for "united action" before trying to get a joint resolution of Congress that would commit the nation to war.

The Secretary lost no time, Within a week Dulles talked with diplomatic representatives in Washington of Britain, France, Australia, New Zealand, the Philippines, Thailand, and the three Associated States of Indo-China—Vietnam, Laos, and Cambodia.

There was no doubt in the minds of many of these diplomats that Dulles was discussing military action involving carriers and planes. Dulles was seeking a statement or declaration of intent designed to be issued by all the nations at the time of the U.S. military action, to explain to the world what we were doing and why, and to warn the Chinese Communists against entering the war as they had done in Korea.

In these talks Dulles ran into one rock of opposition—Britain. Messages flashing back and forth between Washington and London failed to crack the rock. Finally Dulles offered to come and talk the plan over personally with Prime Minister Churchill and Foreign Secretary Anthony Eden. On April 10, just a week after the Congressional meeting, Dulles flew off to London and later went on to Paris.

Whether Dulles told the British about either the NSC decision or about his talks with the Congressional leaders I do not know. But he didn't need to. The British had learned of the Congressional meeting within a couple of days after it happened. When Dulles reached London they were fully aware of the seriousness of his mission.

The London talks had two effects. Dulles had to shelve the idea of immediate intervention. He came up instead with a proposal for creating a Southeast Asia Treaty Organization (SEATO). Dulles felt this was the "united front" he wanted and that it would lead to "united action." He thought that some sort of *ad hoc* organization should be set up at once without waiting for formal treaty organization, and to this, he seems to have felt, Churchill and Eden agreed.

Just what the British did agree to is not clear, apparently not even to them. Dulles, it appears, had no formal SEATO proposal down on paper, while the British did have some ideas in writing. Eden feels that he made it plain that nothing could be done until after the Geneva Conference, which was due to begin in two weeks. But he apparently made some remark about "going on thinking about it" in the meantime.

At any rate, on his return to Washington Dulles immediately called SEATO drafting meeting for April 20. The British Ambassador (who at this point had just read the Nixon off-the-record speech in the newspaper) cabled London for instructions and was told not to attend any such meeting. To cover up, the meeting was turned into one on Korea, the other topic for the Geneva Conference. Out of this confusion grew a thinly veiled hostility between Dulles and Eden that exists to this day. Dulles felt that Eden had switched his position and suspects that Eden did so after strong words reached London from Prime Minister Nehru in New Delhi.

Eden at the Bridge

A few days later, Dulles flew back to Paris, ostensibly for the NATO meeting with Eden, France's Georges Bidault, and others during the week-end just before the Geneva Conference opened.

On Friday, April 23, Bidault showed Dulles a telegram from General Henri-Eugene Navarre, then the Indo-China commander, saying that only a massive air attack could save Dienbienphu, by now under siege for six weeks. Dulles said the United States could not intervene.

But on Saturday Admiral Radford arrived and met with Dulles. Then Dulles and Radford saw Eden. Dulles told Eden that the French were asking for military help at once. An allied air strike at the Vietminh positions around Dienbienphu was discussed. The discussion centered on using the same two U.S. Navy carriers and Philippine-based Air Force planes Radford had talked about to the Congressional leaders.

Radford, it appears, did most of the talking. But Dulles said that if the allies agreed, the President was prepared to go to Congress on the following Monday, April 26 (the day the Geneva Conference was to open) and ask for a joint resolution authorizing such action. Assuming quick passage by Congress, the strike could take place on April 28. Under Secretary of State Walter Bedell Smith, an advocate of intervention, gave the same proposal to French Ambassador Henri Bonnet in Washington the same day.

The State Department had prepared a declaration of intentions, an outgrowth of the earlier proposals in Washington, to be signed on Monday or Tuesday by the Washington ambassadors of the allied nations willing to back the venture in words. As it happened, there were no available British or Australian carriers and the French already were fully occupied. Hence the strike would be by American planes alone, presented to the world as a "united action" by means of the declaration of intentions.

Eden, on hearing all these details from Dulles and Radford, said that this was a most serious proposition, amounting to war, and that he wanted to hear it direct from the French. Eden and Dulles thereupon conferred with Bidault, who confirmed the fact that France was indeed calling desperately for help—though no formal French request was ever put forward in writing.

Eden began to feel like Horatius at the bridge. Here, on the eve of a conference that might lead to a negotiated end of the seven-year-old Indo-China war, the United States, at the highly informal request of a weak and panicky French Government, was proposing military action that might very well lead to a general war in Asia if not to a third world war.

Dulles's Retreat

Eden said forcefully that he could not agree to any such scheme of intervention, that he personally opposed it. He added his conviction that within forty-eight hours after an air strike, ground troops would be called for, as had been the case at the beginning of the Korean War.

But, added Eden, he alone could not make any such formal decision on behalf of Her Majesty's Government. He would fly to London at once and put the matter before a Cabinet meeting. So far as I can determine, neither Dulles or Bidault tried to prevent this step.

Shortly after Eden flew off that Saturday afternoon, Dulles sat down in the American Embassy in Paris with his chief advisers, Messrs. MacArthur, Merchant, Bowie, and McCardle, and Ambassador Dillon. They composed a letter to Bidault.

In this letter, Dulles told Bidault the United States could not intervene without action by Congress because to do so was beyond the President's Constitutional powers and because we had made it plain that any action we might take could only be part of a "united action." Further, Dulles added, the American military leaders felt it was too late to save Dienbienphu.

American intervention collapsed on that Saturday, April 24. On Sunday Eden arrived in Geneva with word of the "No" from the specially convened British Cabinet meeting. And on Monday, the day the Geneva Conference began, Eisenhower said in a speech that what was being sought at Geneva was a "*modis vivendi*" with the Communists.

All these events were unknown to the general public at the time. However, on Sunday the New York *Times* printed a story written in Paris under a Geneva dateline) that the U.S. had turned down a French request for intervention on the grounds Dulles had cited to Bidault. And on Tuesday Churchill announced to a cheering House of Commons that the British government was "not prepared to give any undertakings about United Kingdom military action in Indo-China in advance of the results of Geneva" and that "we have not entered into any new political or military commitments."

Thus the Geneva Conference opened in a mood of deepest American gloom. Eden felt that he had warded off disaster and that now there was a chance to negotiate a peace. The Communists, whatever they may have learned of the behind-the-scenes details here recounted, knew that Britain had turned down some sort of American plan of intervention. And with the military tide in Indo-China flowing so rapidly in their favor, they proceeded to stall.

In the end, of course, a kind of peace was made. On June 23, nearly four weeks before the peace, Eden said in the House of Commons that the British Government had "been reproached in some unofficial quarters for their failure to support armed intervention to try to save Dienbienphu. It is quite true that we were at no time willing to support such action . . ."

This mixture of improvisation and panic is the story of how close the United States came to entering the Indo-China war. Would Congress have approved intervention if the President had dared to ask it? This point is worth a final word.

On returning from Geneva in mid-May, I asked that question of numerous Senators and Representatives. Their replies made clear that Congress would, in the end, have done what Eisenhower asked, provided he had asked for it forcefully and explained the facts and their relation to the national interest of the United States.

Whether action or inaction better served the American interest at that late stage of the Indo-China war is for the historian, not for the reporter, to say. But the fact emerges that President Eisenhower never did lay the intervention question on the line. In spite of the NSC decision, April 3, 1954, was the day we *didn't* go to war.

ATOMIC POLICY: Adaptation to Novelty

A Law Is Passed— The Atomic Energy Act of 1946

BYRON MILLER

An unusually clear example of the role which democratic processes can play in the framing of legislation is presented by the history of the law controlling atomic energy within the United States. Several unique factors combined to deprive the legislator of his comfortable patterns for reaching policy decisions. He was not dealing with a recast of conventional controversy, a labor versus management or debt reduction versus public spending issue, on which his attitudes had long been fixed, his speeches ready at tongue, the public reception and opposition tactics already known. He could not judge by the people lined up on one or the other side, for traditional alignments were criss-crossed. Even commercial special interest groups were largely silent. In short, for most senators and many representatives, atomic energy legislation required an almost pure exercise of judgment. The very same factors also operated to induce a surprisingly wide expression of opinion by the public.

The response of the Congress to this unparalleled necessity for original judgment was not one of imaginative suggestion. Rather, the reaction of many legislators was to escape the entire problem, one senator openly expressing a wish to dump all atomic energy knowledge into the ocean. Most, however, felt lost in a morass of technology, an attitude which appeared to survive the educational hearings. Hence the debates both in and out of Congress all too often exhibited a stubborn tendency to pose choices in terms of conventional opposites which bore little relation to the issues being decided.

The factors responsible for this atypical legislative history can be grouped roughly as follows:

(1) *The Atomic Bomb.* The military and political significance of the A-bomb and the political, social, and economic significance of its civilian counterpart, atomic energy, were problems enough; but they were almost eclipsed by the engulfing emotions of fear

From Byron S. Miller, *University of Chicago Law Review* (Summer 1948, Vol. 15, No. 4).

and awe which then surrounded the subject. The compelling demand for international control was an additional element with a very practical relation to domestic legislation. Each of these factors constituted unique legislative considerations. And the element of fear was not confined to problems bred by the bomb from which it had sprung; rather it diffused through the entire legislative atmosphere in the illogical fashion of a primitive emotion.

(2) *The Newness of the Problem.* Multiplying the problems raised by the special incidents of atomic energy was the total absence of any convenient framework into which the legislative problem could be fitted. The door was open for all manner of entrants into the legislative contest. Fortunately, the universal interest in the subject opened publicity avenues to a degree rarely available to private citizens seeking to make their positions and reasons known.

(3) *The Political Activity of the Scientists.* Into the idea vacuum created by the fear, the stupendous prophecies of atomic energy uses, and the unfamiliarity of the problems presented marched an array of political unknowns, the scientists. These Men Who Made the Bomb personified the factors which had unsettled the legislators. They were awesome creatures indeed to have built the bomb, men of limitless capacity to have harnessed such a colossal new source of energy, and men almost from a different planet, politically speaking. Before the bomb, physical scientists had almost uniformly been silent on public affairs, apparently preferring the precision and predictability of natural forces to the inexact conflicts and compromises of the social world. Yet here they were, mostly young, forceful, and hopeful men and women dealing with old and tired legislators of few ideals, earnest and sure of their subject in contrast to Congressional fear and uncertainty. Matching their energy and capacity to the opportunity, the scientists soon became a major factor in the formulation of atomic energy legislation.

(4) *The Postwar Attitude toward the Armed Forces.* In the wake of victory our armed forces enjoyed a prestige and political strength in Congress then unprecedented in American history. In those quarters, at least, the capacity of the military to control atomic energy in peacetime was demonstrated beyond doubt by their victory in the war. At the same time most veterans, particu-

larly enlisted men, had developed an opposite attitude toward supervisors—the "brass hats"—at least so far as non-military activities were concerned. The general public exhibited attitudes in the full range between these two; but perhaps the larger portion was more readily affected by stories of specific abuses than by the generality of victory. The result may be ungrateful, even illogical; but there can be no disputing the popularity of Mauldin and similar cartoonists.

Each of these factors contributed to make the Congress and the executive branch more susceptible to the wishes of the public than is usually the case. The result was a law unprecedented in scope, in technique and in constructive potentialities. That the ultimate enactment was of such a high standard is a tribute to our means of communication and our human resources—in other words, to our democratic system. This victory was made possible by articulate public opinion; yet the same freedom of expression in the hands of less well-meaning individuals and legislators came uncomfortably close to defeating the will of the overwhelming majority, as the following history indicates.

I. EARLY DEVELOPMENTS: THE MAY-JOHNSON BILL

Until August 5, 1945, when the first atomic bomb was dropped on Hiroshima, neither Congress nor the public knew that an instrument of such vast destructive possibilities was even contemplated. Only the scientists, the military leadership of the Manhattan Project, and the very highest echelon of the Administration knew of the work and of its almost limitless consequences should a bomb be successfully produced. Thus, the secrecy surrounding the project gave these two groups, the scientists and the military, an enormous head start over the rest of the country (and the world) in anticipating the problems created by the release of atomic energy and in developing techniques for meeting these problems.

As early as 1943 the scientists began writing and circulating papers covering such topics as the destructive capacity of the bomb, possible national and international political consequences of its use, and possible peacetime uses of atomic energy. Accounts are available elsewhere of the psychological conflicts which many scientists underwent in trying to live with the knowledge that their goal was the production of a weapon endangering civilization itself. By the end of 1944, however, they had settled upon the need for quick dissemination throughout the world of the few basic facts which would permit an unprepared public to understand the new problems presented by atomic energy. In February 1945 the formation of an organization of atomic scientists was considered but security rules of course precluded action at the time. Finally, the preliminary work of the scientists was gathered together by the Committee on Social and Political Implications, headed by Professor James Franck; this work was incorporated into a special report sent to Secretary of War Stimson on June 11, 1945.

Meanwhile the military leadership had also become active. Shortly after President Roosevelt's death, President Truman was first informed of the atomic project. In May 1945, with the latter's approval, Secretary Stimson set up the Interim Committee to advise the President on the use of the bomb and to recommend legislation that would insure the most advantageous use of this new discovery. The legislative assignment, however, was kept a tight secret.[1] Both the scientists and the Interim Committee considered at length the best way to use the bomb, an effort which culminated in its actual use at Hiroshima and Nagasaki.

Despite contrary assurances from the War Department, no adequate informational measures had been prepared to enable the public to form an intelligent understanding of the significance of the atomic bomb. First reports about the bomb created mental chaos; the few carefully prepared articles were no match for the fanciful speculations put forth by writers, broadcasters, and speakers all over the country. The scientists attempted to fill the information void, but without preparation, without experience in the workings of our mass communications system, and without adequate resources or freedom to reach the bulk of the people before misleading, even harmful, first impressions had been formed. Indeed, it is hard to conceive how any system short of mass censorship during distribution of prepared material could possibly have transmitted the story of the atomic bomb without creating the very first impressions which have since caused so much harm—the notion of "secrets"; the confident expectation of a defense against the bomb; and the assumption that other nations will be incapable of atomic warfare for almost a generation.

[1] Various scientists were told no legislation was yet being contemplated.

The May-Johnson Bill. During these months legislation was being drafted under the supervision of the Interim Committee, behind locked doors and subject to severe security precautions, by General Royall, then Special Assistant to the Undersecretary of War, and William L. Marbury, a well-known private attorney. There is some indication that this secrecy was continued even after Hiroshima; hence the scientists were caught unawares when President Truman sent a special message to Congress on October 3, followed the same day by introduction of the Interim Committee bill in the House by Representative May and in the Senate by Senator Johnson—the May-Johnson bill. There can be no question that the bill reached Congress in unorthodox fashion, since it was not cleared through the Bureau of the Budget, or by the bureau with other departments and agencies as is customary.

The May-Johnson bill was widely denounced as a drive for military control of atomic energy in time of peace, though the bill was sponsored expressly for the purpose of substituting civilian control for War Department supervision. The accusation derives not from explicit grant of authority to the military but from a series of provisions which readily lent themselves to military domination. . . .

The May-Johnson bill was detained at the presiding officer's table in the Senate because of a jurisdictional dispute; in the House, however, it moved smoothly and efficiently into the guiding hands of Andrew Jackson May, chairman of the military affairs committee. While the Senate wrangled over referral to the foreign affairs, military affairs, or a proposed new atomic energy committee, Mr. May opened and closed public hearings on October 9, 1945, and rushed executive committee sessions designed to report the bill out promptly.

Opposition Develops. From the standpoint of the May-Johnson bill's backers such haste was well advised. No sooner was the bill introduced than there rose from atomic scientists throughout the nation an avalanche of outraged criticism that could only have been spontaneous and deeply felt. During the operations of the Manhattan Project in wartime, there had gradually developed a cleavage between most of the scientists and their military supervisors. Without here repeating the many incidents which explain the unenthusiastic attitude of most scientists toward military supervision, it may be sufficient to cite the conclusion of one of the key men in the Project that the military "delayed the bomb by 18 months."

Local organizations of scientists had been formed at each of the principal sites shortly after Hiroshima. Educational efforts directed toward helping the public attain an intelligent understanding of the physical facts of atomic energy and some of their political, social and economic consequences were under way when the May-Johnson bill suddenly appeared on the scene. Immediately, a major share of the scientists' energies was thrown into a fight for more careful consideration of the bill. Led by such outstanding men as Drs. Condon, Szilard, and Urey, they descended upon Washington insisting that a single day's hearings limited to favorable witnesses was a shocking abuse of legislative discretion in dealing with such a momentous and largely uncomprehended subject. When their request for further hearing was initially refused, they met informally with a large caucus of congressmen, then used the hearings of a Senate subcommittee considering science legislation as a sounding board for airing the defects of the May-Johnson bill. Simultaneously, they were calling on prominent private citizens, editors and publishers, on leading figures in the Administration, and on influential senators and representatives. Their efforts so moved Mr. May that he reopened hearings—for a single day. A few witnesses testified against the bill, a few more for the bill, and the committee resumed executive sessions, with General Royall in daily attendance. The bill was reported out with a few amendments, only one of consequence, on November 5. Two Democrats filed dissenting views; nine Republicans voted solidly against government control.

Fortunately for the scientists not all officials in a position to affect the legislation had the stolid single-mindedness of Mr. May. In late October the President began to have misgivings about some aspects of the bill. Indeed, his approval had been given in reliance upon the endorsements of the War Department and the few scientific leaders who served on or with the Interim Committee. He had no notion that scientists would have any serious objection to the proposed law. His concern was echoed by men then occupying key posts under him, such as Budget Director Smith, Secretary Ickes, and Secretary Wallace. In the House of Representatives, Helen Douglas and others had voiced their apprehension so that Speaker Rayburn was of no mind to let the

May-Johnson bill come to the floor until the air had cleared. Newspapers, magazines, and broadcasters throughout the country were charging that the bill was being railroaded through without giving the public a chance to form an opinion on the issues.

The Senate Special Committee. Meanwhile the Senate continued in its disagreement as to committee jurisdiction over atomic energy legislation. The logjam was broken in late October when, after a regular session between the President and Democratic legislative leaders, the Senate voted to establish a Special Committee on Atomic Energy. Following custom, though not without opposition, the sponsor of the resolution creating the committee became its chairman—freshman Senator Brien McMahon. As if to make sure that McMahon was kept in his place, the other ten positions on the committee were awarded to Senator Connally, chairman of the Foreign Affairs Committee, Senator Vandenberg, ranking Republican on the same committee, Senator Johnson, sponsor of the May-Johnson bill and ranking Democrat on the Military Affairs Committee, such conservative stalwarts as Senators Tydings, Byrd, Millikin, Russell, and Austin, and freshmen Senators Hickenlooper and (ex-Admiral) Hart.

The legislative strategy soon emerged. The House bill was to be kept off the floor until the new Senate committee had had an opportunity to study the entire field of atomic energy and to prepare alternative legislation. The heat was off; there was time for the scientists, the public, and the government to settle down to the more difficult task of developing constructive suggestions for the content of atomic energy legislation.

The President's concern over the reception accorded the May-Johnson bill has already been mentioned. Even as he was conferring with legislative leaders, his principal assistant, John W. Snyder, then Director of the Office of War Mobilization and Reconversion (OWMR), came to him with an analysis of the defects of the May-Johnson bill and a preliminary outline of the requirements of a good bill. These suggestions were developed after extensive discussion with the high-ranking scientists who were leading the opposition to the May-Johnson bill and were prepared by James R. Newman, head of OWMR's science division, with the author's assistance. The President was so impressed with these suggestions that he forthwith designated OWMR to act for the Administration in connection with atomic energy legislation. Mr. Newman was shortly appointed special counsel to the Senate Special Committee on Atomic Energy, and Dr. Condon, by then the new Director of the National Bureau of Standards, was named Scientific Advisor to the committee.

Through November and most of December the Senate committee busied itself with the task of learning about the physics, production and potential uses of atomic energy and the military significance of the atomic bomb. Since an examination of the criticisms of the May-Johnson bill had shown that modification by amendment was not feasible because of the many basic changes needed, the drafting of an alternative bill was begun by Mr. Newman and the author under the joint guidance of Senator McMahon and the Administration, and in consultation with the scientists and other agencies of the government. The draft was completed as the general hearings of the Senate committee were nearing conclusion and was introduced by Senator McMahon just before the Christmas recess. The Committee agreed to consider specific legislation when it resumed hearings in January, using the McMahon bill, the May-Johnson bill, and a bill submitted by Senator Ball as the bases of discussion.

II. A BILL EMERGES FROM THE SENATE COMMITTEE

Even as the press was daily reporting the testimony of expert witnesses filling in the general facts about atomic energy and as the McMahon bill was quietly being drafted, the protagonists in the May-Johnson bill controversy were preparing to do battle in the new arena—the Senate Special Committee on Atomic Energy.

The isolated site organizations of scientists were consolidated into a single Federation of Atomic Scientists. A simple word change substituting "American" for "Atomic" sufficed to cover the inclusion of other scientific groups not strictly in the atomic energy field. A small office with a lone secretary was opened in Washington, accessible only by ascent of some four flights of steps. Many of the nation-wide civic, labor, and religious groups banded together to form the National Committee on Atomic Information, devoted solely to the educational task of disseminating the basic physical and political facts about atomic energy, the Committee sharing the Federation's lofty perch. The scientists themselves, unable to afford paid representatives in the nation's capital, inaugurated a relay system whereby a member from each site took a two-week leave of absence, spent it in Washington, and returned only to be replaced by an associate for a similar two-week period. In Washington they worked till all hours of the night, meeting with members of all three branches of the government and influential organizations and individuals, writing speeches and articles, and learning as best they could the political ins and outs in the seat of government. For the most part they avoided political bias. Perhaps their rare combination of a non-partisan attitude and an unflagging devotion to a goal of no conceivable personal benefit explains some of the readiness of political leaders to listen to them. The organizations which had joined in creating the Atomic Information Service merged their legislative activities into the Emergency Conference for the Civilian Control of Atomic Energy sparked by the tireless Rachel Bell. And, to complete the girding for battle, groups of prominent individuals nationally and locally were formed into Emergency Committees for the Civilian Control of Atomic Energy. The national committee roster included, among others, Bishop Oxnam, Beardsley Ruml, William Donovan, Palmer Hoyt, Arthur Whiteside, Percival Brundage, Donald Nelson, Cass Canfield, Harry Emerson Fosdick, Sumner Welles, and John Hay Whitney.

Across the ideological gulf the proponents of military control were not napping. Working quietly, mostly through service officers, they brought their wartime prestige and their hard-earned knowledge of the workings of Congress to bear on the more responsive members of both houses. Even a character assassination here and there was not beneath them. Theirs was a double strategy; preferred was the passage of a bill firmly establishing military control in peacetime, but the alternative of no legislation was almost equivalent since the military would have remained in control.

Thus the lines were forming for the most difficult open contest in the Senate with each development exposed to the eyes of the public, unlike the quick trick tried in the House.

The McMahon Bill. . . . The Senate committee spent four weeks hearing witnesses testifying exclusively with respect to legislation for the domestic control of atomic energy. In the course of these hearings the President sent a special letter to Senator

McMahon outlining the Administration's views on the principal ingredients of desirable atomic energy legislation. With a minor exception, his recommendations paralleled the McMahon bill, thus bringing into the open his change of heart on the May-Johnson bill.

The hearings concluded, the Committee embarked upon a schedule of executive sessions almost unprecedented in legislative annals. For six weeks practically the full membership of the Committee met in almost daily session, combing over the legislative proposals before them. The Committee's first response to the weight of favorable testimony on the McMahon bill came when, after a preliminary skirmish, it voted to use the bill as a working guide. Section by section, the Committee went through the bill three separate times, emerging with a true group product, a bill which, while still bearing a resemblance to the original McMahon bill, nevertheless contained changed in almost every line. Several sections were completely re-written, others substantially overhauled, a few settled by more or less artful compromise. The result was a superior piece of legislation, a testimonial to the latent capacities of free discussion. True, a few provisions are subject to pointed criticism, but rarely has a legislative body making its own decisions emerged with a bill reflecting as high a caliber of statesmanship as did the Senate Special Committee in reporting out its modified form of S. 1717.

The Committee Product. A full analysis of the Committee's changes would not here be appropriate. Some of its evident improvements were: 1) the creation of the post of General Manager, to be appointed by the President and to service the Commission in supervising the four Divisions and other organizational units; 2) the revision of the patents section to provide explicitly that certain inventions were not patentable and to make the availability of utilization patents discretionary rather than automatic; and 3) the addition of section expressly providing that international agreements were to supersede any inconsistent provision of the domestic control law.

Two other provisions, however, received the bulk of the Committee's attention and supplied the fuel for the major controversies within and without the Senate unit. These were the sections dealing first, with the relation between the military departments and civilian Atomic Energy Commission and second, with the determination of appropriate secrecy measures. Though the questions were logically distinct, they were the beaches upon which the civilian and military control proponents engaged, and while the black sand of one issue was distinguishable from the white sand of the other, the heat of the conflict fused them into a single mass of deep disagreement on the special capacity of the military to preserve the national security.

From the time of the President's first offhand statements about preserving our monopoly of the "secrets" of the atomic bomb, the majority of the public, as shown by public opinion polls, accepted the simple notion of "secrets," perhaps subconsciously hoping that preserving these "secrets" would protect us against all danger of atomic warfare. Though later polls showed that most people accepted the intellectual proposition that we could not retain our monopoly, nevertheless their emotional dependence on the concept of "secrets" was probably not seriously affected by the logical inconsistency of such a position.

In this respect members of Congress followed the public pattern. From the early questioning of witnesses on the general subject of atomic energy, there was no question but that the law would contain some provision to preserve the "secrets." Indeed, an early propaganda coup was scored when the words "security" and "secrecy" became interchangeable in this field. Hence, from the outset, few scientists publicly advocated a policy of complete declassification, although many were apprehensive of the evils that had been and could continue to be committed in the name of secrecy.

Assuming, then, that secrecy was not only desirable but vitally linked up with our national security, it was not surprising that one of the principal foci in the civilian versus military control dispute became: "Who could better keep the secrets?" Disclosure of the Canadian espionage story in December and ensuing months, succeeded by dark hints from J. Parnell Thomas of the Un-American Activities Committee that secrets were leaking to other nations from Oak Ridge, were not calculated to let the public forget the issue. Curiously, these stories were urged as proving military control alone could preserve the secrets even though Oak Ridge was still under military control.

Meeting the issue on the same level, the scientists responded with two arguments: first, that only a scientist could know a "secret" from a paragraph of jargon; and second, in many instances War Department secrecy rules had hampered the development of the bomb. Indeed on one occasion it appeared that a whole laboratory might have exploded if one group had not illicitly transmitted information unknown to the group in the endangered lab.

Though the public debate proceeded largely on this level, a few members of the Senate committee had realized that secrecy did not depend on the color of the Commission's coats. More serious to them was Secretary Patterson's objection to the original McMahon bill, that it contained inadequate provision for participation in atomic energy control and development by the regular military departments. Their first plan was to give to the Army Chief of Staff a veto power over acts of the civilian Commission. This "compromise" was discarded when the then Chief of Staff, General Eisenhower, showed no great enthusiasm for the power. Next, they developed the so-called "Vandenberg amendment." This proposed to create a Military Liaison Committee consisting of representatives of the War and Navy Departments with power to advise and consult with the Commission on all matters *it* deemed to affect security, to know of all matters within the Commission and, where it felt any action or proposed action was "inimical to the common defense and security," to appeal the question to the President whose decision would be final. Senator McMahon opposed the amendment, urging instead a compromise as to membership on the Commission. Put to a vote, he was defeated 6 to 1, four committee members being absent. His request for postponement of consideration until the full committee was present was granted, the vote then becoming 10 to 1.

Disclosure of the amendment was the signal for a direct offensive by the scientists, the conference of organizations, the emergency committee of prominent individuals, and the many friends of civilian control in the communications fields and elsewhere. This time the public relations advantage rested with their side. The substance of the amendment was proposed by several other senators; Vandenberg's principal contribution was his suggestion of the final wording. Because it was dubbed the "Vandenberg amendment," however, instead of some shorthand reference, the amendment's fate almost as a matter of senatorial courtesy came to rest with Vandenberg. This was most desirable because he was more responsive to public opinion than some of the other sponsors and it was an election year for him—he could not then know that the November 1946 election was to be a Republican landslide. While the clamor against the amendment steadily mounted (including some influential protests from Vandenberg's home town), the Administration also became concerned. For one thing the proposed amendment by-passed the Secretaries of War and Navy, a result not exactly palatable to them. Shortly, Vandenberg himself indicated a willingness to accept modification. The solution lay in the familiar lawyer's legerdemain of accomplishing fundamental changes in meaning while altering as few words as possible. By limiting the scope of the Liaison Committee's functions to military applications and by restoring regular channels within the military departments, the amended amendment ceased to create an autonomous and powerful military committee and replaced it with an orderly liaison within traditional military department jurisdiction and channels. Vandenberg's acceptance of the changes was readily approved by the Senate committee.

Just as the military control debate merged into the secrecy question, so the fight over the Vandenberg amendment affected the committee's attitude when it reached the section dealing with control of information. There, for the first time, Vandenberg, Hickenlooper, and others sought advice from leading scientists in close touch with the scientists' organizations and made a determined effort to produce a section which would preserve the maximum secrecy consistent with dissemination of enough data not to hamper research. In this instance the basic problems confronting the scientists flowed from the Espionage Act which the committee not unexpectedly was unwilling to touch. The final section, while indulging Senator Austin's penchant for inserting the phrase "to assure the common defense and security," provided explicitly that the Commission should weigh against the policy of security through secrecy first, the importance of freedom of communication in assuring the progress of research and second, the desirability of eliminating restrictions when adequate international controls were established.

With these and lesser modifications, the Senate committee unanimously approved their bill on April 19, 1946. Unanimity in a committee of such conservative composition on a bill authorizing unprecedented government controls was no minor or accidental achievement, as the ensuing history indicates. After an agonizing delay, the reasons for which have never become clear, Senator McMahon seized the opportunity on a peaceful Saturday afternoon to bring the committee bill up for consideration on the Senate floor. The Senate approved the bill unanimously on that day, June 1, 1946.

III. FINAL PASSAGE

The jubilance of the proponents of civilian control over Senate approval soon faded as they analyzed the membership of the House Military Affairs Committee, to which the bill was then referred. Of this 27-member committee, 9 of the Republicans had already gone on record as opposed to government control in voting against the May-Johnson bill. Chairman May, whose "own" bill had been stopped by advocates of the measure now resting on his desk, was hardly likely to press for prompt action in perhaps the last month of the legislative session. A half-dozen of the Democrats had consistently sided with May on pro-military measures. Then, with ironic timeliness, invitations to witness the gigantic atomic demonstrations at Bikini drew off a number of committee members, one of these being Representative Holifield who almost alone had fought the May-Johnson bill in committee.

After a week's delay Chairman May announced public hearings would be held. Two witnesses were invited—Secretary of War Patterson and Assistant Navy Secretary Kenney. Examination of the witnesses by committee members demonstrated beyond doubt the committee's preoccupation with the military use of atomic energy and their unquestioning assumption that only the military departments were qualified to act in the interests of national security. This testimony concluded, the House unit embarked upon section-by-section consideration of S. 1717 in executive session.

The amendment pattern was soon apparent. Chairman May supported three militarizing amendments, one to permit military men to serve in any position, another requiring at least one member of the Commission to be from the armed forces, and a third requiring the Director of Military Applications to be a military officer. These revisions approved, he then fought off a host of disabling amendments proposed by the dissident Republican members, allowing only an occasional one to slip into the bill.

By the end of June, though the amendment process was substantially finished, the bill encountered such parliamentary obstacles that its chances of stillbirth rose alarmingly. House rules designate a majority of the committee's roster as a quorum and require a quorum for formal action if the point is raised. Several members of the committee were off to Bikini, others were ill or out of town, leaving it within the power of eight or nine members acting in concert to prevent a quorum. The same Republican group then followed the practice of coming to meetings, counting noses, and, if a quorum were present, taking turns leaving the committee room. This process continued for several days despite powerful objections from the public,[2] from the Administration, and from the Speaker of the House. Whether these pressures were enough to have ultimately been successful is purely speculative, because at this point fortune intervened from another quarter. The Senate committee investigating the national defense program chose this moment to release its first tentative stories on the May-Garsson munitions undertakings. Though Chairman May did not then appear to be much involved, he must have had some foreboding of what was to follow, because almost immediately thereafter he forced the bill out of committee with that uncanny strength which committee chairmen so often display.

This was July 10. The scene shifted to the Rules Committee, where J. Parnell Thomas[3] sought openly to kill the bill on the ground that continued control by the War Department was essential to the nation's safety, urging the conclusion of his Un-American Activities Committee that secrets were leaking to other nations from Oak Ridge. His contention was being supported by some War Department quarters even then, as appears from two concurrent incidents. The Oak Ridge security officer stated over the telephone that the Thomas Committee was inaccurate in

[2] The Emergency Committee for the Civilian Control of Atomic Energy published two full-page ads in the Washington Post in this period. Their emphasis, as was that of the bill's proponents in the House, was upon the eminence of the men supporting the Senate bill—the Senate Committee, Eisenhower, Baruch, et al. Judging from the attention given these advertisements in later floor debate, they evoked a response which more than justified their expense.

[3] Rep. Thomas was a member of both the Military Affairs and the Un-American Activities Committees.

quoting him as saying "the peace and security of the United States is definitely in danger." Yet he was somehow unable to obtain clearance to reduce his denial to writing for submission to Congress. Furthermore, as has only recently been revealed, a "high officer in the Manhattan Project" sent a special message to Thomas about this time urging him to order the FBI file on the Senate committee's scientific adviser (Dr. Condon) because some indications of disloyalty might be obtained from it. Thomas' effort failed and by July 16, under Chairman Sabath's guidance, the Rules Committee had approved by a narrow margin a rule permitting prompt consideration of the bill on the floor of the House.

The Administration in working for the passage of the Senate bill was now faced with a difficult tactical situation. In floor debate a bill is always maanged by the chairman of the committee from which it emanates—here Mr. May. Opposition time is controlled by the ranking minority member—in this case Dewey Short, who was completely against the bill. Confronted with these obstacles, the Administration depended on Ewing Thomason, next ranking Democrat on the committee, who was personally convinced of the wisdom of the Senate bill. From the outset Thomason set his sights on one goal—House passage of some bill under the number S. 1717, regardless of content or amendments, just so that a bill would go into a conference committee of both houses. Valiantly, he fought against efforts to cripple the legislation: amendments establishing the death penalty for violation of secrecy restrictions; requiring FBI approval of the "character and associations" of all employees and contractors; and replacing patent controls with provisions permitting private patent rights regardless of secrecy requirements. Each of these he lost, but in the final test, a motion to recommit the bill to committee, he won by scant 50 out of 342 votes, and the bill moved into conference.

The House conferees were Democrats May, Thomason, and Durham and Republicans Clason and Thomas. Senate conferees were Democrats McMahon, Johnson, and Russell and Republicans Vandenberg and Millikin. In conference the members of each house vote as a unit; hence the vote of the Senate members cannot overrule the House members or vice versa. The problems in the conference committee were twofold: 1) To what extent would the Senate members now "give in" to House amendments which more closely fitted their normal conservatism? 2) Could a civilian control bill secure the approval of the House delegation if May voted with the Republicans?

In conference committee the Senate delegation soon displayed an impressive unanimity in both substance and tactic. In general, all minor House amendments not inconsistent with the structure of the bill were accepted with few modifications. Two basic issues remained—the role of the military and the patents section. Here, the strength of inner conviction flowing from full consideration and careful decision demonstrated itself. The Senate delegation sustained their own decisions on these points by sheer force of superior knowledge and genuine belief.

Of the two, the patents questions afforded the greater likelihood of departure from the Senate bill. The American Bar Association, the National Association of Manufacturers, a number of Hearst papers, and a National Patent Council had unloosed a violent attack on the Senate patents action *after* the bill had passed the Senate. The chairman of the House Patents Committee had taken the floor to denounce the Senate proposal as the end of the American patent system. A former Assistant Commissioner of Patents, whose current employment by RCA was not revealed by the record, had testified that the Senate provision was modeled after the Russian system. Against a background of Congressional unwillingness to modify the patent system over many years,[4] the intensity of the attack was indeed likely to occasion some or many concessions from the Senate delegation.

To the particular credit of Senator Millikin, a self-designated conservative, the Senate version emerged untouched. After a careful study of the objections raised in the House, he concluded that the Senate section alone could both preserve the secrecy sought by other sections of the bill and serve the public interest in a field developed entirely at taxpayers' expense. After hearing this one-and-a-half-hour speech on the subject in the conference committee, the Senate delegation voted unanimously to resubstitute the Senate patents section and May voted with the Democrats to give the House conferee's concurrence by a 3 to 2 vote.

4 Despite a succession of similar recommendations from presidential commissions and legislative committees, the Senate provision contained almost the first limitations in the last hundred years on patentable inventions and on the freedom of patentees in granting or denying licenses.

The military amendments present a different problem because here May's sympathies were clearly with the House Republicans. In this area, Senator Vandenberg bore the brunt of persuasion. Upholding his revised military liaison committee amendment as a fair adjustment of the civilian versus military control issue, he dominated the conference committee discussions. He conceded the requirement that the Director of the Military Applications Division be an active officer, and strove to eliminate both the requirement that at least one member of the commission also be an officer and the clause exempting all commission posts from the 1870 prohibition against military officers in civilian positions. At this point, May was suddenly afflicted with a severe heart attack. His condition not only prevented his testifying before the Senate committee investigating his transactions with the Garssons; it kept him as well from the crucial sessions of the conference committee. In a story-book scene and with a voice implying he was on his death-bed, May finally whispered his acceptance of Vandenberg's proposal. The conference bill was complete, though J. Parnell Thomas in an unusual move refused to sign the report.

Back again on the floor of the House in the closing days of the session, the conference bill drew the same violent opposition which had met the House committee report. Thomas spoke angrily; Patents Chairman Latham denounced the conference bill; others sprang up to attack the bill as dangerous and socialistic. In last-minute desperation the opposition even spread the rumor on the floor of the House that steel was now fissionable; hence the steel industry would be nationalized under the bill. The break came when Clason, the other dissenting House conferee, announced his decision to vote for the bill. In a few moments the conference report was approved by voice vote in the House. Approved by the Senate the same afternoon, it was sent to the President for signature. On August 1, the Atomic Energy Act of 1946 became law.

CONCLUSION

This review of the history of one of the more significant laws of our time permits a few deductions not peculiar to this legislation. Like all laws receiving wide public consideration, the Atomic Energy Act in its history illustrates: 1) the tendency toward oversimplification of the issues with resultant confusion and concealment of the value judgments actually involved; 2) the effect which the nature of the issue and organized efforts can have upon alignments for and against; and 3) the essentially inconclusive nature of all legislation.

The Issues. In the public eye the principal decision lay in choosing between military and civilian control. . . .

. . . the real "control" question involved decisions as to both the amount and direction of the discretion to be given to those in control and the genuineness of the administrative structure, regardless of who might ultimately be appointed. Was it wiser to give sweeping power with almost absolute discretion to the administering body or to determine initial policy as to research, production, peacetime uses, secrecy, etc., and refine the grants of power to match these decisions? What types of exclusive public ownership, what safeguards for private research, what emphasis upon peacetime uses should the law specifically establish? Would responsibility be effectively lodged in a large part-time commission with outside interests working through a full-time administrator with independent powers? Or would responsibility better match authority in a small full-time commission working through an administrator whose role was primarily executory? These were the "control" issues. Yet no special political astuteness is needed to realize how drab and colorless these questions would have appeared in public debate. No wonder both sides sought support within the framework of the simpler symbols of military versus civilian control. . . .[5]

The Alignments. Political parties have long ceased to be the sole mechanism for organized expression on public issues between elections, if indeed they ever were. Private organizations in bewildering variety supply forums for debate on public questions, take positions, and seek simultaneously to influence and represent the thinking of their members. Business, trade, and farm groups; labor, religious, and civic groups, social, book, and

[5] In a very real sense the debate in oversimplified terms contributed to the content of the final bill. Most of the bill's policy conclusions on freedom of research, emphasis on development of peacetime uses, use of traditional methods to preserve secrecy, protection of the public interest in non-military benefits, and leeway for international control followed from subordinate arguments, invoked in favor of civilian control. The simplicity of the issue made public discussion possible; the discussion itself shaped the actual legislative decisions.

family clubs—all are more or less responsible on matters of public policy.

Over a period of years the more politically active organizations have developed fairly clear policy stands; on a host of conventional controversies their positions can readily be anticipated. Sometimes these positions are described as "liberal" or "conservative"; and repeated organizational alignments have tended to give the groupings themselves liberal or conservative labels.

Mere novelty of an issue is not alone sufficient to break down these habits of alignment, as responses to many of the New Deal innovations demonstrated. The atomic energy controversy, however, supplied proof that established groupings may be redistributed. The issue itself was of course a major factor; but the issue alone would not have broken the momentum if many individuals, scientists and others, had not actively worked toward this objective. The results were roughly as follows:

(1) Organizations such as the Veterans of Foreign Wars, the Farm Bureau, and the General Federation of Women's Clubs joined the League of Women Voters and the Congress of Industrial Organization in supporting civilian control;

(2) The National Association of Manufacturers, the American Bar Association, and similar property-emphasis groups were largely silent until after the Senate had approved its committee's bill; and

(3) A few large corporations worked actively but quietly with the unauthorized military spokesmen who lobbied for military control. . . .

Chapter Eight

INQUIRY AS AN INSTRUMENT OF GOVERNMENT: Information, Supervision

REACTION TO THE DELEGATION OF POWER

Congressional Oversight of Administration: The Power of the Purse

ARTHUR MACMAHON

Legislative oversight of administration is a familiar and well-grounded assumption of responsible government. Accepted, too, is the corollary that the need for such oversight increases with executive initiative in policy and the delegation of discretion under the broad terms of statutes. . . .

Congress shows novel zest for staffs of its own. In various ways, it seeks to attach strings to action. How far can this double tendency be pushed under the presidential form of government without creating ambiguities of administrative responsibility? There is a related and deeper difficulty. Can a legislative body—the institutional virtue of which lies in the recentralized choice and

From Arthur W. Macmahon, *Political Science Quarterly* (March 1943, Vol. LXIII, No. 2, pp. 161-190; June 1943, Vol. LXIII, No. 3, pp. 380-414). Reprinted by permission of the Editors of *Political Science Quarterly*.

diffused responsiveness of its individual members—act on details otherwise than through small groups within itself which, by their special biases, may distort the application of public policy and even destroy its integrity? Public policy must be fused from the localisms inherent in popular representative bodies; it must then be carried out with as much wholeness as possible. Mighty issues appear in the present assertiveness of Congress. Welcome as are the stirrings from the lethargy of its own institutional tradition, its restlessness holds at least as much portent as promise.

I

There has been a significant change of emphasis in the Congressional attitude toward administrative discretion and its control. Originally, legislative suspicion and reluctance were reflected in the detailed character of statute law. But, especially in dealing with the flux of economic relations, leeway for administrative determinations was inevitable. . . . The weight is no longer on the initial insertion of statutory detail or upon judicial review. Rather, the legislative body itself seeks to be continuously a participant in guiding administrative conduct and the exercise of discretion. The cords that Congress now seeks to attach to administrative action are not merely the pre-dawn "leading-strings of statutes" of which Woodrow Wilson wrote in *Congressional Government*. The novel feature of the attempted relationship is its immediacy.

The shift of emphasis just described affects one's perspective on the purposes of legislative oversight of administration. In the theory of the matter, four types of objective have been recognized. First, the objective of legislative oversight may be to check dishonesty or waste. Especially is this important when the stream of supervision within the administrative system is poisoned near its source. Apart from checking malfeasance, moreover, legislators have opportunities to see the results of governmental programs; at times they can serve administration almost as a supplementary inspectorate. Second, the objective of legislative oversight may be to guard against unsympathetic or perhaps merely over-zealous attitudes among officials which produce harsh or callous administration. Third, the ideal of legislative oversight has assumed that the non-special minds of legislators, brought to bear upon the administrative routines, may challenge the means in terms of a broad and realistic sense of ends. It may freshen inventiveness as to the means themselves; at least it may rebuke stupidity. Fourth, the objective of legislative oversight may be to see that there is compliance with the legislative intent as embodied in law. This is the face of the theory that is highlighted by the events of the hour.

Within the notion of enforcing compliance with legislative intent a shift is discernible. Formerly compliance meant legality and this was enforced by methods which were essentially external to Congress: the courts, the General Accounting Office as a vast routinized bureau, the Department of Justice, the Treasury controls, and the departmental fiscal offices. Now the legislative intent that is conceived is one of incompletely resolved policy. Without withdrawing power, the Congress seeks in sundry ways to claim what it gave; it asserts the right of continuous intervention.

It is worth pausing to review in baldest fashion some of the methods by which continuous intervention is now essayed. Clues may be drawn from measures or proposals in Congress since January 1943. (1) The amendment of statutes is a method of oversight; as Dr. Elias Huzar has very cogently shown, there is no sharp borderline between legislation and supervision. Recently amendments to wartime laws have been provoked by particular incidents and have cracked like warning whips. (2) Meanwhile Congressional investigations multiply. There is no novelty in this safeguard of free government, but some persons are agitating for a unification of injuries into the conduct of the war. The thought now is less the convenience of administrators harassed by multiple hearings than the possibility of creating a single instrument of potent influence. (3) The standing legislative committees summon administrators to explain and justify decisions, past and pending. A special House committee investigates the extent to which administrative directives have been inconsistent with law, or arbitrary. Some members of Congress are urging that the standing committees should be permanently empowered to watch and perhaps censor the exercise of administrative discretion in their respective fields of jurisdiction. Others, however, propose more inclusive organs for the exercise of continuous scrutiny. (4) Related in spirit, being a likely opening for intervention in administration, is the preposterous but formidable move to broaden senatorial confirmation of appointments. (5) Meanwhile

Congress begins to talk of staffing, but with many shades of opinion about its nature and nexus: whether the personnel should be permanent or transitory and how appointed, whether the attachment should be to committees, and if so to which committees, or should be to the chambers as wholes but singly, or to joint agencies of House and Senate. (6) But outstanding as practical developments have been steps actually taken to enlarge the facilities and duties of the committees on appropriations. . . .

II

The committee structure of Congress reflects the distinction between authorization and appropriation—between the passage of acts which define purposes, convey power, and authorize appropriations, on the one hand, and the year by year provision of money, on the other. The standing committee system had two elements: the legislative committees and the appropriating committees. The separation of authorization and appropriation has the advantage, among others, that it accommodates itself to the technique of planning, for programs may be laid out broadly, to be implemented annually at a tempo suited to conditions. . . .

The appropriations committees of House and Senate work separately. House members, especially, shy away from formalized joint action; experience, they say, shows that it is likely to subordinate them to the Senators. Custom concedes to the House the right to initiate the appropriation bills. The Senate committee is smaller than that in the House; its members serve upon many subcommittees; the staff has less responsibility. In a sense, the Senate Committee on Appropriations sits in an appellate capacity. It circularizes the departments to find out if they have particular items to present in its hearings. Often the agencies choose to take their small cuts at the hands of the House and let well enough alone. But administrators value the opportunity for appeal that the Senate committee affords. The House members, for their part, regard the Senate group as undisciplined and irresponsible. Institutionally, the weight rests heavily on the side of the House. This explains why (despite a few outstanding bits of wartime supervision attempted by the Senate committee) the emphasis in the pages that follow is so generally on the methods of the House Committee on Appropriations.

III

The realities of the appropriations committees are in subcommittees, in the chief clerk, and in the clerks assigned to the subcommittees. The ideal of a concerted consideration of expenditures has not been attained. The committee as a whole sometimes considers what are called questions of policy common to all appropriation bills . . . But on the appropriation bills themselves, the main committee can hardly be said to act. Bills typically come before the committee an hour or so before they are to be brought on the floor in charge of a subcommittee chairman and his associates. The printed bill and the committee report are ready. Indeed, the report (though still without a number) has been given out bearing the notice that it is "subject to release when consideration of the bill which it accompanies has been completed by the whole committee" and with the request that, before it is released, there be a check "in order to be advised of any changes." Alterations in the full committee are rare. Nevertheless, in addition to the continuity of its small and well-knit staff, the committee is united by a body of procedures and an atmosphere, by the influence of the chairman, and by the constant direct association of the subcommittee chairmen in the subcommittee on deficiencies. . . .

Since the actualities of the House committee's work lie so largely in its eleven subcommittees, great important attaches to the assignments of committee members among these groups. The value of the standing committee device is the combination it affords of some specialization in subject matter with a degree of detachment not likely to be found among administrators. But how much emphasis should be placed upon detachment in the choice of the subcommittees that will deal with particular subjects and departments? The selection is made by the chairman of the whole committee, conditioned by the total play of forces in the House. . . .

Whatever the chairman's view, experience shows that the gravitation of special preoccupations can be delayed but hardly resisted. Given time, men will achieve the subcommittee they especially desire and, once on it, they rise by seniority and may thus achieve the chairmanship. Nor is it always necessary to wait long. . . .

It is not Congress, not the House or Senate, not even the appropriations committee as a whole that should be thought of as abstractions, set against administration. The reality is a handful of men from particular states or districts, working with a particular committee clerk on a multitude of details.

The importance of the staff of the appropriations committees can hardly be exaggerated. The modesty of its scale has been truly amazing. . . .

In the case of appropriations, the smallness of the staff has been offset by its continuity and experience. The House committee has had only three clerks since its establishment in 1865 [to 1943] . . .

In the Senate committee continuity of staff has been nearly as marked as in the House. . . . Thus [from 1873 to 1939] the combined service of two clerks covered sixty-six years. . . .

It is the clerk assigned to a subcommittee who takes the proof of the budget (for hearings may begin on some of the bills before its formal presentation) and draws off its material on the wide-margined committee print of the bill, with the supporting material of the estimates run small below each textual item. It is the clerk who prepares many of the questions to be put at the hearings. Sometimes a dependent chairman follows down his list, virtually reading the questions to the departmental representatives. Perhaps the technical question arises whether a given item contains "legislative" matter ordinarily inadmissible in an appropriation bill. "I will ask the clerk to look into that matter." Or, from another chairman: "I am wondering if it is agreeable to postpone the hearing until tomorrow, as Mr. Sheild [Committee Clerk] and I want an opportunity to go over some of these items." It is the subcommittee clerk who works with the chairman in preparing for the crucial process of "marking up the bill" in executive session. He is a consultant in this process; he must keep track of and embody the changes. Then, under very great pressure, he may be almost wholly responsible for writing the report that will accompany the bill—a document with probably growing importance in legislative oversight of administration. . . . The clerk's judgment shapes what goes into the printed hearings. Through all this it is at once the strength and the weakness of the committee aides that they remain "clerks," even "assistant clerks." Some of the staff's relative self-effacement may reflect personal limitations and the protective convenience of routine. Some of it, as will be said again (for the point is crucial), reflects Marcellus Sheild's awareness of the ticklish problem of duplicating leadership under separation of powers. Meanwhile the staff's esprit de corps and cheerful procedural competence has perhaps offset and even delayed the movement for increased staffing around the focus of appropriations. . . .

The really momentous issue is the extent of the staffing under the Committee on Appropriations which would be consistent with good budgetary relations and an integrated responsibility in administration generally. Staffing might easily be pushed to a point where it would bring a legislative budget method into existence in rivalry with the executive budget. An ambiguous responsibility might develop in the departments. There is need for the most careful consideration, not glib endorsement of the idea of staff and more staff.

There is another reason for caution in staffing in addition to the risk of doubling the lines of authority within administration. The peculiar virtue of the lay element in legislative thinking may be sacrificed. The legislator is immediately in touch with his constituents and this gives him an awareness of government from the side of the public. In wielding oversight of administration, it is his duty to bring this practical public sense to bear. How far must this be personal and immediate, not vicarious? In addition, and quite as important, is the criticism which a robust, imaginative lay mind can bring to bear on technical operations. Something of the value of the mingling of special and non-special minds might be lost if the politician-legislator dealt with administration only through an intermediate legislative bureaucracy. . . .

VI

The formal Congressional hearings on the estimates begin, for some of the bills, before the session opens and before the budget has been presented. Hearings on a routine major bill may run for six weeks of nearly daily sessions. Swelled on the one hand by matter prepared in advance (like the justifications) and by information worked up later at the request of committee members during the hearings (usually inserted at the point where the question appears), the printed hearings have become monumental—more than twenty thousand printed pages of material annually. . . .

The limitations of hearings on appropriations as a method of getting at the facts are admitted by Congressmen who participate in the process. . . . Sometimes committee members reveal a kind of defeatism, for they neither fully trust the professional administrator nor know how to challenge him. . . . "I know that there is no use in asking a fellow who is advocating it whether it is sound or not." . . .

The foregoing comments do not deny the expository value of the hearings. Some of the best interchanges are sheerly explanatory. When a subcommittee has recently acquired jurisdiction over an agency, it may consciously go to school in the agency's methods.

Nor do the shortcomings of the method of question and answer deny the galvanizing effect that the mere fear of embarrassing questions may have on the conduct of administration. Inept though it is, and easy though it usually is to parry questions, the annual cross-examination is an ordeal for administrators. On the whole, it is good for them. Some officials at departmental headquarters say that an experience of bureau representatives before a committee teaches more to careless heads of units than lecturing within the department on administrative proprieties. The risk, of course, is that the reflex makes for caution rather than courage. This danger could be lessened by more stress in the hearings on essential results, rather than on methods, provided legislators would make allowance for the extent to which the fruits of governmental action are long-run and indirect. . . .

Consideration of bills in the whole Committee on Appropriations—customarily an affair of an hour or so—is virtually telescoped with the floor debate. A vast majority of the measures —perhaps ninety per cent—are taken up in the House on the same day on which they are considered by the main committee. . . . Certainly the ideal of a broad congressional consideration of major measures—to say nothing of a whole budgetary program—has not been realized. . . .

VII

The reports of the committees on appropriations, especially of the House, are prime instruments of legislative control. These reports command increasing notice by administrators, while they raise problems of responsibility that deserve more analysis than they have yet received.

Each bill is accompanied to the floor by a report. This is a pamphlet which, in the case of the regular appropriation bills in the House, runs from twenty-five to fifty pages, including tables. The report is the work of the subcommittee. The full Committee on Appropriations seldom alters a document which, indeed, has already been printed provisionally. More particularly, the report is the handiwork of the subcommittee chairman and of the assistant clerk regularly assigned to the group. Their respective parts in the actual preparation of a report vary with personalities and circumstances. The role of the clerk is necessarily heavy; the writing is apt to fall to him. The product must be appraised in the light of the fact that, in the exigent rhythm of appropriations, an assistant clerk (who often covers two subcommittees, each with jurisdiction over many agencies) has at the most a week of day-and-night work in which to frame the report after the subcommittee has "marked up" the bill in executive session.

In drafting the report, the departmental officers are sometimes consulted. In at least one case in recent years, the departmental budget officer sat through a week-end with the committee clerk in framing many parts of the report. Under these circumstances, naturally, the report is likely to contain remarks that later will provide fulcrums whereby the department can exercise leverage upon its self-assertive parts. Such a nexus of departmental leaders and committee clerks is more than interesting. It is highly significant, for it illustrates two things: first, that the disciplinary strains in government are not a simple alignment of administration as a whole against the legislative body; second, that the pressure of the legislative body may be exerted in fortifying the central machinery within the administration itself. . . .

The efficacy of committee reports is the fact that disregard of them may lead to a cut in appropriations in the following year. A follow-through is the more likely because, amid the vastness of the governmental operations as presented in the estimates, committees are repetitive; members repeat old questions and pursue old strictures. . . .

Sometimes the strictures in the reports merely put administrators under notice that certain results are expected and that information on them must be submitted in the future. There is endless variation, of course, in the nature of the compulsion applied, the response expected, and the time allowed. Thus notice is often served that, as a condition to the approval of funds for the year beyond that for which appropriations are being made, specified information must be presented to the subcommittee. The span of appraisal may be longer than a year. In the report a few years ago on agricultural appropriations the committee said of the four regional laboratories set up especially for the discovery of new outlets for farm products: "At the hearings the Department representatives were challenged to achieve results within ten years which will consume sufficient surpluses and be of sufficient commercial advantage to justify the expenditures under this head and if not to discontinue the laboratories. . . ."

Enough has been said to show the range of intervention in administration through language in reports to the appropriations committee. Much ambiguity attends this method of oversight. Several factors affect the degree to which an administrator must regard any particular bit of verbiage as mandatory. How precise is it? Was the point raised in the hearings and, if so, was it dwelt upon? Did the administrator himself make any admission or commitment? Did the legislative body give any especial attention to the item in question? Especially, was there a vote upon it, as in the rejection of an amendment not desired by the subcommittee? The foregoing are some of the circumstances which the administrator must consider. His exercise of judgment is apt to be harder because he must reckon with two chambers.

VIII

The discussion thus far has mainly concerned direct relations between subcommittees and administrators when appropriations are being made. It is appropriate to consider interim contacts during the year. As a background, it is necessary first to comment on the nature of appropriations in the national government of the United States.

The form and content of appropriating legislation in the national government have received very little analysis, official or academic. It has been the accretion of practice, for the most part stubbornly repetitive, but shaped in the past by countless forgotten situations. The result is highly uneven; there is no standard unit. Within the Department of Agriculture, as Verne Lewis has pointed out, some of the items "were as small as $5,000; other items were as large as $500,000,000."

Once a breakdown of appropriation items has become customary, the tendency is to perpetuate it. Comparison from year to year is aided by repetition, which indeed is encouraged by the law and by the Budget Bureau's instructions. Sometimes, where appropriations have been segregated, efforts at simplification are defeated by outraged subcommittee members who cling to items that have a local habitation and a name. . . .

The prevailing type of breakdown in national appropriations truly evades definition. "Lump sum" is hardly the term for it, apart from some emergency appropriations. But the usual categories are broad. Because of the scope of the ordinary item, the appropriation language itself leaves wide administrative leeway. A crucial question, therefore, is the continuing force of the highly detailed preparatory material: the estimates, the justifications, and remarks made by the administrators in the hearings. . . .

This is a difficult, highly empirical field for practical judgments by administrators on the nature of their obligation. The agencies differ in the degree to which they seek to stick literally to the estimates. Some find it easier than others; much depends on the tempo and the need for adjustment. . . . The attitude of different units varies with their experience. The head of a bureau which has been caught and chastised is jumpy and watchful. Some years ago the estimates meant less than they do now, but recently enough administrators have been in trouble to put all on guard. Sometimes, when consultation seems necessary in the face of a need to disregard the plan of expenditure in the estimates, the Bureau of the Budget is visited. But on occasion it is deemed advisable to clear with a House appropriations subcommittee.

Discipline may follow a departure from the estimates without prior consultation with the subcommittee. . . .

What is impressive, in tendency if not as matured fact, is the extent to which administrators meet with appropriations subcommittees in *ad hoc* sessions during the year. Sometimes the administrators themselves seek the contact as a safeguard; sometimes they are summoned for admonition or worse. The subcommittees vary in the degree to which they engage in such activity.

Much depends upon the chairman. But generally speaking, interim supervisory relationships are increasing.

IX

What has been said about continuous control leads directly to the relations of the appropriating groups to the Budget Bureau and generally to the organs of administrative management.

The degree of exactness with which the amounts of the annual appropriations follow the Budget estimates is beside the point of the present inquiry. Negatively, at least, a Budget recommendation is almost an absolute prerequisite of House action. Indeed, members of the Senate appropriations group complain that House conferees frustrate the Senate's initiative by standing in conference against any item that has not been recommended by the Budget. But this does not mean that the subcommittees are unwilling to go behind the Budget figure. Fairly typical was the question put by a subcommittee chairman to the representative of the Civil Aeronautics Authority: "We will start off by asking you how much you asked the Budget for." . . .

. . . The committees (ran the argument) need the complete and first-hand knowledge possessed by the bureau chiefs. Since "under our Budget plan, the function of the Executive is to propose and that of the legislative branch is to dispose, . . . the right to interrogate any and all witnesses on any pending matter of legislation and that of having such witnesses give responsive answers thereto is fundamental and inherent in the legislative branch." All this was put down "to clarify the minds of those in the Department who may have been entertaining unfounded misapprehensions. . . ."

There has been not a little Congressional sniping at the Bureau of the Budget. The subcommittees have at times seemed to be provoking the bureaus to revolt against Budget control. . . .

But collaboration is not absent between the Bureau of the Budget and the appropriations committees. An especially fruitful pattern of cooperation has been followed at times when the whole committee has become aware of a problem common to many of the appropriation bills and has requested the Bureau of the Budget to report on a solution. Thus in 1939 the question of a general policy about administrative promotions was handled in this way. The Bureau's study became the basis of a statute, reflected in turn in subsequent appropriation acts. The Bureau of the Budget has made other inquiries at the instance of the appropriating groups. The act of 1921 provided a broad basis for such requests. . . .

What about closer cooperation in the routine handling of the annual appropriations? Some informal contact already exists between the staffs of the Budget Bureau and the committees on appropriations. But further intimacy, especially if institutionalized, must be developed cautiously. A practicable minimum step would be to have the committee clerks attend the annual hearings before the estimates division of the Budget in the late summer and fall. The clerks, however, should not remain for the executive sessions in the afternoons wherein the Budget examiners discuss and decide tentatively upon revised figures for the units they have had before them in the morning. Even the first-mentioned step would require enlarged permanent staffs for the committees on appropriations. A reasonable minimum would be one experienced assistant clerk for each regular appropriation bill.

No amount of legislative staffing could take the place of executive supervision. Fitful legislative intervention is no substitute for controls within administration. The most valuable contribution of legislative oversight is to galvanize the disciplines of administration itself. It is significant that the reports of the appropriations committees abound in recommendations to administration that it investigate its procedures and organization, sometimes at the bureau or departmental level, sometimes above. The committees frequently disclaim competence for detailed constructive inquiry in these matters. The staff necessary for continuous inquiry could be maintained only at the risk of a harmful division of responsibility, while such a staff would still lack a first-hand sense of operations.

The hazard is that a body like Congress, when it gets into detail, ceases to be itself; it acts through a fraction which may be a faction. This, among other lessons, is a moral to be read in the work of the committees on appropriations.

THE PURSUIT OF A LEGISLATIVE PURPOSE

The Development of Congressional Investigative Power

NELSON MC GEARY

The history of congressional investigations in the United States is a record of a slowly but steadily broadening implied power of the national legislature. Although the authority of Congress to conduct inquiries and to compel the disclosure of information has at times suffered setbacks—including a serious rebuff from the United States Supreme Court in 1881—any ground lost has been recovered and eventually even extended.

The Investigatory Power

In 1792, within three years of the establishment of the new United States government, the House of Representatives provided for the first congressional investigation. A special committee of seven members, with power to send for persons and papers, was directed by a resolution to inquire into the reasons for the failure of the northwestern expedition led by Major General St. Clair against the Indians.

The members of the House did not doubt their power to conduct this investigation. Precedent for such inquiries, they felt, was readily available both in the British Parliament and in the legislatures of the American colonies. They believed that the power to appropriate implied the power to determine how appropriations were spent.

It is reasonable to estimate that during the century and a half since the St. Clair inquiry, as many as six hundred investigations have been conducted. For several decades the House of Representatives was the chief inquisitor; in the first forty years the House conducted seven or eight times as many inquiries as the Senate. In the 1920's, however, it could be said that the Senate had become the principal inquisitor; one writer went so far as to label the House as "impotent." This predominance of the role of the Senate, especially evident in the 1920's and 1930's, can be traced to the absence of effective cloture in that body inducing

From Nelson McGeary, *University of Chicago Law Review* (Spring 1951, Vol. 18, No. 3).

the approval of investigations sponsored by a minority. Although a tightly led majority in the House may throttle some inquiries, this, at present, by no means reduces the House to a minor role; in each of the last four sessions of Congress (1947-50), for example, the House has authorized more investigations than the Senate.

For almost a hundred years following the St. Clair investigation, congressional inquiries were subject to little supervision or control by the judiciary. And although the Senate got a later start than the House, both chambers frequently used the investigatory power, not only to inquire into the honesty and efficiency of the executive branch of the government, but also to obtain information to assist Congress in its task of legislating wisely and intelligently. In addition, a number of inquiries aided one or the other house to perform duties relating to its own members, such as judging the qualifications and conduct of individuals elected to Congress, and punishing persons attempting to bribe members.

Little opposition ever developed in Congress itself to its right to authorize investigations into the administration of the law or into "membership" matters. But there were differences of opinion concerning the legality of inquiries directed at obtaining information to help in the enactment of laws. It was not until 1928 that the House established the precedent of vesting in a committee the power to compel witnesses to testify in a law-making investigation. When the resolution providing for this extension of the investigatory power was being considered in the House, considerable opposition arose. Following lengthy debate, however, the victory went to those representatives who argued that only through the compulsion of testimony could the necessary facts be learned. The acute division of opinion was nevertheless revealed in the vote of 102 for the resolution and 88 against.

Investigations to aid in legislating also were strenuously opposed in the Senate, where no inquiry of this type was approved until 1859, at which time the upper house established a special committee to inquire into the facts "attending the late invasion and seizure of the armory and arsenal at Harper's Ferry."

Although not all congressional investigating committees need the power to compel the attendance and testimony of witnesses, numerous inquiries would be fruitless if the power to compel disclosure were not exercised. Both the House and Senate, accordingly, from the early days of their inquisitorial careers, have granted to many investigating committees the power to send for papers and persons. For some decades Congress enforced this authority by means of its common-law power to punish for contempt. Witnesses who remained recalcitrant when brought before the bar of the Senate or House were on occasion imprisoned and also fined. But the length of a prison sentence could not extend beyond the close of the legislative session during which the contempt occurred.

Partly because of this limitation, Congress in 1857 enacted a statute providing that a witness who, having been summoned, refused to appear or to answer pertinent questions or produce papers before an investigating committee, was guilty of a misdemeanor, punishable by "a fine of not more than $1,000 nor less than $100 and imprisonment in a common jail for not less than one month nor more than twelve months." Whenever a witness failed to obey a summons, a statement of the facts was to be certified by the President of the Senate or the Speaker of the House, as the case might be, to the "appropriate United States attorney, whose duty it shall be to bring the matter before the grand jury for its action."

If either house of Congress finds it difficult or undesirable to seek punishment of a witness by means of this statute in the courts, it can fall back on its own common-law authority to punish. Moreover, the United States Supreme Court has held that both forms of punishment can be inflicted on the same individual.[1]

The 1857 contempt statute was not used extensively at first. Three years after its enactment, for example, when the Senate chose to punish one Thaddeus Hyatt for his refusal to appear before the committee investigating the raid on Harper's Ferry, it invoked its own inherent power, not the statute, to commit the witness to jail. After the United States Supreme Court in 1880[2] decreed that the courts could review the congressional power to punish for contempt, however, both houses made increasing use of the statute. At the present time, therefore, when either house wishes to punish a recalcitrant witness, the usual procedure calls for a certification of the facts for court action. That Congress still occasionally relies on its own power is illustrated by the action

[1] *In re Chapman,* 166 U.S. 661, 672 (1897).
[2] *Kilbourn* v. *Thompson,* 103 U.S. 168 (1880).

of the Senate in jailing a Washington lawyer who, after being served with a subpoena *duces tecum* for papers relating to air mail contracts, first allowed clients to remove several letters from his files.[3]

Kilbourn v. Thompson and After

The congressional investigating power, after almost a century of relatively calm sailing, during which time it was shored up by a mass of precedent and by a number of contempt cases in the courts, suddenly ran into a serious judicial storm. In *Kilbourn v. Thompson,* one of the two major pronouncements on the power of congressional investigation, the Supreme Court sharply narrowed the scope of the power.

The occasion for this decision was an inquiry by a special House Committee into the nature and history of a "real estate pool" and transactions involved in the bankruptcy of Jay Cooke & Co. The House resolution, which granted the Committee the power to compel testimony, stressed the government's interest in the case as a result of "improvident deposits" of public money having been made with the London branch of the bankrupt company. The manager of the pool, Hallet Kilbourn, who had been brought before the Committee to testify concerning the pool, refused to produce certain papers and declined to answer the question: "Will you state where each of the five members reside, and will you please state their names?"

Kilbourn, arrested by the sergeant-at-arms of the House of Representatives, was brought before the bar of the House where he still refused to comply with the Committee's requests. The House thereupon approved a resolution declaring him to be in contempt and directed that he be kept in custody until he was ready to produce papers and answer the question. Remaining in the common jail of the District of Columbia for forty-five days, he then was released in habeas corpus proceedings by the Chief Justice of the Supreme Court of the District of Columbia. After unsuccessfully suing the sergeant-at-arms, as well as the Speaker of the House and members of the Committee, for false imprisonment, Kilbourn appealed to the United States Supreme Court.

Mr. Justice Miller, speaking for the Court, vigorously attacked the House resolution. "To inquire into the nature and history of

[3] *Jurney* v. *MacCracken,* 294 U.S. 125 (1935).

the real estate pool," he exclaimed, "[how] indefinite!" He denounced the resolution as containing

no hint of any intention of final action by Congress on the subject. . . . Was it to be simply a fruitless investigation into the personal affairs of individuals? If so, the House of Representatives had no power or authority in the matter more than any other equal number of gentlemen interested for the government of their country.

The Court argued that the House had assumed a "clearly judicial" power which "could only be properly exercised by another branch of the government." And, to drive home further the point that Congress' investigative powers are limited, the Court refused to "concede that the Houses of Congress possess this general power of punishing for contempt. The cases in which they can do this are very limited." Kilbourn's imprisonment, said the Court, had been unlawful.

The *Kilbourn* decision, therefore, required of all investigations a clear and precise constitutional purpose. At the same time it seemed to support the thesis that a broad area of the private affairs of citizens is immune from congressional scrutiny. Even more important, perhaps, the Court doubted the existence of a power to inquire and punish for contempt "to enable either House of Congress to exercise successfully their function of legislation. . . ." The issue was side-stepped, however, when Justice Miller explained that "[t]his latter proposition is one which we do not propose to decide in the present case, because we are able to decide it without passing upon the existence or nonexistence of such a power in aid of the legislative function." The net result of the decision, therefore, was that for almost half a century serious doubt was cast on the very existence of a congressional power to compel testimony for the principal purpose of obtaining information to assist Congress in drafting legislation.

In spite of this grave doubt, both houses of Congress zealously continued to investigate. In most instances the motives of the inquiries were mixed. Many investigations continued to have the principal purpose of helping the legislature to discharge its function of holding administrative officers to a strict accountability; such inquiries ranged all the way from a deliberate attack on an administrator or an executive agency to an ascertainment of the needs of a department. An administrator's knowledge that at some future time he and his activities might be subjects of congressional investigation has probably been the principal external deterrent to wrong-doing in the executive branch. Probably the bulk of the inquiries, however, were conducted for the principal or supplementary purpose of obtaining facts which would suggest to the legislators what, if any, legislation was desirable. Moreover, as means of mass communication developed throughout the nation, congressmen became increasingly aware of the potentialities of investigations as useful tools for disseminating facts and ideas and for moulding public opinion. This shaping of opinion, which generally is an aim collateral to the effort of Congress to enact legislation or to supervise the executive branch, may sometimes remedy any wrongs exposed without the necessity of passing legislation. In any event, many committees conduct their investigations in such a way as to try to generate public opinion behind recommended statutes. While congressional committees have always made use of inquiries to shape opinion, the techniques of doing so were most fully developed in the twentieth century.

Investigation and Administration

The first major high point of congressional investigative activity had occurred in the Grant Administration when free-flowing charges of corruption had brought a surge of investigation into the executive branch. Another period of swell came in the latter part of Woodrow Wilson's Administration, when the majority of Congress was of a different party then the President; during the last two years of Wilson's second term, fifty-one inquiries were in progress. It was in the days of the Teapot Dome scandals during the Harding Administration, however, that congressional investigations reached heights of importance and public attention which have never been exceeded. Led by men like Senators Walsh and Wheeler, the Senate occupied the predominant role in this inquisitorial epoch.

A somewhat subtle change in the emphasis of congressional investigations took shape in the 1930's after the election of President Roosevelt. From the very first inquiry in 1792, one purpose of many investigations had been to embarrass the Administration or to hold it in check. Congressmen, when they investigated the executive branch, not infrequently were politically motivated; they sought electioneering ammunition with as much earnestness as they delved for information to aid in legislating. Chief Executives, on their part, had always been aware of the possibilities of using sympathetic committee investigators as "vehicles of vindication" for the Administration. A peak for investigations calculated to curb the Administration was reached in the 1920's when malfeasance and misfeasance had entered administration. But the early days of the New Deal—when, in contrast to the previous decade, a strong congressional majority, led by the President, was committed to a program of social change—witnessed a demonstration of the possibilities of direct aid to an Administration by means of investigation. Thus some inquiries were neatly arranged to reinforce recommendations by the President concerning major legislation. The exposures in 1933 and 1934 by the Senate committee investigating stock exchange practices and banking, for example, contributed markedly to the enactment of such Administration-supported legislation as the Banking Acts of 1933 and 1935, the Securities Act of 1933, and the Securities and Exchange Act of 1934. Other possibilities of co-operation between an investigating committee and the Administration were suggested when the Senate Committee on Interstate Commerce conducted an inquiry into the financing of railroads partly for the purpose of acquiring information which the Interstate Commerce Commission felt it did not have the power to obtain. . . .

McGrain v. Daugherty and After

One of the inquiries of the 1920's provided the occasion for the United States Supreme Court to record its second major opinion on the subject of the congressional investigative power. The doubts which had existed as a result of the *Kilbourn* case, as to the right of the legislature to unearth facts to assist in the framing of legislation, were dispelled by *McGrain v. Daugherty.*

The controversy in this case arose in the course of an investigation by a Senate Select Committee into the administration of the Department of Justice under ex-Attorney General Harry Daugherty. The Senate resolution providing for the inquiry referred to the alleged failure of Mr. Daugherty to prosecute and defend cases wherein the government of the United States was interested. The appellee in the case was Mally S. Daugherty, the president of an Ohio bank and the brother of Harry Daugherty. During the hearings the Committee served a subpoena on Mally

Daugherty requiring him to appear and testify and to bring with him certain of his bank's records. When he failed to appear, a second subpoena ordered him to come before the Committee, but made no reference to records or papers. Again the witness did not comply; nor did he offer any excuse.

An aroused Senate thereupon approved a resolution ordering that Daugherty be brought before the bar of the Senate to answer questions pertinent to the investigation. "The appearance and testimony of the said M. S. Daugherty," stated the resolution, "is material and necessary in order that the committee may . . . obtain information necessary as a basis for such legislative and other action as the Senate may deem necessary and proper."

Following the arrest of Daugherty by John J. McGrain, deputy sergeant-at-arms of the Senate, however, the Cincinnati federal district court in a habeas corpus proceeding discharged Daugherty from the custody of the deputy.

The Supreme Court, although it heard the case argued late in 1924, did not hand down its decision reversing the lower court until early 1927. The unanimous opinion, written by Mr. Justice Van Devanter, brushed aside the contention of Daugherty that the *Kilbourn* case strongly intimated, if it did not actually hold, that neither house of Congress has power to make inquiries and exact evidence in aid of contemplated legislation. The justices recognized Congress' power of investigation by clearly approving inquiries conducted to help Congress legislate. "The power of inquiry—with process to enforce it—is an essential and appropriate auxiliary to the legislative function," insisted Mr. Justice Van Devanter. Either house of Congress

> has power, through its own processes, to compel a private individual to appear before it or one of its committees and give testimony needed to enable it efficiently to exercise a legislative function belonging to it under the Constitution. . . . The power is so far incidental to the legislative function as to be implied.

The Court declared that the administration of the Department of Justice which was the subject of the investigation in question, was "[p]lainly [a subject] on which legislation could be had." The original resolution creating the committee did not expressly state a legislative intent and the justices believed such a statement was unnecessary.

McGrain v. Daugherty did not grant to Congress an unfettered power of investigation. Justice Van Devanter carefully pointed out that limitations do exist. He affirmed *Kilbourn v. Thompson*, for example, by agreeing that "neither house is invested with general power to inquire into private affairs and compel disclosures," and that "a witness rightfully may refuse to answer where the bounds of the power are exceeded or the questions are not pertinent to the matter under inquiry." These limitations, however, have been employed very little by courts in recent years to restrict congressional investigating committees.

The courts, in the instances where they have had occasion to discuss the congressional investigative power, have been liberal in allowing committees to proceed unmolested; and, almost without exception, they have supported the committees in their contests with witnessess. Still it has never been determined precisely how far a committee may search into the private affairs of a citizen. The Fourth and Fifth Amendments to the Constitution of course serve as checks on the methods used by committees but courts seem to be increasingly unwilling either to refuse to sustain a committee's actions or to interfere with inquiries in any way.

That the courts are now holding only loose rein on congressional investigators is nowhere more clearly demonstrated than in the opinion by Justice Holtzoff in *United States* v. *Bryan.* The case resulted when Helen R. Bryan and three other persons refused to produce papers subpoenaed by the House Committee on Un-American Activities. In the opinion are interesting comments relating to the general power of Congress to investigate. Justice Holtzoff readily acknowledged that Congress cannot compel the divulgence of information for the purpose of learning whether a crime was committed, to be used as a basis for a criminal prosecution; but he went on to explain that if the same information is wanted for use in connection with legislation, Congress has a right to demand it.

If the subject under scrutiny may have *any possible relevancy and materiality, no matter how remote,* to some possible legislation, it is within the power of the Congress to investigate the matter. Moreover, the relevancy and the materiality of the subject matter must be presumed. The burden is on one who maintains the contrary to establish his contention. It would be intolerable if the judiciary were to intrude into the activities of the legislative branch of the Government, and virtually stop the progress of an investigation, which is intended to secure information that Congress deems necessary and desirable in the proper exercise of its functions, unless the lack of materiality and relevancy of the subject matter is clear and manifest [emphasis supplied].

If this quoted paragraph can serve as an accurate delineator of the congressional power of investigation, it is difficult to conceive of many subjects which would not be valid fields for inquiry. It is a well known fact that the powers of Congress enumerated in the Constitution, especially the commerce power and the spending power, have been so drastically expanded by court interpretation as to permit national legislation in fields of almost boundless variety. And each time that Congress' power of legislation is broadened, it follows that the power of investigation is similarly expanded. If, in accordance with the *Bryan* case, Congress may secure information "unless the lack of materiality and relevance of the subject matter is clear and manifest," and if the Senate and House are permitted to make inquiries into subjects "no matter how remote" their relevancy to legislation, the restrictions on the permissible fields of inquiry are extremely loose.

Although the courts frequently reiterate that the congressional power of inquiry is not unrestricted, they appear to be most reluctant to hold that a particular investigation has gone beyond proper bounds. A majority of the United States Court of Appeals of the District of Columbia, for example, in holding that a congressional committee could require an individual to answer whether he was a believer in communism or a member of the Communist Party, waved aside evidence which was critical of the behavior of the House Un-American Activities Committee:

The remedy for unseemly conduct, if any, by Committees of Congress is for Congress, or for the people. . . . The courts have no authority to speak or act upon the conduct by the legislative branch of its own business, so long as the bounds of power and pertinency are not exceeded.[4]

The "bounds of power and pertinency" are so indistinct, however, that congressional committees can apparently now conduct investigations with little fear that the courts will throw a tight harness over them. Yet it is not true that committees always obtain the information they seek. Some refusals by witnesses to

[4] *Barsky* v. *United States*, 167 F. 2d 241 (App. D.C., 1948), cert. denied 334 U.S. 843 (1948).

testify or to produce subpoenaed papers pass without serious challenge. A committee may choose not to press for an answer because the same information is available from another source or because the members decide that the procurement of the information from the witness is hardly worth the time and trouble of obtaining Senate or House approval of a resolution providing for coercive or punitive proceedings. A committee which insists, however, likely will get the information it seeks or will have the satisfaction of seeing the recalcitrant witness punished.

The Separation of Powers Limitation

There is one major exception, however, to the general rule that a persistent congressional investigating committee can pry loose the information it seeks. Because of the separation of powers, it is not entirely clear how far Congress can go in requiring testimony and papers from the executive branch of the government. On occasion, when a committee runs into a direct collision with the President, the former returns empty handed. Such conflicts are relatively infrequent, but American history has been spotted with them from Washington to Truman. The first President's cabinet set precedent, when called upon for papers, by asserting "that the executive ought to communicate such papers as the public good would permit and ought to refuse those the disclosure of which would injure the public."

When Congress asks for information the executive branch usually complies; to do otherwise might create unnecessary and damaging suspicion of the motives of the administrator. Moreover, Congress, through its control over appropriations, can exert powerful pressure on an administrator to submit requested information. But Wolkinson, in an admittedly incomplete compilation, lists refusals by seventeen Presidents and their heads of departments to comply with requests from Congress or its committees for information and papers. When a President declines to divulge information, it has become customary for him to state that the disclosure "would not be compatible with the public interest." Such replies may not satisfy the Senate or the House; angry legislators may rise to the floor to blast the Chief Executive or other administrators. But although both houses of Congress have always asserted their right to procure information from the executive branch, they have never forced a final showdown on their power by persisting in their demands. Actually, the question involved here may not be justiciable.

Although a number of Presidents on occasion have declined to submit information to Congress, such refusals, as has been seen, have been relatively rare. Probably no one President stands out as the chief withholder, although Andrew Jackson's refusal to supply requested information remains one of the most significant incidents. It is of interest in the present day, therefore, that at least one Senator currently complains that "the number of occasions in which Congress has met with executive rebuff has greatly increased in recent years." This situation is in direct contrast to the 1930's and President Roosevelt's first two terms, when, as has been noted, congressional inquiries were directed more at aiding than at supervising the Administration. Under President Truman the emphasis of some investigations shifted partially to an attempt to embarrass or discredit the Administration. In such an atmosphere the Administration on several occasions refused to comply with congressional requests for information. Most, if not all, of the requests that were turned down were aimed at obtaining copies of reports by the Federal Bureau of Investigation and other investigative agencies of the executive branch concerning the loyalty of certain government employees. The President, early in 1948, clarified his position in a memorandum to all officers and employees of the executive branch:

> The efficient and just administration of the employee loyalty program, under Executive Order No. 9835 of March 21, 1947, requires that reports, records, and files relative to the program be preserved in strict confidence. This is necessary in the interest of our national security and welfare, to preserve the confidential character and sources of information furnished, and to protect Government personnel against the dissemination of unfounded or disproved allegations. It is necessary also in order to insure the fair and just disposition of loyalty cases.
>
> For these reasons, and in accordance with the long-established policy that reports rendered by the Federal Bureau of Investigation and other investigative agencies of the executive branch are to be regarded as confidential, all reports, records, and files relative to the loyalty of employees or prospective employees (including reports of such investigative agencies), shall be maintained in confidence, and shall not be transmitted or disclosed except as required in the efficient conduct of business.
>
> Any subpoena or demand or request for information, reports, or files of the nature described, received from sources other than those persons

in the executive branch of the Government who are entitled thereto by reason of their official duties, shall be respectfully declined, on the basis of this directive, and the subpoena or demand or other request shall be referred to the Office of the President for such response as the President may determine to be in the public interest in the particular case. There shall be no relaxation of the provisions of this directive except with my express authority.

This statement of policy has formed the basis for refusals of information to at least three congressional investigating committees.

The alleged power of the chief executive to decide whether the disclosure of a specified report or other information is or is not compatible with the public interest represents in practice an important limitation on the congressional power of inquiry.

The Need for Restraint

Although the executive branch may erect troublesome road blocks on the paths of congressional investigations, those committees which seek information from private citizens apparently may pursue their courses with a minimum of judicial control. True, the Bill of Rights of the United States Constitution has not been repealed. But if the resolution providing for an inquiry expressly states or at least implies a legislative intent, however remote, the restrictions which remain on the congressional investigatory power seem to be almost meaningless.

Even casual observers of American government are aware of the barrage of criticism that in recent years has been hurled at the procedures of congressional investigating committees. While a portion of this censure is of the sore-head variety, much of it is thoughtful and obviously justified. Many committees conduct their inquiries with a proper amount of decorum and with concern for the rights of those citizens who are being investigated, but a minority of the investigations deserve strong condemnation for their excesses. In some inquiries, for example, no effort is made to establish the credibility of witnesses, and an accused person has no opportunity to present evidence in his own behalf.

It has become increasingly evident since the case of *McGrain v. Daugherty* that the major responsibility for preventing misuse of the power of investigation rests on Congress itself. Among some senators and representatives there appears at the mid-century to be increased concern over the injuries which unbridled investigations are inflicting on the prestige and dignity of Congress. Members of Congress as well as outside observers have offered a variety of proposed codes of procedure to govern Senate and House investigators. Whether or not such a code is enacted, however, some reliance must always rest on the sense of justice and restraint of individual investigators.

THE FUSION OF POLICY AND OVERSIGHT

Congress and the Atom

HENRY M. JACKSON

Few students of government would acknowledge the birth of the atomic age as a landmark in the history of American constitutional law; yet the pattern of relations which has evolved between the Congress and the executive branch in atomic energy is almost as unique as the splitting of the atom itself.

The ordinary government agency functions in a glare of publicity. Through the sheer force of public opinion, the people can themselves often shape official policy. But not so in atomic energy. The world of the atom is covered with a veil of secrecy. And even if secret data were more widely circulated, few laymen could understand their full import unless prepared to spend long and arduous hours in a study of atomic problems and issues. Against this background, five Atomic Energy Commissioners, whose only tangible link with the American people is their appointment by the President and their confirmation by the Senate, have been empowered to make decisions which not only affect our hopes for material advancement, but which may very well determine our national survival.

Responsibility of the Joint Committee on Atomic Energy

These were the considerations in the mind of the Congress when, seven years ago, it created the Joint Committee on Atomic Energy to oversee the national atomic energy program on behalf of the Congress and the American people. The McMahon Act of

From Henry M. Jackson, *The Annals of the American Academy of Political and Social Science* (November 1953, Vol. 290, pp. 76-81), American Academy of Political and Social Science, Philadelphia.

1946, which established the civilian Atomic Energy Commission, also created the Joint Committee and required it "to make continuing studies of the activities of the Atomic Energy Commission and of problems relating to the development, use, and control of atomic energy." In turn, the Commission was required to keep the Joint Committee "fully and currently informed" concerning its programs.

As long as one speaks in the traditional language of constitutional law—with its black-and-white divisions between co-ordinate and coequal branches of the government—it is difficult to define the Joint Committee's precise role in atomic policy-making. This watchdog group has been accused both of running the atomic energy program, and of acting as a mere captive of the Commission. Neither view is correct. In truth, the Committee and the Commission jointly run the atomic program. Fundamental policy, though normally originating within the Commission, tends to be made with the advice and consent of the congressional committee. And in the case of certain vital policy decisions, the urging from the Joint Committee has played so powerful a role that it can be said the Committee made the decisions, with the advice and consent of the executive branch.

Some may lament this dual responsibility, arguing that it blurs vital divisions of authority between legislators and administrators. Others may insist that, in atomic energy, the power of Congress must be very great, in order to offset the immense authority afforded the executive branch in the McMahon Act. However history may judge this unique Committee-Commission relationship, it cannot be doubted that it now merits the closest possible examination by students of political science.

The McMahon Act entitles the Committee only to be kept "fully and currently informed" concerning the activities of the Commission. This mere right to know, with no legal authority to direct or supervise, may seem at first glance a frail foundation for Committee authority. Yet in atomic energy, this simple right to know highly classified information in and of itself confers immense powers of moral suasion upon the Committee. Here, in a most literal sense, knowledge is power.

Apart from the highly classified documents which the Atomic Energy Commission regularly transmits, the Joint Committee itself originates many secret papers covering all phases of the atomic program. It keeps in daily and intimate touch with the defense establishment, the State Department, the Central Intelligence Agency, the Federal Bureau of Investigation, and the National Security Council. Every effort is made, through a twenty-four-hour armed guard over the Committee offices and through appropriate use of vaults, safes soundproofing, electronic devices, exclusion areas, FBI investigations of staff personnel, and the like, to maintain standards of security vigilance at least as high as those maintained within the executive branch.

Role of the Joint Committee

The great fund of secret knowledge entrusted to the Committee has created a number of dilemmas for its membership. From a strictly legal standpoint, the watchdog group is required only to keep itself abreast of atomic developments. Should it therefore play a passive role, accepting the information furnished it and expressing no opinions of its own? Or should it assume an active role? If the latter, should it pass judgment on decisions of the executive branch only after they are made? Or should the Committee take a position before far-reaching issues are decided? And if the Committee is to regard its mandate in this active sense, where should it draw the line in intervening in the affairs of the executive branch—where does prudent stewardship end and destructive meddling begin?

The question may be asked in specific ways. Should the Committee urge the building of certain plants which it feels that the interests of national security require? The Committee has in fact made such urgings. Should the Committee have access to confidential FBI reports on atomic employees?" The Committee in fact has such access—the only group of Congress that does. Should the Committee insist upon seeing the internal staff papers of the Commission and the minutes of the Commission's meetings? The Committee has never so insisted, because the members respect the Commission's need for a certain privacy in its internal functioning. Should the Committee be informed of Commission decisions before they are reached, or only afterward? In actual practice, it knows about the big issues well in advance of any solution, but on lesser matters it is often advised following a decision.

How about the awarding of contracts, the hiring of Commission personnel, and the selection of plant sites? Should the Committee participate in these matters? In practice, it has not participated. It has followed a strictly hands-off policy—and rightly so, I believe.

Common-Sense Wisdom

It may be wondered how the Committee—composed as it is of laymen—can possibly know enough about the technical facts of atomic energy to formulate sensible policy conclusions. The Committee, true, has come to rely upon the advice of its small but highly trained professional staff. Yet I do not believe this goes to the heart of the matter. If the Joint Committee members can make rational decisions on high questions of atomic policy—as I believe they do—it is, I think, primarily because laymen may well be better qualified than specialists to play the role of basic policy-makers. After having worked with atomic problems for some years, I am deeply convinced that wise policy—in the sense of basic programmatic decisions—depends far less than most people imagine upon an exquisite technical acquaintance with atomics. A minimum understanding of the specialized lore of atomic energy is of course indispensable. Yet such knowledge can be translated into rational public policy only by decision-makers who can relate it meaningfully to the totality of human and historical experience.

A few examples may help to make my point. Just a few years ago, many technically trained people insisted that the supply of uranium raw materials was rigidly limited, and that such fixity of supply placed a sharp upper limit on the output of atomic weapons. Not a single member of the Joint Committee possesses a mining degree. But even as laymen, they knew that in the case of copper or iron or gold or almost any raw material which can be named, greater exploration and mining effort pays off in greater production. So, the views of many technicians to the contrary notwithstanding, the members of the watchdog group concluded that our nation could procure uranium in far greater quantities if it was willing to pay the necessary price; and of course this turned out to be so.

Again a few years ago, many military experts insisted that atomic bombs could never be carried by fighter planes against tactical targets; they argued that the bomb simply could not be made small enough or light enough. Once more, no member of the Joint Committee really understood the intimate details of weapons technology. But as laymen, they could recall no piece of ordnance within human experience which could not be refined or improved or reduced in size. In addition, they sensed that even the experts in the infant science of atomics had no more final knowledge about atomic weapons than the experts had final and complete knowledge of aerodynamics at the time the Wright brothers flew at Kitty Hawk. Many of the Committee members therefore urged—years before the doctrine gained wide acceptance in the Pentagon—that atomic weapons could and should be adapted to tactical uses.

Perhaps this is only another way of saying that the congressional watchdog committee has served as the guardian of the obvious in atomic energy. It has tried to make sure that the simple propositions and the everyday truths are not overlooked in the world of atomics, as they can be so easily in a subject which is synonymous with complexity. Ours is an age, if I may be permitted a philosophical digression, which revels in complicated technics and subtle philosophies. We peer into the most distant reaches of the universe and try to divine the ultimate meaning of things. But in so doing, we may sometimes overlook what is standing directly in front of our faces. The memorable admonition of Justice Holmes, that the vindication of the obvious is as important as the elucidation of the obscure, has not lost its relevance in this atomic age.

Leading Rather than Restraining

Not that the history of these first years of the atomic era will ever be entitled "The Joint Committee was always right." Far from it. Although the Committee has consistently led the executive branch in its insistence on an all-out weapons production program, I regret that it did not press for an expanded effort even earlier and even more vigorously than it did. And the same holds true on the peacetime side of the atom. The Committee's present chairman, to his great credit, is urging that our nation achieve a practical demonstration of useful atomic power as soon as is humanly possible.

This much, at any rate, is clear: This watchdog group simply does not conform to the popular stereotype of a congressional committee. Most people think of legislative committees as veto groups—as bodies overridingly concerned with holding the executive branch in check and preventing capricious acts. This is of course one of the vital jobs of the Joint Committee, and it performs it as best it can. More often than not, however, the Committee finds itself saying to the executive branch not "Do less; do it more cautiously," but "Do more; do it more boldly." And for every time the members ask "Isn't this program too ambitious?" they find themselves asking a dozen times "Isn't this program too cautious?"

This often surprises newcomers to Washington and to the executive branch. Having been reared on the doctrine that the executive branch proposes and the Congress disposes, they appear for the first time as Joint Committee witnesses, expecting to earn their battle stripes through defending their plans against charges of excessive boldness. But, to their surprise, they normally find themselves winning their Purple Hearts while fending off charges of excessive timidity.

Procedure and Leadership

The Committee is not very often in the headlines—which, I believe, is all to the good. Its work proceeds informally, with a minimum of fuss and feathers and klieg lights. In conformance with necessary security requirements, about three-quarters of the hundreds of meetings the Committee has held have taken place in executive session. The members have heard testimony from virtually every ranking government official, scientist, and military man connected in any way with atomic energy. At least once a year members or staff representatives inspect each field installation of the Commission, of which there are dozens. Trips to such major sites as Hanford, Oak Ridge, Los Alamos, Savannah River, and Paducah occur routinely at much more frequent intervals.

The performance of any congressional committee in large part reflects the quality of its chairman. On this score, the Joint Committee has been singularly fortunate. It is impossible to overestimate the contributions of the late Senator Brien McMahon to the national atomic energy program. He will be long remembered as sponsor of the Atomic Energy Act of 1946, and as a magnificently able chairman of the Joint Committee. Senator

Bourke Hickenlooper, the first chairman of the Joint Committee, earned this nation's gratitude for his largely single-handed—and successful—fight to save the atomic energy appropriations during the waning hours of the Eighty-second Congress. Congressman Carl Durham took the initiative in pressing for hearings on atomic power. The Committee's present chairman, Congressman Sterling Cole, has already won the respect and admiration of his colleagues on both sides of the aisle. In the Joint Committee, this aisle has become of less and less significance; the Committee has a firm, long, and growing tradition of bipartisanship.

Appropriations Procedure

When the McMahon Act was under consideration, Congress tended to believe that both international control and industrial power from the atom might soon become realities. It therefore seemed sensible to furnish sweeping authorization for the appropriating of funds, since such authorization, besides smoothing the path of the civilian Commission in its first year or two in office, might shortly give way to different provisions. But what may have made sense in 1946 does not necessarily make sense today.

The Joint Committee, even now, is not empowered to report out authorizing or enabling bills—to the great detriment, I think, of the atomic program. If the Department of Defense wishes to construct a radar network or a new air base, four steps are necessary to secure congressional approval. The relevant legislative committees—that is, the Armed Services Committees of the House and the Senate—must report out an enabling or authorizing bill, which the Congress must pass. The Appropriations Committee must then report out a bill providing funds for the project in question, and the Congress must also pass this.

The wisdom of such a procedure has been demonstrated again and again. The relevant legislative committees which first evaluate a new construction program of the executive branch are uniquely equipped, through their specialized knowledge and experience, to decide whether it is desirable. If these committees place their seal of approval on the project through a favorable authorizing bill, the Appropriations Committees are subsequently assisted in considering the project from the point of view of how much money should be voted on its behalf, and how such sums will fit into the nation's over-all budget. The legislative committees, in these cases, serve as programmatic experts in their respective fields, and the Appropriations Committees serve as general fiscal experts.

The logic of such a procedure would seem especially compelling in atomic energy. Here, it is simply impossible to estimate the desirability of Commission-sponsored construction programs unless one has great familiarity with the atomic project—a familiarity which can be acquired only through day-by-day contact with the program. Although they are men of great judgment, ability, and experience, the members of the Appropriations Committees have immense demands on their time, and they have not acquired specialized competence in matters atomic. For the most part, their acquaintance with the program is transient and casual.

The ensuing difficulties can be illustrated by a hypothetical case. Suppose the Commission plans a reactor development program which may ultimately cost hundreds of millions of dollars. Suppose the Joint Committee, after holding detailed hearings, believes that the program is undesirable. Suppose it believes that construction of the proposed reactors is premature at this time. Let us even suppose that the Committee becomes convinced, on the basis of expert scientific testimony, that building the reactors would represent an extravagant waste of resources, or that the possibility of a radiation accident might endanger the lives of people living near the reactor sites. In any such cases the Commission would remain legally free (so broad is its present authorization) to proceed as it saw fit, provided it secured funds from the Appropriations Committees.

The resultant danger of ill-advised action is less acute in the Senate than in the House. Senate rules permit three members of the Joint Committee to sit as ex officio members of the Senate Appropriations Committee when the atomic budget is being considered. The regular members of the Appropriations Committee have come to heed the counsel of their ex officio colleagues, and the Senate has exhibited great responsibility and rare discrimination in its handling of atomic energy appropriations.

Efforts to institute a similar arrangement on the House side have so far proved unavailing. Fearing encroachments upon its prerogatives, the House Appropriations Committee has denied requests for ex officio participation in its deliberations by Joint Committee members when the atomic budget is being studied.

The House approach to appropriations in the atomic field has accordingly suffered, and on several occasions dangerous cuts have been restored only when the appropriations bills of the two Houses have been reconciled in conference.

Last year, for instance, the House Appropriations Committee —with the laudable objective of encouraging economy, but with mistaken notions of how to bring it about—reported out an atomic energy appropriations bill whose restrictive riders would have seriously delayed completion of the vast plant expansion program which had just been launched by the executive branch. The Senate—thanks in good part to the missionary work of its Joint Committee members—resisted the House-endorsed bill. After a dramatic all-night debate which delayed the adjournment of the Congress, the Senate view prevailed and the atomic expansion program was permitted to go forward unimpaired.

"The Atomic Equation"

It would be both impractical and unnecessary to desire that every legislator acquire in atomic energy the kind of competence possessed by Joint Committee members. The whole point of the committee system of operation, after all, is to provide for specialists in public policy—for experts whose knowledge of some particular field transcends that of their congressional colleagues. So it should occasion no alarm if not all legislators are qualified to decide whether the Commission should build plant X or plant Y, or whether it should concentrate on developing this or that model of atomic weapon.

What can and must be asked, however, is that every last member of the Congress understand the meaning of "the atomic equation"—the terrible portent of the growing stockpiles of atomic weapons now being amassed on both sides of the Iron Curtain. What can and must be asked is that every member of the Congress recognize the imperative necessity of maintaining and increasing our atomic lead over the Soviets. What can and must be asked, finally, is that the entire Congress recognize that the atom has two sides—that the same materials which can destroy society in the form of atomic weapons can immeasurably enrich our lives if harnessed in the form of perceptive applications of atomic energy.

SECTION V *The Meaning of Modern Representative Government*

Chapter Nine

ASPECTS OF THE CONTROVERSY: Mobocracy, Power Elite, Benevolent Myth

BEWARE THE LEGISLATURE

The Devitalization of Executive Power

WALTER LIPPMANN

1. *The Elected Executive*

Our inquiry has shown, I believe, that we cannot take popular government for granted, as if its principles were settled and beyond discussion. We are compelled to agree with Sir Henry Maine who wrote, some seventy years ago, that "the actual history of popular government since it was introduced, in its modern shape, into the civilized world," does "little to support the assumption that popular government has an indefinitely long future before it. Experience rather tends to show that it is characterized by great fragility and that since its appearance, all forms of government have become more insecure than they were before."

We have been dwelling upon the devitalization of the executive power as the cause of the fragility that Maine speaks of. It is, I have been saying, the disorder which results from a functional derangement in the relationship between the executive power on the other hand, the representative assemblies and the mass electorates on the other hand.

Democratic states are susceptible to this derangement because congenitally the executive, when dependent on election, is weaker than the elected representatives. The normal drainage of power in a democratic state is away from the governing center and down into the constituencies. And the normal tendency of elections is to reduce elected officers to the role of agents or organized pluralities. Modern democratic governments are, to be sure, big governments, in their personnel, in the range and variety of their projects, the ubiquitousness of their interventions. But to be big is not necessarily to be strong. They are, in fact, swollen rather than strong, being too weak to resist the pressure of special interests and of the departmental bureaucracies.

As a rule competition in the electoral market works like Gresham's law: the soft money drives the hard money out of circulation. The competitive odds are heavily against the candidate who, like Burke with the electors of Bristol, promises to be true to his own best reason and judgment. The odds are all in favor of the candidate who offers himself as the agent, the delegate, the spokesman, the errand boy, of blocs of voters.

In a modern democratic state, the chief executive office must be elective. But as heredity, prescription, consecration, rank and hierarchy are dissolved by the acids of modernity, the executives become totally dependent on election. They have no status and no tenure which reinforce their consciences, which invest them with power to withstand the tides of popular opinion and to defend the public interest.

They hold their offices for a short time, and to do this they must maneuver and manipulate combinations among the factions and the pressure groups. Their policies must be selected and shaped so as to attract and hold together these combinations. There are moments, the "finest hours," when communities are lifted above their habitual selves in unity and fellowship. But these moments are rare. They are not the stuff of daily life in a democracy, and they are remembered like a miracle in a dream. In the daily routine of democratic politics, elected executives can never for long take their eyes from the mirror of the constituencies. They must not look too much out of the window at the realities beyond.

2. *The Protection of the Executive*

During the nineteenth century good democrats were primarily concerned with insuring representation in the assemblies and with extending the control of the assemblies over the executive power. It is true that the problem of the inadequate executive, ovrridden and dominated by the assembly, was very much in the minds of the Founding Fathers at the Philadelphia convention, and it has been a continuing concern of the critics and opponents of democracy. But until the twentieth century the problem was not sharply and urgently posed. That there was such a problem was well known. But it was not the immediate problem.

For some generations before 1914, the West enjoyed fine political weather. Moreover, the full force of the coming enfranchisement, emancipation, and secularization of the whole population had not yet worked its consequences. Governments still had authority and power, which were independent of the assemblies and the electorates. They still drew upon the traditional sources of authority—upon prescription, hereditary prerogative, and consecration.

Yet the need to protect the executive and judicial powers from the representative assemblies and from mass opinion has long been understood. Many expedients have been devised to soften, to neutralize, to check and to balance the pressure of parties, factions, lobbies, sects. The expedients have taken, says Bryce, two general forms, the one being to put constitutional restrictions upon the assembly and the other, "by a division of the whole power of the people," to weaken it. This has been done by electing the legislature and the executive separately, or by having the legislative bodies elected by the differing constituencies and at different times.

The constitutional mechanisms have never themselves been sufficient to protect the executive. And much invention and reforming energy have been applied to finding other ways to insulate the judicial, the executive and the administrative functions from the heavy pressures of "politics" and "politicians." The object has been to separate them from the electoral process. The judiciary must be independent of fear and favor. There must be no connection between the judgment of the courts and the election returns. The civil service, the military services, the foreign service, the scientific and technical services, the quasi-judicial administrative tribunals, the investigating commissions, the public schools and institutions of learning, should be substantially independent of the elections. These reforms were inspired by the dire effects of the spoils system, and they were pushed as practical remedies for obvious evils.

Yet implicit in them there is a principle which, if it can be applied deeply enough, gets at the root of the disorder of modern democracy. It is that though public officials are elected by the voters, or are appointed by men who are elected, they owe their primary allegiance not to the opinions of the voters but to the law, to the criteria of their professions, to the integrity of the arts and sciences in which they work, to their own conscientious and responsible convictions of their duty within the rules and the frame of reference they have sworn to respect.

3. *The Voters and the Executive*

The implied principle may be defined in other terms by saying that while the electors choose the ruler, they do not own any shares in him and they have no right to command him. His duty is to the office and not to his electors. Their duty is to fill the office and not to direct the officeholder. I realize that, as I have stated it, the principle runs counter to the popular view that in a democracy public men are the servants (that is, the agents) of the people (that is, of the voters). As the game of politics is played, what I am saying must seem at first like a counsel of perfection.

There are, however, reasons for thinking that it is not an abstract and empty bit of theorizing. One is that until comparatively recent times, it has been the principle on which the election of rulers—lay and spiritual—has usually been carried out.

In the early church, says Acts VI, the twelve apostles called the multitude of the disciples to them and said, "Look ye out among you seven men of honest report, full of the Holy Ghost and wisdom, whom we may appoint over this business." When these men had been chosen, and had prayed, "the apostles . . . laid their hands upon them." Having been ordained, they were not the servants of the multitude who had elected them, but of God.

This principle applied to the election of Popes. As Suarez says, "The Pope is elected by cardinals, yet he receives his powers from God immediately." The same principle applied to elected kings. After the electors had chosen the king, he was crowned and anointed. Then his duty was to his own vows and not to the electors. The act of election did not bind the ruler to the electors. Both parties to the transaction were bound only to the office; the electors to designate a king worthy of the office, the king to fill the office worthily.

If we look closely at the matter, we find, I believe, this must be the principle of election when the electors are choosing, not someone to represent them to the government, but the governors themselves. Though it is not too well recognized, there is a radical difference between the election of an executive and the election of a representative. For while the executive is in honor bound not to consider himself as the agent of his electors, the representative is expected to be, within the limits of reason and the general public interest, their agent.

This distinction has deep roots in the political experience of Western society, and, though unrecognized in principle, it is implicit in our moral judgments. Everyone who has a case in court is entitled, we believe, to be represented by a lawyer who, within the law and the code of professional practice, is expected to be the partisan and advocate of his client. But this presupposes not only that his opponent will be effectively represented too, but that the case will go to a court where the judge is not an advocate and has no clients. The judge is bound by his judicial vows. The same ethical standards are recognized, though they are applied less rigorously, in the executive branch of the government. No President or head of a department could afford to admit that he was using his office to further the interests of a client or of a pressure group, or even his party. His acts must be presented as taken in obedience to his oath of office, which means taken disinterestedly and rationally. He must never in so many words admit that in order to gain votes he sacrificed the public good, that he played "politics." Often enough he does just that. But fealty to the public interest is his virtue. And he must, at the very least, pay it the homage of hypocrisy.

When we move over to the representative assembly, the image

is different, and the ethical rule is applied, if at all, loosely and lightly. The representative is in some very considerable degree an agent, and the image of his virtue is rather like that of the lawyer than of the judge. There are, of course, occasions when he is in fact the holder of one of the great offices of state—as when he must speak and vote on a declaration of war and the ratification of a treaty. But in the general run of the mundane business which comes before the assembly, he is entitled, indeed he is in duty bound, to keep close to the interests and sentiments of his constituents, and, within reasonable limits, to do what he can to support them. For it is indispensable to the freedom and the order of a civilized state that the voters should be effectively represented. But representation must not be confused with governing.

4. *The Enfeebled Executive*

In the effort to understand the malady of democratic government I have dwelt upon the underlying duality of functions: *governing*, that is, the administration of the laws and the initiative in legislating, and *representing* the living persons who are governed, who must pay, who must work, who must fight and, it may be, die for the acts of government. I attribute the democratic disaster of the twentieth century to a derangement of these primary functions.

The power of the executive has become enfeebled, often to the verge of impotence, by the pressures of the representative assembly and of mass opinions. This derangement of the governing power has forced the democratic states to commit disastrous and, it could be, fatal mistakes. It has also transformed the assemblies in most, perhaps not in all, democratic states from the defenders of local and personal rights into boss-ridden oligarchies, threatening the security, the solvency, and the liberties of the state.

In the traditions of Western society, civilized government is founded on the assumption that the two powers exercising the two functions will be in balance—that they will check, restrain, compensate, complement, inform and vitalize each one the other.

In this century, the balance of the two powers has been seriously upset. Two great streams of evolution have converged upon the modern democracies to devitalize, to enfeeble, and to eviscerate the executive powers. One is the enormous expansion of public expenditure, chiefly for war and reconstruction; this has augmented the power of the assemblies which vote the appropriations on which the executive depends. The other development which has acted to enfeeble the executive power is the growing incapacity of the large majority of the democratic peoples to believe in intangible realities. This has stripped the government of that imponderable authority which is derived from tradition, immemorial usage, consecration, veneration, prescription, prestige, heredity, hierarchy.

At the beginning of our constitutional development the King, when he had mastered the great barons, was the proprietor of the greatest wealth in the realm. The crown was also the point from which radiated the imponderable powers to bind and to command. As the King needed money and men for his wars, he summoned representatives of the counties and the boroughs, who had the money and the men he needed. But the imponderable powers, together with very considerable power in land and in men, were still in the King's own hands. Gradually, over the centuries, the power of the Parliament over the supplies of the government grew larger. They had to appropriate a larger proportion of a much greater total. At the same time, in the white light of the enlightenment and the secularization of men's minds, the imponderable powers of the crown diminished.

Under the stress and the strain of the great wars of the twentieth century, the executive power has become elaborately dependent upon the assemblies for its enormous expenditures of men and of money. The executive has, at the same time, been deprived of very nearly all of his imponderable power: fearing the action of the representative assembly, he is under great temptation to outwit it or by-pass it, as did Franklin D. Roosevelt in the period of the Second World War. It is significant, I think, certainly it is at least suggestive, that while nearly all the Western governments have been in deep trouble since the First World War, the constitutional monarchies of Scandinavia, the Low Countries, and the United Kingdom have shown greater capacity to endure, to preserve order with freedom, than the republics of France, Germany, Spain and Italy. In some measure that may be because in a republic the governing power, being wholly secularized, loses much of its prestige; it is stripped, if one prefers, of all the illusions of intrinsic majesty.

The evaporation of the imponderable powers, a total dependence upon the assemblies and the mass electorates, has upset the balance of powers between the two functions of the state. The executive has lost both its material and its ethereal powers. The assemblies and the class electorates have acquired the monopoly of effective powers.

This is the internal revolution which has deranged the constitutional system of the liberal democratic states.

BEWARE THE EXECUTIVE

Congress: The Middle Level of Power

C. WRIGHT MILLS

More and more of the fundamental issues never come to any point of decision before the Congress, or before its most powerful committees, much less before the electorate in campaigns. The entrance of the United States into World War II, for example, in so far as it involved American decision, by-passed the Congress quite completely. It was never a clearly debated issue clearly focused for a public decision. Under the executive's emergency power, the President, in a virtually dictatorial way, can make the decision for war, which is then presented to the Congress as a fact accomplished. "Executive agreements" have the force of treaties but need not be ratified by the Senate: the destroyer deal with Great Britain and the commitment of troops to Europe under NATO, which Senator Taft fought so bitterly, are clear examples of that fact. And in the case of the Formosa decisions of the spring of 1955, the Congress simply abdicated all debate concerning events and decisions bordering on war to the executive.

When fundamental issues do come up for Congressional debate, they are likely to be so structured as to limit consideration, and even to be stalemated rather than resolved. For with no responsible, centralized parties, it is difficult to form a majority in Congress; and—with the seniority system, the rules committee, the possibility of filibuster, and the lack of information and expertise —the Congress is all too likely to become a legislative labyrinth. It is no wonder that firm Presidential initiative is often desired by Congress on non-local issues, and that, in what are defined as

From *The Power Elite*, by C. Wright Mills (pp. 255-267).

emergencies, powers are rather readily handed over to the executive, in order to break the semi-organized deadlock. Indeed, some observers believe that "congressional abdication and obstruction, not presidential usurpation, has been the main cause of the shift of power to the Executive."

Among the professional politicians there are, of course, common denominators of mood and interests, anchored in their quite homogeneous origins, careers, and associations; and there is, of course, a common rhetoric in which their minds are often trapped. In pursuing their several parochial interests, accordingly, the Congressmen often coincide in ways that are of national relevance. Such interests seldom become explicit issues. But the many little issues decided by local interest, and by bargain, by check and balance, have national results that are often unanticipated by any one of the locally rooted agents involved. Laws are thus sometimes made, as the stalemate is broken, behind the backs of the lawmakers involved. For Congress is the prime seat of the middle levels of power, and it is on these middle levels that checks and balances do often prevail. . . .

. . . As a political actor, the Congressman is part of the compromised balances of local societies, as well as one or the other of the nationally irresponsible parties. As a result, he is caught in the semi-organized stalemate of the middle levels of national power.

Political power has become enlarged and made decisive, but not the power of the professional politician in the Congress. The considerable powers that do remain in the hands of key Congressmen are now shared with other types of political actors: There is the control of legislation, centered in the committee heads, but increasingly subject to decisive modification by the administrator. There is the power to investigate, as a positive and a negative weapon, but it increasingly involves intelligence agencies, both public and private, and it increasingly becomes involved with what can only be called various degrees of blackmail and counter-blackmail. . . .

There is another way of gaining and of exercising power, one which involves the professional politician in the actions of cliques within and between the bureaucratic-like agencies of the administration. Increasingly, the professional politician teams up with the administrator who heads an agency, a commission, or a department in order to exert power with him against other administrators and politicians, often in a cut-and-thrust manner. The traditional distinction between "legislation" as the making of policy and "administration" as its realization has broken down from both sides.

In so far as the politician enters into the continuous policy-making of the modern political state, he does so less by voting for or against a bill than by entering into a clique that is in a position to exert influence upon and through the command posts of the executive administration, or by not investigating areas sensitive to certain clique interests. It is a member of quite complicated cliques that the professional politician, representing a variety of interests, sometimes becomes quite relevant in decisions of national consequence.

If governmental policy is the result of an interplay of group interests, we must ask: what interests outside the government are important and what agencies inside it serve them? If there are *many* such interests and if they conflict with one another, then clearly each loses power and the agency involved either gains a certain autonomy or is stalemated. In the legislative branch, many and competing interests, especially local ones, come to focus, often in a stalemate. Other interests, on the level of national corporate power, never come to a focus but the Congressman, by virtue of what he is as a political and social creature, realizes them. But in the executive agency a number of small and coherent interests are often the only ones at play, and often they are able to install themselves within the agency or effectively nullify its action against themselves. Thus regulatory agencies, as John Kenneth Galbraith has remarked, "become, with some exceptions, either an arm of the industry they are regulating or servile." The executive ascendancy, moreover, has either relegated legislative action—and inaction—to a subordinate role in the making of policy or bends it to the executive will. For enforcement now clearly involves the making of policy, and even legislation itself is often written by members of the executive branch.

In the course of American history, there have been several oscillations between Presidential and Congressional leadership. Congressional supremacy, for example, was quite plain during the last third of the nineteenth century. But in the middle of the twentieth century, with which we are concerned, the power of the Executive, and the increased means of power at its disposal, is far greater than at any previous period, and there are no signs of its power diminishing. The executive supremacy means the relegation of the legislature to the middle levels of political power; it means the decline of the professional politician, for the major locale of the party politicians is the legislature. It is also a prime indicator of the decline of the old balancing society. For —in so far as the old balance was not entirely automatic—it was the politician, as a specialist in balance and a broker of contending pressures, who adjusted the balances, reached compromises and maintained the grand equilibrium. That politician who best satisfied or held off a variety of interests could best gain power and hold it. But now the professional politician of the old balancing society has been relegated to a position "among those also present," often noisy, or troublesome, or helpful to the ascendant outsiders, but not holding the keys to decision. For the old balancing society in which he flourished no longer prevails. . . .

In the old liberal society, a set of balances and compromises prevailed among Congressional leaders, the executive branch of the government, and various pressure groups. The image of power and of decision is the image of a balancing society in which no unit of power is powerful enough to do more than edge forward a bit at a time, in compromised countervailance with other such forces, and in which, accordingly, there is no unity, much less coordination, among the higher circles. Some such image, combined with the doctrine of public opinion, is still the official view of the formal democratic system of power, the standard theory of most academic social scientists, and the underlying assumption of most literate citizens who are neither political spokesmen nor political analysts.

But as historical conditions change, so do the meanings and political consequences of the mechanics of power. There is nothing magical or eternal about checks and balances. In time of revolution, checks and balances may be significant as a restraint upon unorganized and organized masses. In time of rigid dictatorship, they may be significant as a technique of divide and rule. Only under a state which is already quite well balanced, and which has under it a balanced social structure, do checks and balances mean a restraint upon the rulers.

The eighteenth-century political theorists had in mind as the unit of power the individual citizen, and the classic economists had in mind the small firm operated by an individual. Since their time, the units of power, the relations between the units, and hence the meaning of the checks and balances, have changed. In so far as there is now a great scatter of relatively equal balancing units, it is on the middle levels of power, seated in the sovereign localities and intermittent pressure groups, and coming to its high point within the Congress. We must thus revise and relocate the received conception of an enormous scatter of varied interests, for, when we look closer and for longer periods of time, we find that most of these middle-level interests are concerned merely with their particular cut, with their particular area of vested interest, and often these are of no decisive political importance, although many are of enormous detrimental value to welfare. Above this plurality of interests, the units of power—economic, political, and military—that count in any balance are few in number and weighty beyond comparison with the dispersed groups on the middle and lower levels of the power structure.

Those who still hold that the power system reflects the balancing society often confuse the present era with earlier times of American history, and confuse the top and the bottom levels of the present system with its middle levels. When it is generalized into a master model of the power system, the theory of balance becomes historically unspecific; whereas in fact, as a model, it should be specified as applicable only to certain phases of United States development—notably the Jacksonian period and, under quite differing circumstances, the early and middle New Deal.

The idea that the power system is a balancing society also assumes that the units in balance are independent of one another, for if business and labor or business and government, for example, are not independent of one another, they cannot be seen as elements of a free and open balance. But as we have seen, the major vested interests often compete less with one another in their effort to promote their several interests than they coincide on many points of interest and, indeed, come together under the umbrella of government. The units of economic and political power not only become larger and more centralized; they come to coincide in interest and to make explicit as well as tacit alliances.

The American government today is not merely a framework within which contending pressures jockey for position and make politics. Although there is of course some of that, this government now has such interests vested within its own hierarchical structure, and some of these are higher and more ascendant than others. There is no effective countervailing power against the coalition of the big businessmen—who, as political outsiders, now occupy the command posts—and the ascendant military men—who with such grave voices now speak so frequently in the higher councils. Those having real power in the American state today are not merely brokers of power, resolvers of conflict, or compromisers of varied and clashing interests—they represent and indeed embody quite specific national interests and policies.

While the professional party politicians may still, at times, be brokers of power, compromisers of interests, negotiators of issues, they are no longer at the top of the state, or at the top of the power system as a whole.

The idea that the power system is a balancing society leads us to assume that the state is a visible mask for autonomous powers, but in fact, the powers of decision are now firmly vested within the state. The old lobby, visible or invisible, is now the visible government. This "governmentalization of the lobby" has proceeded in both the legislative and the executive domains, as well as between them. The executive bureaucracy bcomes not only the center of power but also the arena within which and in terms of which all conflicts of power are resolved or denied resolution. Administration replaces electoral politics; the maneuvering of cliques replaces the clash of parties.

THE BENEVOLENT MYTH OF REPRESENTATIVE GOVERNMENT

Restoration of the Representative System

GAETANO MOSCA

Specialization in the various political functions and cooperation and reciprocal control between bureaucratic and elective elements are two of the outstanding characteristics of the modern representative state. These traits make it possible to regard that state as the most complex and delicate type of political organization that has so far been seen in world history. From that point of view, and from others as well, it may also be claimed that there is an almost perfect harmony between the present political system and the level of civilization that has been attained in the century that saw it come into being and grow to maturity. That civilization may perhaps have shown itself inferior to some of its predecessors as regards the finer perfections of artistic and literary forms, as regards depth of philosophical thought and religious sentiment, as regards appreciation of the importance of certain great moral problems. But it has shown itself far superior to all others in its wise organization of economic and scientific production and in its exact knowledge and shrewd exploitation of the forces of nature. There can be no question that the political system now prevailing has won over the spontaneous energies and wills of individual human beings the same victory which the complex of institutions, instruments, knowledge and aptitudes that form the culture and the strength of our generations has won over the forces of nature.

Certainly, it was possible yesterday, and it is possible today, for the special interests of small organized minorities to prevail over the collective interest, paralyzing the activity of those whose duty it is to safeguard the latter. But we must realize that the state machine has grown so powerful and become so perfected that never before in Europe or in the world has such a mass of economic resources and individual activities been seen to converge upon the attainment of collective purposes—the [First] World War has recently supplied a terrible but irrefutable proof of that. If it be objected that some ancient cities, and perhaps some of the medieval communes, on occasion exerted no less effort in proportion to their size, the answer is that the smaller the organism, the easier it is to coordinate the activities of the cells that compose it. Athens, Sparta and certain medieval communes that were large for their day had territories and populations a hundredth the size of the average modern state. Rome only, at the time of her Punic Wars, and again during the first two centuries of the empire, when she was successfully extending her language and civilization over all of western Europe, obtained results which are comparable in magnitude to the results that the political organizations of our day obtain, on which in some respects may be of greater magnitude.

But every human organism, whether individual or social, the

modern representative state included, bears within itself the germs which, if they ripen, may bring on its decline and destruction. Let us mention here just a few such germs of decay, the main ones, that is, which already can be clearly seen at work.

Apparent at this moment in many countries in Europe is a considerable economic decline of the middle class, the prosperity of which made the advent of the representative system possible. If the economic decline of that class should continue for a whole generation, an intellectual decline in all our countries would inevitably follow. According to Aristotle, a certain distribution of moderate property ownership was an indispensable requisite for the proper functioning of the Greek city. So the existence of a moderately well-to-do middle class is necessary today for the normal livelihood of the modern representative system. So true is this that in countries and regions where such a class is not very well developed, or is without the requisites for maintaining its prestige and influence, the modern representative system has yielded its worst results. If the decline in question should be accelerated, or merely continue, the forms of our present organization might be observed for some time still, but really we would have either a plutocratic dictatorship, or else a bureaucratic-military dictatorship, or else a demogogic dictatorship by a few experts in mob leadership, who would know the arts of wheedling the masses and of satisfying their envies and their predatory instincts in every possible way, to the certain damage of the general interest. Worse still, there might be a combination of two of these dictatorships, or indeed of all three. It is interesting to note that this danger was clearly perceived by Rousseau: "Taking the term in its strictest sense," he wrote, "there has never been a real democracy and there never will be. It is against the natural order that the great number should rule and the small number be ruled."

This danger would seem to be all the greater in that it is linked with another, which is a logical consequence of the system of ideas that has supplied the moral and intellectual basis for the representative system. We allude here to the frame of mind, so widely prevalent hitherto, that has made the introduction of universal suffrage almost inevitable. During the first decades of representative government the bourgeoisie was disposed to compromise with the dogma of popular sovereignty on which the representative system had been founded, and adopted varieties of restricted suffrage almost everywhere. But later on, swayed more by force of logic than by any upthrust that came from the lower strata of society, and constrained especially by the necessity of seeming to be consistent with the principles which it had proclaimed and in the name of which it had fought and overthrown absolutism, the bourgeoisie adopted universal suffrage. Universal suffrage came first in the United States, then in France, in 1848, and after that in all other countries that were governed by representative systems.

Now never have the many, especially if they were poor and ignorant, ruled the few, especially if they were fairly rich and intelligent. The so-called dictatorship of the proletariat, therefore, could never be anything more than the dictatorship of a very restricted class exercised in the name of the proletariat. Perhaps some perception of that truth may have penetrated more or less clearly into the consciousness, or subconsciousness, of the ruling classes and inclined them to accept universal suffrage without very much resistance. But once everybody has acquired the right to vote it is inevitable that a clique should detach itself from the middle classes and, in the race to reach the better posts, try to seek leverage in the instincts and appetites of the more populous classes, telling them that political equality means almost nothing unless it goes hand in hand with economic equality and that the former may very well serve as an instrument for obtaining the latter.

That has come about and is still coming about all the more easily, in that the bourgeoisie has been, in a sense, the prisoner not only of its democratic principles but also of its liberal principles. Liberalism takes it to be an axiomatic truth that every belief, every opinion, has the right to be preached and propagated without hindrance. Certainly liberalism and democracy are not the same thing, but they have a certain common foundation in an intellectual and emotional current which started in the eighteenth century on the basis of an optimistic conception of human nature or, rather, of the sentiments and ideas that *ought to prevail* in associations of human beings. Just as democracy, therefore, has to admit that the best government is the government that emanates from the consent of the numerical majority of citizens, so liberalism has to believe that the good sense of the people is enough to distinguish truth from error and to treat harm-